JOURNALISM: NEWS COVERAGE

JOURNALISM:

News Coverage

(For PG Diploma & Degree Courses in Journalism & Mass Media)

Shahzad Ahmad

ANMOL PUBLICATIONS PVT. LTD.
NEW DELHI - 110 002 (INDIA)

ANMOL PUBLICATIONS PVT. LTD.
4374/4B, Ansari Road, Daryaganj
New Delhi - 110 002
Ph.: 23261597, 23278000
Visit us at: www.anmolpublications.com

Journalism: News Coverage

First Published, 2005

PRINTED IN INDIA

Published by J.L. Kumar for Anmol Publications Pvt. Ltd., New Delhi - 110 002 and Printed at Mehra Offset Press, Delhi.

Contents

Preface

In Modern world, Journalism is one discipline, which attracts people like any thing, but, it is equally challenging and drastic in cases. Particularly, under the new world order and in current global scenario, its value has increased manifold.

Apart from being a glorious profession, Journalism, today is a full-fledged subject, mastery of which leads one to a successful career and an all powerful status in society.

As a discipline, Journalism requires proper training and a comprehensive course, if possible. Although, there is no defined qualification for appointment as a journalist, in any capacity, in any media organisation, yet it is always better to be properly qualified and well-equipped with all essential knowledge.

Of course, there are books on Journalism but not in a great number. And, if one goes selective, then only a few books would rest in hand, as there is still a dearth for exclusive and exhaustive books on several streams of Journalism.

This series of books on Journalism is an effort to fill the abovesaid vaccum only. Here are books on all subjects and topics, related to Journalism. The undersigned is confident enough that this humble endeavour would prove to be worthy on the basis of its merits and receive a warm acceptance by students of journalism, scholars and the working journalists, as well.

— Editor

1

Introduction

In two centuries of independent journalism, the art of divining the meaning of the news has been at once the most challenging and the most frustrating to seasoned professionals. William Bolitho once compared the process to "seeing through a brick wall," which has nothing whatever to do with the relatively easy business of differentiating between events and pseudo-events. It is, inessence, the separation of the truth from the news.

This is, by all odds, the least likely of all the journalist's practices to win him the administration of a mass public in these dangerous times, although it is one of the most essential. If he is right, he is, as the saying goes, only doing his job, and what is so remarkable about that? Yet, when he is wrong, his detractors take pains to point out for his benefit that scholars are still worrying about the meaning of events in the seventeenth century, with perhaps a bit of apprehension over what happened in ancient Greece, so why all the rush? As for those timid souls who invariably do not know or cannot say, and have access to no one who might be able to help them, they are not journalists. This may seem utterly unreasonable, but it is a recognized way of journalistic life and some actually enjoy doing it.

In those shrinking areas of primarily Western civilization where the journalists still is permitted reasonable liberty of movement and expression, his work necessarily involves him in difficulties that are almost unavoidable. The gathering and distribution of the news in a reasonably impartial and accurate manner are in themselves complicated processes, as a rule. It takes somewhat more than good will and academic honours including the Ph.D. to cope with the basic reporting of the ordinary processes of life and self-government in an open society and the administration of justice, let alone such extraordinary events as civil disturbances, panics, disasters, national emergencies, and wars. When the journalist in addition is called upon to disseminate instant wisdom while great events are unfolding, he knows that he is often laying himself open to furious challenge, primarily from his own kind. Therefore, unless he is a syndicated columnist or another imposing personality who commands the unique trust of his proprietor and editor, the system under which he operates requires him to qualify, to hedge, and to dredge upon-persons as his sources.

There is, unfortunately, no way of hedging gracefully. Taking refuge in the cliches of American journalism, many back into the interpretation of events with an apologetic. It is believed ...or, "It is said.." Others, seeking support from threadbare mystery, adopt the time-worn formula of crediting or blaming the up-person with such expressions as, "Sources here indicate ..." or "In authoritative circles it is felt..." Finally, a few will take a bolder line by forthrightly stating the opinion of impartial observers, generally meaning themselves. Only a handful can be read with the admiring exclamation of a Ralph Waldo Emerson, upon perusing *The Times* of London in the mid-nineteenth century: "It is so!"

The ailment is endemic to the journalism of the space age, when the generalist may be rendered helpless by events he does not understand and the specialist may be too muscle-bound to move quickly enough to service the news media. In one sense, the American journalist superbly fulfills his function by quickly organizing and presenting the factual developments surrounding great events, from space shots to war, and from national elections to the civil rights crisis. As long as the news is hard and hot (shop talk terminology that makes sense to the journalist if no one else), he usually does his work with consummate professional skill. But where the news is based on rival propaganda claims, exaggeration for striking effect, or deliberate untruths put forward by eminent persons, groups or nations, then the press is at a disadvantage because it has as yet devised no machinery for consistently dealing with such matters. Occasionally, a newspaper simply will refuse to publish mendacious material, regardless of the prestige of the source. In one instance, celebrated within the profession, a determined reporter crumpled a statement handed out by a distinguished American ambassador and told his colleagues in cold fury. "This is a goddam lie and I refuse to send it to my paper." But generally the rule that is followed, as stated in various forms by authorities from John Milton to John Knight, requires publication of truth and falsehood alike on the hopeful assumption that the public will recognize the former and turn its back on the latter.

Aside from these ethical considerations, the news itself is often difficult for the average citizen to comprehend (and that sometimes includes the average editor). It is not un-known for sources to add to the complications by deliberately putting a construction on the news that is favourable "to some particular interest, public or private. Moreover, the journalist himself may add to the process of distortion quite innocently with his selection of a fact to be featured and headlined in a complicated article. Or, he may omit comparatively dull material that is important but requires too much space or time to explain. The two-line quote, the brief angled description, the loaded word or phrase, and misplaced emphasis all can be dangerous. But the journalist who sins the most against the public interest is the one who writes or speaks to appease his superiors' set notions of what is going on or to conform to the policies of his organization.

There is no question that experienced journalists are generally able to handle these difficulties in their daily routine, but even they cannot hope for perfection. As for the television newscasters, the demands of the clock and the lack of picture possibilities restrict their interpretive reporting in regular news programmes. A minute or two is not sufficient to explain the meaning of such things as the struggle in China, the decline of NATO, the meaning of "black power," or the "death of God," and the machinery of Medicare. But it is in the news magazines, which generally do not receive sufficient credit for their good work, that the temptation is greatest to make the angle the message.

Sometimes the angling is harmless and even amusing. Newsweek's cover story on Pop Art, a passing fad of the mix-sixties, began with a breathless glorification of the trivial in this manner:

> It's a fad, it's a trend, it's a way of life. It's pop. It's a $5,000 Roy Liethenstein painting of an underwater kiss. It's a SI poster of Mandrake the Magician.... It's 30,000,000 viewers dialing 'Batman' on ABC every week. It's Superman zooming around on the Broadway stage. It's Pow! Bam! commercial on TV..."

The historic cure for this kind of writing is to force the culprit to read it out loud before an audience of fellow journalists and take the consequences. It has no dubious intent, nor can intelligent people take it very seriously. Usually, it can safely be ignored or, once read, forgotten.

But the same exaggerated technique, applied to a serious subject, can have a quite different result. As Great Britain was wrestling with a grave economic crisis. Time gaily head-lined a cover story: "London : The Swinging City." In glib and colourful language, the account reported as follows on the state of affairs in the capital of the United Kingdom.

It was one thing for one of Britain's angry men, John Osborne, to equate the highest British values with down-and-out vaudeville in his play. "The Entertainer," It was quite another for Time to present the image of Britannia in a miniskirt, an aging and hefty grand dame miscast in the role of a go-go girl. The British were not pleased by the effusive, schoolgirl prose in the leading American news magazine.

Henry Fairlie, a British journalist who attracted an admiring following of American editors because of his talent for insult, responded with measured invective: "If I were given to conspiracy theories, I would believe that there is a plot to denigrate Britain by praising everything in it which is mindless and nasty, which is senseless and corrupting, which is meaningless and deadly. "It was perfectly true, he agreed, that a small section of highly publicized British life was giving the impression that Britain seems destined to sink giggling into the sea" "But he argued that it was a distorted picture. The headlines announcing the Wilson government's devaluation of the pound soon confirmed his astringent analysis. It was just about as accurate for *Time* and others to cast all Britain in the Beatle mold in the late 1960s as it had been for the Hearst newspapers and others in the 1930s to welcome John Bull into the Cliveden Set as an appeaser of Hitler.

When Prime Minister Wilson clapped on a wage-price freeze, it became difficult if not impossible foe any responsible publication to sustain the happy and carefree image of a swinging Britain American tourists, curtailing their own spending, found the British people anything but switched on. The fact was that the British were deeply concerned over the chronic economic problems of their great and ancient land; with money tight, and little hope of relief in sight, the average Britisher was aş far from "the scene" as his quiet neighbourhood pub. Of course, extreme fashions were being vended with promotional skill on Carnaby Street and a thin, bony teenager dubbed Twiggy caused American fashion houses to fall over themselves to engage her services as a model. There were prostitutes in Soho and effeminate, long-haired boys in Piccadilly. Strip clubs were operating and most Britishers continued to be enthusiastic smalltime gamblers. But none of this was really news. As Herbert L.Matthews observed, those who knew Britain and the British could scarcely conclude that their national character had changed.

The daily newspapers, of course, have their own troubles with both the glorification of trivia and the dangers of distortion in dealing with the news. While no one can know all the faults and virtues of 1,750 newspapers at any particular time, it is readily apparent from the most sketchy and unscientific examination that not all editors are bemused by great events and even fewer are patient with seemingly insoluble issues of overwhelming importance. In considering the future of disarmament negotiations, for example, some editors published a column by Holmes Alexander on the subject which began : "Genocide is a horrid crime but sometimes it is tempting. What a better world we would have if we could put a merciful quietus on our Utopians, those persons who look for perfectabilily in man." The New York Daily News could become apoplectic over the hurt feelings of girls who received obscene telephone calls from strange men, devoting a whole tabloid page of advice to the ladies (Point 1 : "Hang up!") while summarizing the passage of Britain's drastic wage-price freeze law in one paragraph buried on Page.

Even in the prestige newspapers there can be awkward moments, such as Ambassador Edwin O. Reischauer's fare well interview in Japan which the Washington Post headed "Reischauer Backs U.S. Viet Policy," while The New York Times headline was, "Reischauer Critical of Viet Policy," The ambivalence of editorial thought, as evidenced in New York and Washington, produced a certain amount of grim humor in a Senate Foreign Relations Committee hearing room when it was publicly displayed by Leonard Marks, director of USA.

The hard-working wire services, always comparatively easy targets because of the tremendous volume of news they handle under great pressure and tough competitive conditions, also have made their share of errors for various reasons. When James H. Mereditch was shot by a roadside sniper in 1966 outside Hernado, United Press International correctly reported he had been slightly wounded and taken to a hospital while the Associated Press through a reportorial misunderstanding filed a bulletin that he was dead. The erroneous information was retracted after a half-hour.

The failure of both American wire services and Reuters, the British agency, to file prompt reports on the death of United Nations' Secretary General Dag Hammarskjold in 1961 was an even more striking instance of reportorial error. Newsmen at the airport at Ndola, Northern Rhodesia, (now Zambia) had mistaken a visiting British official, Lord Lansdowne, for Hammarskjold and had a bulletined his arrival on a Congo cease-fire mission at a time when he already was dead. As the agencies discovered to their charge in hours later, the Hammarskjold plane had crashed before he had ever reached Ndola. It was sadly recorded in the AP Log thereafter that AP men should "never assume to be a fact what they did not know to be a feet."

Although the Hammarskjold case emphasizes the vulnerability of the independent news media to wire service errors, this has given rise too few signs of concern either among journalists or the public at large. The disposition is to accept the occasional factual error as "just one of those things". Actually, it would be a mistake to assume that the relatively rare instances of bad factual reporting on major stories has hurt the credibility of the American news media. The evidence is all to the contrary. The celebrated nature of each of these cases, and the controversy that surrounded them, points up the comparatively isolated nature of factual errors that mar the reporting of big-news in the United States.

These are generally not the things that bother the journalist about his news organizations and their performance. Nor do many knowledgeable persons inside or outside the profession take stock any longer in the outdated criticism in Upton Sinclair's Brass Check. As Walter Lippmann once stated the position: "If the press is not so universally wicked, nor so deeply conspiring, as Mr. Sinclair would have us believe, it is very much more frail than the democratic theory has yet admitted. It is too frail too carry the whole burden of popular sovereignty, to supply spontaneously the truth which democrats hoped was inborn."

There are several ways in which this frailty of the press manifests itself, one of the most important being the treatment of the substance of a controversial issue in the news columns. A.T, Steele, a distinguished correspondent in the Far East for many years and scarcely a devotee of the Brass Check school of criticism, has singled out the coverage of Communist China for close examination. He believes that the editorial orientation of a newspaper is a "factor of importance" in the handling of news about China. "Indeed", he contends, "it can be argued that the generally conservative attitude of the American public on China is more attributable to this influence than to any other Newspapers of conservative outlook-and they are predominant in the smaller cities and towns-tend to give prominence to news and to background stories that favour their point of view. They also tend to use columnists of a predominantly conservative viewpoint. The total impression of China conveyed week after week to the readers of such a newspaper is likely to be different from that conveyed by a militantly liberal or independent newspaper".

As for television, there is so little of substance that appears on the networks outside the regular news programmes and their hasty expansion for big stories that every innovation is greeted with somewhat muted applause. Thus, a documentary on China, the Middle East, the Cong, Harlem, Watts, or Appalachia becomes a matter for enthusiastic comment. A long and perhaps wearisome documentary on foreign policy may be regarded as just short of a triumph. Where so skimpy a diet is generally available, a small addition makes the regular fare seem like a banquet — and perhaps sometimes it actually is. Yet, few can doubt that the burden of presenting the substance of the news, fairly or not, is still the job of the press.

Because this is so, what thoughtful journalist do and say about their own situation becomes something more than mere shop talk to a discerning public. It is a matter of record, documented at professional meetings and other public occasions too numerous to mention, that those not under compulsion to remain silent are becoming increasingly concerned, not only over slanted interpretations of the news but also over the manner in which such material is obtained. The "background" system, under which officials and others freely offer their views of the news in return for a pledge of anonymity, has proliferated beyond anything imagined by its founder, Earnest K. Lindley The "background" session, originally intended to be a quiet private talk between an official and a reporter or small group of reporters at most, has become a weekly event in which large numbers of correspondents hear the Secretary of State or the Secretary of Defense State opinions, but not for attribution to them.

In a similar manner, Secretary of State Dean Rusk invented a term called *deep background* instead of the regular background, which could be attributed to an informed source or some other unperson, he held his "deep background" conferences only for an elite list of "trusties," the British term for correspondents who are particularly in the government's confidence. In such sessions, the Secretary of State would cover extremely sensitive situations but only in return for the correspondents' pledge to use the material without any attribution whatever. This was, in its purest form, what James Reston once called "compulsory plagiartism"— the acceptance of an official view as one's own.

Such abuses of what was once recognized as a perfectly reasonable reportorial device have had serious consequences in Washington and elsewhere. Respected public figures of the stature of McGeorge Bundy and Bill Moyers have called for a more principled stand by both journalists and public officials in their dealings with each other. Some of the major correspondents for the better newspapers have refused publicly to use, for attribution to unnamed sources, the kind of material that should be labeled with the name and position of the official issuing it. As Max Frankel of *The New York Times* once told a State Department briefer at a White House background conference. "There's no reason why most of this can't be on the record. The *Times* will not print this story unless it's on the record." It went on the record."

Alan L. Otten of the *Wall Street Journal* called reporters who attended background conferences the "prisoners of the system." He pointed out that once they committed themselves, they were well-nigh obliged in most cases to rush into print with the government's unattributed material because of competitive pressures. Like so many others, he also ridiculed the supposition that any source in Washington could be kept secret for very long after putting out news or views that made major headlines. Nor could it be successfully argued that the device in all cases divested the government of responsibility for what was said and done under the fragile seal of journalistic confidence. Too often, such confidences proved to be a contradiction in terms.

Dsespite the somewhat mild rebellion, it should not be imagined that backgrounders are out of style or that the practice is on the point of being abandoned. For both professional and personal reasons, some understanding must be maintained between the journalist and his sources that will make it possible for them to talk together, even to argue, without guarding the utterance of every word. Long before Lindley dreamed up his World War II system of journalistic protocol, the better reporters and editors of the nation maintained such confidential relationships with some of the most important figures in public and private life. They still do. A negligible part of the many private conversations between reporters and their sources reaches print or the broadcast media in attributable form; under a kind of unspoken gentleman's agreement, which varies from source to source, the reporter generally knows what he can use and what he must pass up for the time being. If all background conference were abandoned, it would not hurt the skilled professional one bit because he has gained the trust of his sources and they are scarcely likely to abandon a beneficial two-way relationship. Under today's mass background conference routine, therefore, the only ones who really benefit are the junior reporters without sources, the lazybones who would rather pick an official's brains than use their own and do some independent work, and- the numbskulls who worry more about the exact form of a quotation than the meaning behind it.

There is no law in the land that requires any source in government or out of it to trust all reporters; in fact sheer prudence would rule against it. True, formal announcements or other news developments must be given to all the media representatives on a fair and equitable basis; however, when it comes to discussing the meaning of the news, every source is going to pick the reporters be trusts and who are likely to be of most benefit to his interests. Those who are shut out will not like it. On occasion, they may kick up such a fuss that they will break their way into the circle of journalistic "trusties" on their own terms. That kind of rivalry always has existed, regardless of the growth of the system of handling out background information and opinion, and it is bound to continue.

Despite the abuses of the backgrounder, all available evidence indicates that the use of material derived from it is increasing steadily in the American news media and abroad. The wire services and the newspapers syndicates are making available a great deal more explanatory material today than they did a decade or two ago and many more newspapers are using it. Such interpretation may on occasion be faulty, windy, or difficult to understand, but editors need not run it if they do not approve of it. The imperfections of the system, in short are not sufficient reason for abandoning the effort to explain the news.

Of course, editors still exist in the United States who conceive it to be their duty to play Horatius at the Bridge and keep out of the paper all notions that run contrary to their own pure beliefs. They are a hardy breed; although their numbers are dwindling in the space age, they still have a considerable influence in the far right wing of American journalism. If there were a far left with more than token access to print, undoubtedly the situation would be the same but there have been no far left publications of significance in the nation for many years. In consequence, the "play it safe" school of journalism flourishes primarily in places where editors either do not care about the meaning of the news or do not dare arouse local opposition by presenting views contrary to prevailing sentiment.

It is extraordinary, on balance, for so many inside the profession to adopt so critical an attitude on the problem of interpreting the news. In view of the long and undistinguished record of the American press in stubbornly facing down its critics, the movement toward greater realism in dealing with both the news and its sources is healthy and heartening. The mere acceptance of interpretation as a proper function of journalism, achieved after so many years of argument, is not enough. The methods of achieving it cannot be exactly defined; nor, for that matter, can they ever be expected to attain perfection. No computer is ever going to be invented that will emit acceptable explanations of the news at the touch of a button. No magic formula can be devised by science for clarifying, in one blind flash of revelation, the meaning of the convulsive upheaval of peoples and values in the world of the declining years of the twentieth century. Like the companion arts of exposition and illustration, interpretation has to be worked over, developed, and guarded against abuse and excess. Nor can it be assumed that everybody in journalism automatically inherits the right to interpret the news by the mere declaration that he is a journalist.

Conscientious editors rightly attempt to restrict the interpretation of events to those who have the ability, the background, and the experience to attempt it. Even so, there are many pitfalls before the qualified interpreter. What is true one day in a rapidly developing situation is not necessarily so the next, but often only the passage of time will cause the difference to be revealed. It took two years for the Communist hierarchy in Moscow to dump Nikita S. Khrushchev as premier after his failure to keep Russian rockets in Cuba aimed at the United States. It was even longer before the average American editor realized that there really was a split between the Soviet Union and Communist China. On September 30, 1965, the Western correspondent who flew into Djakarta could assume with reason that Indonesia was becoming allied with Peking: next day, with the failure of a Communist uprising, the opposite was the case although it was some time before the new position was clarified.

Writing of an equally difficult stage of the Vietnam War, Vermont Royster pointed out in the *Wall Street Journal* ; "The deficiency is inherent in the situation. Therefore, there is probably no way to remedy it." " This is so often true that it is pointless to try to define preciselsy the position of interpretation between the function of reporting, on the one side, and editorializing, on the other. Many editors have tried to do it, some even believe the process can be compartmentalized. However, no set of compartments or definitions can dispose of difficulties that are, as Royster has said, inherent in the situation. For as all able journalists know, interpretation uses both the techniques of reporting and editorial writing without finally being either a report or an editorial. It is, by and large, an honest judgement of the meaning of events, suitably documented by whatever evidence of fact or opinion that can be marshaled to support it.

The identity of the writer or commentator, and the integrity of his organization, are the only guarantees that can be provided to the public of the good faith behind the interpretation. Usually, it is sufficient. The notion that the public will be satisfied if an analysis is labeled as such really means very little, for the news columns are replete with unlabeled interpretation in the prestige press. More to be desired is the absence of any sign in the work of an analyst that he is an advocate of one cause or another, or that he has any special interest to advance. The same is true of his organization. There should be only one advocate — the editorialist. It is not seemly for the interpreter to try to persuade or to exhort: once he does, he sheds his assumption of disinterest which is all that separates him from the editorialist.

The current tendency to dramatize non-essentials, to oversimplify complex questions, and to imply U.S. importance one day and omnipotence the next has helped foster a national mood of confusion and frustration.

Such attitudes naturally encouraged some of the rivals of the daily newspaper, particularly the journals that aspired to give a more acceptable meaning to the news than the press. As a group they had long since adopted an adversary philosophy. Marya Marines, a critic for *The Reporter* magazine, spoke for example of the "tragedy" of the "decline of public confidence in the daily press" and warned that the public would turn to television for something better. However, despite Miss Mannes's prophecy, there has been no perceptible mass movement to follow the intellectual leadership offered by either television or the magazines in the United States.

The truth is that no element of the news media in the United States has any ground for complaency today. All are under critical scrutiny by informed public opinion as never before some more than others. If there is a single continuing issue that tests the public's belief with its news and communications system, it is by all odds the handling of the civil rights crisis. While there have been instances of superb work by all sections of the news media on this story in every part of the nation, the record on the whole is not one that satisfies most thoughtful journalists. More heat may be generated by the livery debate over free press and fair trial, but bench and bar are well able to fend for themselves in the rough and tumble of the democratic arena. This is not necessarily so as far as the protagonists in the turbulence over civil rights are concerned. Their leaders by and large, do not command the kind of respectful attention from the news media that is invariably accorded the American Bar Association and its distinguished spokesmen. The fair reporting of the civil rights story, in all its confusing aspects, depends in effect on the good faith of the news media as a whole.

Some of the editors and publishers in the South have refused to let anything prevent them from telling the truth about non-compliance with the law in all its unlovely aspects. Some reporters, photographers, and newscasters of impectable Southern lineage have repeatedly exposed themselves to mob violence in order to cover the news of their own and neighbouring communities. Yet, there is no doubt that in the beginning and to some extent even today — many Southern newspapers have qualified before the rebellious majorities in their communities the threat of terrorism.

Their editorial pages have condoned resistance to the law, even when it meant the endorsement of crimes up to and including murder.

There are still resolute journalists in the South who uphold the tradition of personal responsibility — Ralph McGill and Eugene Patterson on the *Atlanta Constitution.* Barry Bingham and Norman Isaacs on the *Louisville Times* and *Courier-Journal,* Hodding Carter on the *Greenville* (Miss.) Delta Democrat-Times, J.O. Emmerich on the *McComb* (Miss.) *Enterprise-Journal,* and others in a number of trouble centres. By their example, they have caused a substantial part of the press in the South to lift its standards in handling the news of America's great social crisis.

It is true that there is still little encouragement that can be given to the smaller and weaker papers in segregationist centres. Ira B. Harkey. Jr., a symbol of defiance in Mississippi, had to sell his *Pascagoula Chronile* and turn to teaching journalism. Hazel Brannon Smith, who made her weekly *Lexington Advertiser* respected every where except in Mississippi, led a precarious existence for years. Consequently, relatively few cared to follow her forthright example.

Although a segregation-minded populace continues to buy complying newspapers in the deep South and patronizes their advertisers, this scarcely implies respect for the press. In Germany where might made right, Bismarck also was able to force newspapers to do his biddsing but he referred to them contemptuously as the "reptile press," crawling on its belly before him. Naturally, the average Southern editor and publisher would consider such terminology a mortal insult, especially in the deep South where segregation remains an article of personal faith for the majority. But even a community of the most violent segregationists can measure the stature of a newspaper that prints only what its readers want to see and voices only editorial sentiments that can be applauded by the crudest and most vicious elements. It is not an image that registers on the poll-takers pad, but it is there, nevertheless, for all to see.

Rightly or wrongly, with the rise of civil rights violence across the land, the news media have often been as unwelcome in the ghetto as the police and other elements of the Establishment. This was particularly true in the Newark and Detroit riots of 1967. Reporters never know when they are likely to be jumped upon. Photographers with still or television cameras cannot be sure of their own safety, let alone their equipments. The relatively good record of most of the news media in covering disturbances does not seem to count for much. Nor have the excellent and often sympathetic documentaries about the civil rights movement on television made any significant impression on the militancy of the Negro masses. In effect, the lack of belief attached to the segregationist press in the deep South has also encompassed a considerable part of the press elsewhere among the ghetto-dwellers of the land. The difference in the motivation of the more liberal elements of the press has not loosened the growth of a belief among the extremists, white and Negro; that the news media constitute a symbol against which an effective protest may be registered.

The frailty of the press is very much in evidence in the civil rights issue. It is, in fact, no exaggeration to say that the press has been made a part of the issue. While accepting some of the failures in the South and the neglect of dangerous conditions in a number of cities elsewhere until they exploded into rioting, most working journalists do feel that they have done a decent and considerate job on the whole in telling the civil rights story. Outside the deep South, the record generally sustains them. But no one can persuade the militant Negro that this is so. He does not believe it. To him, the news means something entirely different than it does to the press he calls "white" because he will not acknowledge it as his own.

This state of mind, and the civil disorder it breeds, has shaken some of the complacency out of the news media and to some extent, forced its more progressive elements to re-examine their methods. What mob coverage does to inflame rioters to even greater acts of looting and sabotage will be examined later in this book, together with the general problem of controlling herd journalism.

Historically, journalism is not a profession that is founded on starry-eyed optimism: It glorifies its Cassandras and ridicules its Pollyannas. It scorns the uplifter as much as it suspects the reformer, having had grievous experience with both in the course of its daily dealings with human affairs. As an echo to events, it cries woe's knowing full well that such an automatic reflex action has a better chance of being right than wrong. The journalist who predicted 19 times at the opening of League of Nations meetings that this one would be its last had the dubious satisfaction of seeing events bear him out at the 20th session. Such a philosophy glorifies the prophet of doom as he and his followers are being consumed by the flames they themselves have kindled.

Clearly, the journalist needs a different approach to the reporting of a controversy such as civil rights that goes to the very roots of national existence. As the position was stated by George Hunt, managing editor of Life, it is no longer sufficient to practice "blind adherence to news for new's sake, and playing it for all it's worth." Such laissez-faire philosophy is out of date. Nor can it be propped up by some new gimmick in presenting the news, or a tricky method of writing interpretation to get more people to read it. What is required is a greater degree of editorial commitment — the decision, for example of editors in Rochester. N. Y. to go out and look for signs of progress in civil rights as well as the daily yield of bad news, the publication, as a further example of an enormous volume of material on crisis areas by editors in Los Angeles. Philadelphia, Kansas City, St. Louis, Hartford, and other cities. The telling of the Story of the City is the No. 1 assignment in American journalism today.

What this means, in short, is that the more progressive journalists at length have realized that there are both civic and national responsibilities that come ahead of their normal professional duties. Merely telling and printing the news is not enough; nor is it sufficient to keep chanting a litany about interpreting the news without finding better people, better ways, more space, and more time to do it before a crisis makes it imperative. The journalist is no longer justified in wrapping himself in the guise of a philosophical anarchist and pretending that he is someone set apart with a mission beyond that of ordinary men. For the fact is that he no longer is a mere news gatherer; often, in the act of gathering news, he makes it and even influences the course of events. Surely, the time has come for him to recognize it. He is not part of a gigantic shadow play; he is one of the principal actors, and what he says and does can have a substantial influence on its outcome. He must face up to his responsibilities as a good citizen first, a good journalist second.

Whether the journalist likes it or not, this is the standard by which the public is judging him and will continue to judge him and his works. His are the responsibilities of the innovator and leader, not merely of the critic, and he must exercise all of them if he is to continue to exert his right to give meaning to the news.

2

Various Aspects

The contents of a newspaper can be broadly divided into four parts-news; articles and features; opinion pieces such as editorials, comments, letters to the editor, reviews, columns; and advertisements.

News constitutes about 60% of the space in a newspaper. It pertains to some recent event which is a matter of interest to readers or listeners. News implies new thing or latest information.

The Concepts

A few definitions of 'news' are:

> "News may be defined as any accurate fact or idea that will interest a large number of readers."
>
> "News is anything timely that is interesting and significant to readers in respect of their personal affairs or their relation to society, and the best news is that which possesses the greatest degree of this interest and significance for the greatest number."

"News may be defined as an accurate, unbiased account of the significant facts of a timely happening that is of interest to the readers of the newspapers that print the account."

"News is the first report of significant events which have interest for the public."

"News is an account of a current idea, event or problem that interests people."

"News is the record of the most interesting, important and accurate information obtainable about the things man thinks and says, sees, describes, plans and does."

According to Mr. B.G. Verghese, former Editor-in-Chief *The Hindustan Times*, "the standard definition that only 'man bites dog' is news is obsolete and inaccurate. In view of the 'communication gap' in a democratic society that which is reported becomes news and that which is not reported remains non-news. Sensationalizatlron, disaster, fraud and the like is news but it is not 'sole news or the highest news'." Mr. Verghese advocates reporting of more constructive developments and trends in great social, economic and political changes, technological advances, modernization processes rather than concentrating only on political news.

News Stories

News stories are particularly of two types-straight news and interpretative *or* explanatory or opinionated writing. A straight news story gives factual account of what has happened in a simple, clear and accurate manner. This type of story never distorts, misrepresents or gives wrong facts. It draws no conclusions, makes no accusations, offers no opinions and does not indulge in any speculation. Interpretative news story, on the other hand, reports happenings in depth, gives all sides of the picture, provides background and puts some meaning into the news so that the reader can better understand and appreciate the event.

Most of the definitions of news agree on the point that news is which is of interest to the public. The interest, however, differs from person to person and place to place. Some other characteristics of news are immediacy, proximity, oddity, conflict, suspense, curiosity, and consequences.

The following are the important elements of news:

1. Immediacy or timeliness is of great importance. The new thing: or latest information makes all the difference. As news ages, it lose its potency. The nearness of an event in time is vital to daily newspapers.
2. Truth and objectivity is another quality of news. The balanced picture of an event or a happening or accuracy in reporting events enhances the value of news.
3. Nearness or propinquity, i.e., closeness in space, is yet another element of news. The newsworthiness of an event is in direct ratio to its physical nearness to the public served by the newspaper appraising it. An accident or a crime near at home has much greater news value than a bigger accident or crime abroad.
4. News should be of interest or concern or significance to readers. The interest, however, differs. It may be of interest to a section of the community or of local, regional, national or international interest.
5. Names of individuals also make news. The person may be widely known because of his position, wealth or status. Even an unknown person can make news because of some oddity, eccentricity or unusual occupation or some other factor.
6. Timing and place of occurrence of an event are also important elements of news. The hour of an event may decide its news importance, so also where the thing happens is important. Suicide in a city may not be big news, but in a small place such news may hit the headlines.

7. Numbers and size make news. An accident in which a large number of people have died or injured makes news. If very few people are involved in the accident and nobody died, the news value becomes less important.
8. Suspense and mystery adds to the value of news. It holds readers' interest in the news. The more the suspense, the greater is the curiosity of readers in the news.

The other elements which are dominant in news stories are action, movement and mobility; combat, struggle, contrast, rivalry; sex and scandal; beauty and romance; adventure and pathos including exploration, discovery, excavation, invention; novelty and humour; and stories about children and animals.

In brief, news is associated with something new or something novel; or relates to a famous person; or of importance to a large number of people; or pertains to conflict, mystery, crime; or reveals something confidential; or forecasts the future; or deals with a funny situation; or romance; or sex, suicide, murder, etc.

Job of Reporters

To be a successful reporter, one must have news sense or flair or nose for news. He should have the ability to recognize the news value in ordinary things. The qualities necessary in a reporter are: patience and perseverance to get a story; eye for details; capacity for hard work; gift of imagination; skill for clear and concise presentation of news and views; and spirit of enterprise and adventure.

The reporter has to work with great speed under stress and strain. He will succeed only if he has an understanding of time value and necessary flexibility and adaptability to change himself to the changing situation.

The reporter must report the news accurately and fairly without prejudice and personal opinion. The following remarks of the late Mr. Frank Moraes, Editor-in-Chief of the *Indian* Express, about the qualities necessary in a news reporter are very pertinent:

"What do I regard as the most important quality in a news reporter? I would unhesitatingly say-accuracy. This, and the ability to express himself clearly and concisely. The average newspaper reader is a man in a hurry. He should never be required to read a sentence twice to get its meaning."

To sum up, the essentials of good reporting are-accuracy, balance, brevity and speed. Loose writing and unverified details create a number of difficulties and should be avoided.

Reporters cover a variety of assignments-accidents, court cases, crime, proceedings of legislatures, communal incidents, demonstrations, deaths, etc. besides political, social, economic and cultural events and sports.

In covering accidents, a competent authority, an identifiable official spokesman should be quoted. The time, place and cause of the accident and if possible an eye witness account is to be given. The reporter should give the names of casualties only if he can verify their accuracy. He should show respect to the dead and avoid horrid details. Legal complications would arise if a person is reported to have 'died', but who is actually alive. The nature of accident should be described accurately. He must attribute his report to some authority. The source should be identified at the very start. The context in which the announcement of the accident is made, for instance, 'Press Conference' or 'Interview' as the case may be, should be mentioned.

In reporting court cases, care is to be exercised in not giving cause to libel or contempt. Anything that reflects directly or indirectly on the personal character or conduct of identifiable persons or institution or criticises or hinders the process of law should be scrupulously avoided. The report should be 'a fair summary' of evidence tendered, the statements made by the counsel and the ruling given by the court. If charges made by the prosecution are reported, the reply of the defendant must also be incorporated in the story. The onus of proving that the report was in public interest will be on the agency or newspaper.

In reporting crime, murder, suicide, fire, sabotage, etc. the statement pertaining to the name of the person involved, motive, cause, etc. should be attributed to police or an appropriate source. The term 'arrest' is different from 'taken into custody' or 'detained' for interrogation and as such, correct nomenclature should be used. A person is presumed to be innocent until he is found guilty by a court. So it is advisable to use expressions like 'alleged assailant and ,allegedly stabbed'. All information provided by police should be attributed to them. A reporter should refrain from making comments or speculating the circumstances under which the crime was committed, nor should he draw any conclusion or support or discount a particular theory.

The communities are generally not identified as 'Hindus' or 'Muslims' while reporting communal clashes. Generalized allegation and accusation of being anti-national should not be made against a whole community. Fullest verification is necessary before giving any facts and figures. Nothing should be included in the report which will whip up communal passions. The source from which casualty figures, etc. are taken should be indicated. If the figures are not confirmed, the report must indicate that the figures are 'unconfirmed'. News of efforts aiming at resolving peace and harmony should be highlighted.

The death story should include the cause of death, its time and place. Age of the dead and by whom survived, as well as the name of the disease are to be mentioned. If the name of the disease is not intelligible to readers, it should be explained in layman's language.

In, demonstrations and meetings, avoid adjectives and superlatives. Give as far as possible a factual account.

In covering presentation of budgets in Parliament and Assemblies, the new tax proposals, deficit, surplus, comparison between the past and present budget tax proposals, new schemes, reactions, etc. are to be reported. In reporting debates, the name of the speakers are followed by their party affiliations. In reporting-question-hour, identification is not necessary. The report of the proceedings show be fair and objective and remarks, if any made, should be in public interest. The expunged portions should not be included in the report.

The reporter has to interview people for news. He should study the subject and should have at least a broad background of it before conducting interview, particularly on specialized subjects. Knowledge of shorthand and typing will help him a great deal. While interviewing people, he should be a good listener and keep up a pleasant and cheerful disposition. The reporter should have mastery over the techniques of interviewing people.

The reporter should also clearly understand the difference between the classifications of news. 'Flash' is a one-line news item about an event of major significance. It has an element of suddenness and tells about something unexpected. 'Snap' is used for important sports or commercial news. 'Top priority' story consists of one or two paragraphs, while 'priority' story may run upto three or more paragraphs.

Press correspondents and reporters, possessing press authority from newspapers or news agencies, can send press telegrams including flash press telegrams to the concerned paper or agency. The rates charged for ordinary and express inland telegrams for minimum first. 50 words are Re. 1 and Rs. 2 respectively, and for every 5 additional words Paise 10 and Paise 20 respectively. The flash telegrams are limited to a maximum of 100 words, and are charged at the same rate as that of inland express private telegram. The press telegrams may be accepted without payment, if the newspaper or news agency had obtained previous sanction from the postal authorities.

The news story must be written effectively. The introductory sentence or paragraph, the lead or the beginning, is crucial to the story. The function of the lead is not only to summarize the story but also to attract readers to the story. It sets the tone and the temper of the story. The news story should have the most important points in the first paragraph, but the temptation to 'tell' too many things in the introduction should be avoided.

Brevity is the quality of presentation of news. In the news story there is not much scope for subsidiary and background material. The news is written in terse, concise and matter-of-fact manner. There is not much room for colour, ornamentation, or dramatization. It is a hurriedly written piece to meet the deadline. Since it is limited to time and place, no attempt should be made to make it a self-contained story.

Typical Style

Every news agency or newspaper follows its own 'style'. But a few general guidelines, in regard to the style of writing, are given below:

1. Use short words, short sentences, short paragraphs-and produce a clean copy.
2. Avoid needless adjectives so that the risk of exaggeration or under-estimation is eliminated. Distinguish between factual and propagatory material which is available from your sources whether official or non-official.
3. Guard against word-wasting abstractions.
4. Where there is no risk of ambiguity or awkwardness, drop the point from groups of initials such as CIP, SP, IAF, PIB and AIR. But where confusion may occur, use points as in U.N. (United Nations), U.S. (United States), W.H.O. (World Health Organization).
5. Do not abbreviate names, use Mohammed (not Mohd.), Choudhary (not Ch.).
6. The standard abbreviations are:

   kg, km, kw, kv (for both singular and plural); Mr., Mrs., Dr. (preceding a name); Jr., Sr. (following a name); Academic degree: B.A., M.A., M.S., Ph.D., M.D.; M.P. (Member of Parliament); GMT (Greenwich Mean Time),

(Indian Standard Time), Hrs. (hours); For ships: M.V. JAL JAWAHAR (Motor Vessel) or S.S. AKBAR (Steamship); I.P.C. (Indian Penal Code), Cr. P.C. (Criminal Procedure Code).

7. Do not abbreviate the days of the week, and the months of the year in the body of the copy. Similarly, use Rupees, not Rs. except in tables.

8. Use the following abbreviations for Service ranks: Lieutenant—Lt; Lieutenant Commander—Lt Cdr; Commander—Cdr; Captain—Capt; Major—Maj; Lieutenant—Colonel—Lt Col; Colonel—Col; Brigadier—Brig; Major General—Maj Gen; Lieutenant General—Lt Gen; General—Gen; Flight Sergeant—Flt Sgt; Flight Lieutenant—Flt Lt; Squadron Leader—Sqn Ldr; Wing Commander—Wg Cdr; Group Captain—Group Capt; Commodore—Cmdr; Warrant Officer—WO.

   In the first instance, the rank should be given in full.

9. Except May, June and July, the months are to be abbreviated in dateline: JAN, FEB, MAR, APR, AUG, SEP, OCT, NOV, DEC.

The months of the year and the days of the week are, however not abbreviated in the body of the copy.

10. Use October 30 and not 30th October as a way of style.
11. Calendar years to be mentioned in full: 1966 (not 66) and financial year: 1976-77.
12. Except in quotes, the time should be rendered on the basis of 24 hour cycle. Use 1115 hrs and 2130 hrs.
13. GMT time should be converted into IST and both should be mentioned-occurred at 1100 hrs IST (0530 hrs GMT).
14. All editing should be done in capital letters only. Heavily edited copy should be retyped.
15. Type 'no' and 'now' twice. Also type twice uncommon names of persons and places, Example: "He said now

now..." This is to ensure "now" does not appear as 'no' in transmission, which happens quite often.

16. Numbers up to eleven should be spelt out and beyond that in figures. For money use lakhs and crores, not millions. However, for expressing the number of men and other things use millions. For example: A grant of rupees five lakhs.. ., but 5,00,000 people (in figure)... six million shoes... 96.50 million tonnes of foodgrains.
17. Except when confusion is likely to result, the following are not put in quotes: names of newspapers or magazines; trade names; makes or models of cars and aircraft; sports events or trophies; fictional or stage character; ships or pets; names of royal, official or historical houses and castles.
18. The following are normally put in quotes: nicknames or pennames; titles of books, poems, songs, plays and films; private houses or properties in general.
19. Avoid abbreviations like i.e., e.g., n.b., viz., etc. and use their equivalents: that is; for example; note carefully; namely; and so forth.
20. Do not use in the copy trade names for the products of the same type manufactured by others. Use words like detergent powder (not surf); transparent wrapping (not cellophane); vacuum flask (not thermos); synthetic fabric (not terylene); petroleum jelly (not vaseline); aspirin (not aspro) and edible oil (not vanaspati).

Released News

The term press release is generally used for releases covering news. The press release should contain worthwhile material which has some news value. It will not only mean unnecessary expenditure but will also damage the reputation of the concerned Publicity/ Information Department if the release is based on a very trivial matter.

A press release should be written in journalistic style. It should provide facts or information of interest to the readers and should attempt to cover all aspects of a specific subject. There should not be any loose end. The press release should be on a current subject or which is in news. The release should not be generally lengthy. It should be concise and to the point. It has not much scope for subsidiary or background material. The release should be a piece of clear writing without any ambiguity, without any effort towards colour or ornamentation. The drafting should be done in a manner that if the last paragraphs are deleted by the newspaper, no damage is done to the news story in the press release.

The introduction or lead should be in a summary format as we have in a news story. The relative value of the various ingredients of the subject in the press release are weighed and evaluated and the most pertinent portion of them are included in the lead.

The releases should have a consistent format. Generally, the name of the organization from where the release emanates, is given on the top. The date and place are indicated on the top right side. The release should have a title and a sub-title also, if necessary. It should have a suitable introductory paragraph. In the case of releases from non-official organizations, it is also desirable to mention the designation of the person issuing the release and his telephone number.

The press releases covering news in the case of government are mainly of four types-Press Communiques, Press Notes, Hand-outs, and Unofficial Hand-outs.

The press communiques are issued when some important government decisions or announcements are made, such as cabinet appointments, conclusion of the foreign dignitaries' visit, international agreements, etc. The press communique is formal in character. It carries the name of the Ministry or Department and place and date at the bottom left hand corner of the press release.

Generally, the press is expected to reproduce the press communique without any substantial change. No heading or sub-heading is given.

The second category of press release is press notes. The press notes are less formal in character. These are also issued on important official matters, e.g., raising or lowering of tariff rates, etc. The press note also carries the name of the Ministry or Department and place and date at the bottom left-hand corner. Headings or sub-headings are given in press notes. Unlike the press communique, the newspapers can edit or condense the press note. Both the press communique and the press note are the responsibility of the government department and not that of the Press Information Bureau (PIB), the Central government agency which deals with the press on behalf of all ministries and departments of the Government of India, nor that of they State Directorates of Public Relations/ Information, which deal with the State government departments.

The third category of press release is hand-outs. The hand-outs are issued on a variety of subjects like the day-to-day activities of the ministry or departments, VIP speeches, questions and answers in Parliament, etc. The hand-out is a less formal type of release and not issued under the government's formal authority. It covers the name of the PIB or other releasing agency on the top without any mention of the ministry or department to which the release pertains. One of the important common categories of hand-outs relates to speeches of ministers or other high officials. Hand-out is issued only when the speech is related to the governmental activity. No official hand-out is issued, if the minister has spoken in his personal capacity as a member of a political organization. The place and date are indicated on top at right-hand side.

The speech, when released to the press in the form of a hand-out, is summarized and properly edited. Formal introductory and concluding remarks, are omitted and redundant and repetitive material taken out. Proper title and sub-title are given. The important aspect or aspects, which are to be stressed, are included in the introductory paragraph or in the lead. The full text of the speech is not released unless the subject is of very great importance.

While covering inaugural and other functions, where VIPs make speeches, the press release should stress on the significance of the function, and try to spell out in concrete terms the benefits it gives to the community rather than reproducing the speech. For instance, the opening of a new branch of a bank or of a power house at a particular place should be an opportunity to the communicator to bring out in the press release the specific gains which would accrue to the people of that area rather than spotlighting on the dignitary and his speech.

The speech of the Prime Minister or of a very important dignitary, on formal occasions or at important gatherings, is generally released in full to ensure correct reporting. The full text is also helpful to the editors and column writers. It is also utilized for reference purposes in the future. If the speech of the Prime Minister or the dignitary is extempore, advance arrangements will have to be made for reporters and tape-recorders.

Unofficial hand-outs are issued on a subject where the government would not like to assume official responsibility in the matter, but feels that there may be a positive advantage in making the information public unofficially. These hand-outs are supplements to oral briefings. These are given across the table to press correspondents and no general release is made. The unofficial hand-outs would not have the imprint of the PIB or other releasing agency. The date and place are indicated at the bottom left-hand corner.

The Press Information Bureau and the State Information Departments handle press relations work on behalf of the Central and State governments respectively. The PIB provides information to the press on government activities; it feeds Indian and foreign correspondents with news and background material, and keeps the government informed of press and public reaction to governmental activities. It endeavours to give special assistance to small newspapers in regional languages.

There is a positive advantage in having centralized releases on behalf of the different departments at one point. It is convenient to press representatives. It also guards against release of material pertaining to one ministry or department, which is critical or contradictory or not in good taste of other departments. The Press Information Bureau and the State Public Relations Departments are in a position to take an overall view of the functioning of the government, and as such can provide effective coordination.

Various Handouts

There are many other forms of releases, which do not cover news but give information in an indirect way and help in building the image of the government or an organization. More widely-known releases of this type are backgrounders, biographical sketches, contradictions, articles and features, newsletters, releases on reports, broadcast talks, etc.

Contradiction or denial of news story is to be issued only when - there is a serious mistake or the facts in the story are patently incorrect. Since denials give more publicity, it should be avoided as far as possible, particularly when the story is substantially correct. The best way for the publicist is to publish a positive story after a lapse of some time. The opportunity should be utilized to present a correct statement of facts without referring to what has been incorrectly published in the past. Negative statement or refutation of a news story, except in very exceptional circumstances, is not a good strategy.

Background material providing additional information and useful details is essential for journalists, newspapers and periodicals. Events should be anticipated and necessary background material is prepared well in advance. It may also be supplied on ad hoc requests. The backgrounder should be a self-contained release as far as possible. It would be useful for leader and column writers. The backgrounder should give a detailed run-down for better appreciation of decisions or activities.

Whenever the government or other reports are to be given to the press, it is necessary that a summary should also be released, which should be brief. The constructive side of the report is to be highlighted in the summary. Out of these reports, self-contained items can be taken out and released separately. If a report that is to be presented to Parliament, it should be ensured that it is not given to the press before it has been distributed to members of Parliament, or laid on the Table of either House of Parliament.

The press release from business houses also follows more or less the same format. It should also include the name of the organization, address, name of the concerned officer, telephone number, etc. to facilitate the work of the newspaper representative to get speedy clarification and additional information, if required.

No payment is required to be paid to newspapers if the releases, discussed above, are published in newspapers.

In these releases, the name of releasing agency is given at the top. The place and date are indicated on top right-hand side. The type of release is mentioned in a box on top left-hand side. Title and sub-title are also given.

One important point to remember is about the timing of the releases. If the publicist wants to reach both 'dak' ('dak' editions are meant for outstations and up-country centres and, therefore, printed earlier in the evening) and city editions of the newspapers, the release must be in the hands of the news editor by noon, latest. Even when the objective is to get into city edition only, it is a good policy to send the release before 1500 hrs. In certain cases, the copy can be sent a day in advance with an embargo put both at the top and at the bottom of the release. Embargo is to be indicated in either of the two ways: (i) For publication/ broadcast on or after___________hours on___________20 ;or (ii) Not to be published/ broadcast before___________hours on___________20

Newspapers have a lot of prepared material for the magazine section of their Sunday editions. As such, it will not be in the publicist's interest to send unimportant items on Saturday, Sunday and other holidays. It is preferable to send such items on other than these days for publication. Through the technique of embargo, the publicist can release his story simultaneously from different centres in the country. While putting the embargo, the requirements of radio should also be taken into consideration. For instance, when it is desired that the embargo story is to appear in papers, say, on Saturday morning, the embargo should only be for the Friday evening, so that the news can be used in radio news bulletins on Friday evening.

3

Sources of News

In the last two decades there has been a lot of controversy regarding the journalist and his professional privileges. The most interesting and controversial of these is "should a journalist publishing any information be compelled to disclose in a court of law, the source of his information, when it has been given to him in confidence and with the implied understanding that the source would not be disclosed?" This question has caught the attention of people in the profession, the courts, academicians and others. Simply stated the controversy seems to be between the duty of a citizen to give evidence in a court of law on matters relevant to the trial in that court and the duty of a journalist to his own profession.

The Awareness

All well-informed citizens are aware that they should support the administration of justice by attending the courts and giving evidence when duly summoned. In our country this is implicit in the scheme of the Indian Evidence Act, 1972. The duty to testify at judicial proceedings has been recognised early in the development of English Law. Even the Supreme Court of the U.S.A. has acknowledged it. However, there also exists a conflicting duty for the journalists, which requires the source of their information to remain undisclosed, at least when it is supplied in confidence.

If we examine the issue further, we find that the conflict is neither between lawyers and journalists, nor between newspapers and courts, but between courts and news reporters. Both believe themselves to be dedicated to one object, "discovering the truth." It is as agonising for a judge to have relevant information withheld from him, on a plea of crown privilege, as it is for the reporter to find facts, painfully elicited by him on a promise of secrecy, ruthlessly laid bare in a court. While there are different types of "privileges," in the field of evidence, a privilege is said to exist when "one is not obliged to answer particular questions or to produce particular documents." Evidentiary privilege has a long history. During the Roman Empire, neither advocates, nor physicians were allowed to testify during trials of former clients. Clergymen were also not compelled to appear in courts because of the high social status enjoyed by them. This practice was adopted by Anglo-Saxon England, continuing till the late eighteenth century. After that, the only privileged relationship that became a part of the English common law and continues till today, is the professional relationship between the attorneys and their clients.

Scene in Different Countries

In the Indian Evidence Act, 1872, a witness is compilable to answer all relevant questions pertaining to particular litigation in a court of law. This Act confers no privilege on a reporter in regard to disclosing the source of his information. Therefore, a reporter or any other journalist cannot, in a court of law, claim such a privilege. Although, there are probably no reported decisions on the subject, the legal position is fairly well established and is borne out by at least two incidents that took place in India in the past where journalists preferred court punishment rather than reveal the identity of their contributors. In one such case, Kaliprasanna Kavyavisharad, Editor of the *Hitavada* declined to disclose the name of the writer of a poem published in his paper for which he was charged with lebel. The manuscript was produced in court, with the portion bearing the name of the author torn off. He was consequently jailed for nine months.

The other case was of Bipin Chandra Pal, who was sentenced to six months imprisonment because he refused to disclose the author of an article for which Aurobindo Ghose was being tried for sedition. Pal was sent to jail for six months for refusing to depose as to the above fact though Aurobindo Ghose was subsequently acquitted.

Position in England and Australia : In England, there is no privilege for a journalist in regard to his source of information. Recently, there have been some cases in which journalists had to face the legal consequences of their professional obligation. In 1963, two journalists—one from the *Daily Sketch* and the other from the *Daily Mail* preferred to go to jail for defying the order of the Radcliffe Tribunal. They refused to disclose the source of their information about the leakage of certain Admiralty secrets in the famous "Vassal Scandal." When the case was reported to the High Court, the Lord Chief Justice Parker sentenced both the correspondents to six months imprisonment, though recognising the conflict between the sense of honor of a journalist and his duty to the State.

After the Vassal case there was a move in England to confer legal immunity on journalists, but nothing substantive has been done so far. In 1971, a BBC reporter went to jail rather than disclose the identity of an IRA member interviewed by him. The House of Lords has ruled as recently as August, 1980 that Granada Television, one of the major commercial companies of Britain, must name the informant relating to the case against state owned British Steel Corporation. Though Granda Television maintained it would appeal to the European Court of Human Rights, the House of Lord's decisiop was widely regarded as a major setback for investigative reporting in Britain, already badly hampered by stringent libel and contempt laws and security curbs.

In Australia it has been held that a journalist has no privilege against the disclosure of information to a Royal Commission, which has the power to demand such disclosure under the Evidence Act, 1928.

Position in U.S.A. : The existence and scope of a newsman's right as regards the disclosure of his source of information has received much attention in U.S.A. recently. There has been no federal legislation so far conferring the privilege on journalists although there have been many proposals on the subject.

Till 1970, sixteen States in the U.S.A. had made the legislative determination that "protection of the identities of newsmen's informants from disclosure before judicial and legislative proceedings was necessary in order to maintain a flow of information to the public and it would not unduly hamper the Judicial and Legislative process." The statutes enacted in the various States generally protect the confidential sources of persons connected with, engaged on, or employed by specified news media, while only three have defined the term "Newspaper." Three others apply the privilege to other periodicals also, seven apply it to Press Associations, six to Radio Stations. In twelve of the States recognising the privilege, it is absolute.

As there is no federal law as yet on the subject in America, an interesting case could be quoted. "The Caldwell Case" arose out of a statement made by the Black Panther leader Mr. David Hillard which appeared in the December, 1969 issue of the *New York Times,* under the byline of Earl Caldwell, a Black correspondent for *The Times,* who specialised in covering the Panthers. Two months later, a federal Grand Jury in San Francisco, investigating a broad range of Panther activities, served a subpeona on Mr. Caldwell ordering him to testify before the Grand Jury and to bring with him notes and tape recordings of his interviews with Panther leaders. Caldwell refused on the ground that he could not testify without irreparably damaging the confidential source relationships he had built up over the months. This was soon confirmed when Black militant sources in several cities refused to talk to the journalists from *The Times, Newsweek* and A.B.C. The federal district court judge ruled that "Mr. Caldwell was obliged to appear before the Grand Jury, but need not reveal confidential sources, associations or information, unless such statements or information were given to him for publication or public disclosure."

In the "Branzburg Case," Mr. Justice Douglas in his dissenting opinion observed, "The function of the press is to explore and investigate events, inform the people what is going on, to expose the harmful as well as the good influences at work."

As against all this, there has been criticism also of the privilege that "it might hinder the search for truth." But such hindrance from time to time would have to be endured in the greater public interest of protecting the source in order to invite the type of information that can only be secured confidentially. Secondly, the fact that even now journalists prefer to go to jail rather than disclose sources indicates that the mechanisms used are rather ineffective. A statute granting such privilege would be a declaration of public approval of confidential sources.

Furthermore, the privilege would be unique and different from other privileges. In all other privileges, it is the "communication" which is privileged, whereas in the case of a journalist, it is the "source" which is meant to be kept confidential. This may also be more helpful to the investigative process in the long run and to the administration of justice. In instances of Governmental corruption, the value of the press as a recipient of such information is particularly important.

To sum up, we could say that in all fairness to society and in the greater public interest such a privilege must be conferred on the newsmen in order to:—

(1) make a flow of free and undiluted information available to all times about matters of public interest.

(2) make the legal position of such informers secured.

(3) protect the people from State high-handedness or corruption in order to preserve the ideals of a true democracy.

(4) create an atmosphere of truth and forthrightness in the society to protect its people from all forms of corruption, exploitation and encroachment.

In order to achieve all these, the law must try to find a just compromise between conflicting interests, so that the journalist can conform to both of his duties as a citizen and as a professional person. The privilege should be carefully phrased in order to avoid its being misused.

The peace of 1919 was made in an atmosphere of hatred and the desire for revenge; economists saw that its financial provisions were unworkable, and that its vindictiveness would breed war. Mr. J. L. Garvin in the *Observer* was one of the few to point out publicly these and other disabilities. His prophecies have mostly been fulfilled by the rise of Nazi-ism, intensified nationalism and rearmament. There is the same difference Today between the views of the experts and those which appear in the Press. The most Nelsonian optimist can see that there are several problems needing a quick solution—unemployment, slums, traffic mortality, to say nothing of matters of foreign policy. Most educated people believe that workable solutions for our material ills exist: but they do not stand much chance of being tried, because the mass of voters who decide upon the character of our governments have never even heard of them. For this the Press is largely responsible, because it suppresses or distorts all but 'safe' views and accepted theories.

The question is sometimes asked "What can be done about it" and it would be cowardly to say that there is no answer and that nothing can be done. To say that the first thing is to understand it fully sounds platitudinous, but a clear understanding of the problem shows some of the directions where a start can be made. "The real problem of the 'stunt Press' consists not in the mischievous ingenuity of this or that journalistic pander, but in certain social, psychological and industrial conditions." It is often said: "A single person can do nothing about it; it's hopeless." If it is hopeless, it is because so many relapse into that attitude. The shirking of responsibility adds power to the Press. It flourishes on acquiescence. The Press can become an insult to its readers, but because readers take this treatment lying down they help to perpetuate it. The longer the Press continues in its present ways, the more difficult it will be to improve. It has created a taste for, its product, and it reinforces and mobilises emotions and attitudes which had never found such a mouthpiece before. The problem is not simple, but unless each person plays his or her part, nothing can be done. (Compare the accident problem on the roads.) The ways in which he will exert his influence will differ. The Press is a public institution for which we pay willy-nilly; we should aim at making it provide as good service as the Post Office. Some people will try to follow up the implications of Norman Angell's dictum, just quoted. Some will be able to note cases of inaccuracy, suppression and other practices, and will make these known to the papers themselves, both the guilty one and its rivals. Newspaper managements are sometimes very sensitive to public opinion, and a number of determined readers could make them more so. (The churches and other bodies are feeble here; the three of an organised boycott of the products advertised in a particular paper would soon modify its behaviour.) Others will find opportunities in education. Journalists themselves, as is shown by one of the examples in the Case Book, are aware of the defects of the Press, but the controllers' ideas of what the public wants prevent them from doing much to improve the papers they work for.

The Expectations

It is also important that we should decide what we want from the Press. First of all, news, and if necessary, a context of information to make the news intelligible. That sounds obvious enough, but, as I hope to show, the presentation and selection of news is not satisfactory. Selection there must be, because of the great bulk of matter which comes into the office; but we should require that the selection should be made in accordance with an intelligent standard of what matters and what does not. Ideally we would expect that papers of opposed views should choose the same items for the main page; and that they should withhold no relevant information. The paper's political and economic views should be expressed mainly in the editorial columns or special articles, without colouring the news. We need hardly expect a paper to be impartial—that is impossible—but we have the right to know from what angle the news is selected, and what interests the paper is serving. In short the news should give an accurate and balanced account of what is happening, and the comment enable the reader to come to an opinion without suspending rational judgment.

"The *Morning Post*—Independent of Everything" (an advertisement).

"Newspapers which are not free are much better unpublished." *Daily Mail*, 3 May, 1926.

"The *Daily Express* is not run for the prime purpose of making profits. This newspaper is a public institution, which in the national interest sacrifices money to the main plan of serving the public." (Advertisement, signed 'Beaver brook.')

Newspapers do not exist to give news. Their purpose is to make profits from advertisement revenue, which enables a paper costing two-pence to be sold for a penny. All consumers lose by this; those who buy dailies get something which is not exactly a newspaper, though it can be argued that advertisements pay for a news-collecting machine of amazing technical efficiency. Those who never buy papers pay for them all the same every time they buy their advertised stockings or soap. To get advertisements large circulations are needed, and the policy of the paper tends to be determined by the fight for readers. Some provincial papers, however, are not interested in raising circulation, as in their case of increased cost of printing more copies would necessitate the raising of advertising rate higher than they could afford to maintain them. The chairman of Allied Newspapers put it in a more dignified manner when he said, at a company meeting: "A great group such as Allied Newspapers must be run on sound financial and commercial lines. In other words, I recognise that our first duty is to our shareholders." After that his Lordship discussed the responsibility of the Press toward national life. In the struggle for circulation important considerations receive less attention than they ought to—truth, quality of comment, sometimes even the foibles of the controller. There are of course exceptions to these generalisations; there are one or two small circulation papers run at a loss or a very small margin.

Another feature of the modern newspaper, exemplified especially in the *Daily Express* and its success, is that it tries to do far more for its reader than the news-sheet of a hundred years ago. It gives him not only news and comment, but also free insurance, notes on motoring and gardening, how to keep fit, how to look beautiful, how to behave in courtship, marriage and relations with other people, guides to reading and entertainments, crossword puzzles and so on, besides pages of advertisements. All this has a bearing on the making of opinion; readers' interests are affected by the amount of space given to various items. The pages taken up by sport fill columns which might be given to more important news and articles; they develop in the reader too great an attention to sport and keep him from vital contact with the world. This interest has been so developed that the news agencies have been known to instruct their correspondents to cut down important foreign news because a test match was in progress.

There is obviously something to be said for this widening of the newspaper's scope, but the disadvantage is that we get less real news, less explanation and comment upon it. The main happenings are often very well reported, though how little news is obtainable under difficult conditions was shown in the Abyssinian War. But however accurately events may be reported, such news means little by itself. During that war some weeklies of comparatively small circulations did supply what was wanted, articles filling the background and explaining its meaning in terms of Italy's economic problems and Mussolini's political needs and its implications for British Interests. Some of the daily and Sunday papers gave the impression that the issue was simple— between Christianity, equated with western civilization, and backward and brutal heathenism. It is easy to list more recent examples; it was not easy in 1938 for an unprejudiced reader to get a clear view of the rights and wrongs of the Sudeten problem, and after Franco's victory it was still more difficult to come across any information about the state of Spain.

Whole Truth

No newspaper can give the whole truth even if it wants to. A wealthy newspaper will have correspondents in most of the capitals, and many of these have done excellent work, but for the bulk of foreign news it must depend upon the agencies. Some of these may have an interest in emphasising or concealing certain items, they may be influenced by a particular government and will try to make the news fit that government's policy. Or an agency may have connections with financial or advertising interests.

In foreign crises most papers have their own correspondents on the spot, and they often send in excellent reports. Frequently, however, the accounts have to be sent ready coloured to match the character of the paper which commissions them. The demand for speed and yet greater speed means that unverified reports are printed in large type, with no mention of the qualifications that the correspondent may have stressed. Often such reports are proved next day to be baseless or exaggerated, but the denial or correction, if any, will be put in small print in a neglected corner of the paper, if it is published at all. It is the impression made on the reader by the original rumour that nearly always remains. Tension between nations is only one result of this manipulation of the news at the source.

Recently for example it was reported that Germany had presented an ultimatum to Rumania, and that Englishwomen had been evacuated from Malta. Neither report was confirmed, but both contributed a little to the nervousness which makes it easier for wars to start. The remedy for this is not suppression or censorship of news, such as the dictators would like to see operating in the democracies. The correspondents on the spot are not necessarily to be blamed for misleading reports; they depend for their livelihood on supplying the demand for human interest, coloured news, and above all, speed.

The case of the Zinovieff letter exemplifies the way in which the publication of a false or unconfirmed report may alter the course of history. In 1924 the newspapers printed an account of a letter supposed to have been sent to the British Communist Party from the Executive Committee of the Communist International. In the words of the Foreign Office, it contained "instructions to British subjects to work for the violent overthrow of existing institutions in this country, and for the subversion of His Majesty's armed forces as a means to that end." The previous year the Soviet Government had undertaken not to support in any way agencies which aimed at spreading discontent in the British Empire and as the Communist International was in close touch with the Russian Government the letter if genuine was evidence of Russian bad faith. The Soviet representative denounced the document as a gross forgery and argued that on internal evidence it was a tissue of absurdities. The Labour Party in this country had been anxious for closer relations with Russia and the publication of the letter gave its opponents valuable and timely ammunition; "the utter defeat of the Labour Government at the elections was unquestionable in substantial measure furthered by the discovery." (A. B. Keith, editor of *Speeches and Documents on International Affairs, 1918-1937*.)

In the newspaper office all news has to pass through the hands of the sub-editors, who are nearly as important as the advertising department. They select, reject, or present the news to suit the policy of their paper—or rather its requirements; because one or two popular papers are guided not by policy but by the need to provide entertainment. In the arrangement of the news the Press has very great power, and few papers use it scrupulously. News which might depress the shares of a company associated with the particular paper will not be printed—unless it is so important that competitors stress it, in which case it will be given a quiet corner off the main pages. A daily may be linked with the banks; no adverse criticism of the banking system will ever appear. The big industrial assurance companies, too, have sufficient influence on the Press to ensure that nothing damaging to them is ever published. Again there may be exceptions to this if the news is interesting enough; the case of Mrs. Borders against a building society was featured by newspapers which draw revenue from the advertisements of such societies.

The whim of the controller may cause the works of a novelist, clergyman or economist to be excluded from mention, though in the case of very prominent figures an occasional slighting notice has to be permitted. As Lord Baldwin observed a few years ago, "The newspapers conducted by Lord Rothermere and Lord Beaver brook are not newspapers in the ordinary acceptance of the term. They are engines of propaganda for the constantly-changing policies, personal wishes, personal likes and personal dislikes of two men. What are their methods. Their methods are direct falsehood, misrepresentation, half-truths, the alteration of the speaker's meaning by putting sentences apart from the context, suppression and editorial criticism of speeches which are not reported in the paper. What the proprietorship of these papers is aiming at is power, but power without responsibility—the prerogative of the harlot throughout the ages."

The degree of personal control is a little exaggerated here. The controllers do of course influence their papers' policies, and may for instance telephone twelve words to be written up into an article or leader by the staff. But they will always change their tunes if circulation or other considerations demand it. It was entertaining to watch the face-about of certain penny papers when they realised that Hitler's aims were not all compatible with the interests of the British Empire; it was as complete and rapid as that of Mr. Churchill, who at the time this is being written is demanding a firm and immediate alliance with the government which a few years ago he denounced as "this foul reptilian regime."

The nominally respectable journals are not always more careful in this respect than the so-called gutter press. Or worse, because few people trust the popular paper, whereas the soberer organs can trade on their reputations to mislead their readers. "Critic" of the *New Statesman and Nation* wrote:

> General Crozier would have been furious at the patronising evasions of *The Times* obituary notice of him. What business has *The Times* to say that "In kindness to him his last book, *The Men I Killed*, which appeared last month, is best forgotten?" It said clearly

> what Crozier wanted this generation to understand. After a lifetime of fighting he wanted people to know that the horror of war lies not so much in its suffering as in its indiscriminate stupidity; he wanted people to know that it had been his duty as a much decorated and very brave soldier (which even *The Times* admits him to have been) to shoot his own men as well as the Germans. Such things happen in war. *The Times* also slurred over the facts about his retirement. He left the army (thereby just forfeiting his pension) because he insisted on punishing British looting in Ireland during the black-and-tannery period, and was overruled by the British Command which did not then apparently mind what was done to the Irish or what happened to the morale of the British Army. *The Times* also says that Crozier "became a professional lecturer and writer for the League of Nations," and says nothing of the fact that he was a strong opponent of the League of Nations, who during the last period of his life spent his entire time working with Dick Sheppard on the Peace Pledge Union. During the last years of his life Crozier put the whole of his tough fighting energy into building a movement to fight all war. I suppose *The Times* objects to facing the fact that war experience may make a man a pacifist. It would still like to pretend that pacifism is a synonym for cowardice.

It should be added that there were numerous protests against this notice, and that *The Times* eventually published a correction. In this connection it may be mentioned that on the other side the pacifist *Peace News* appeared at one time to lay too much stress on news excusing Hitler's attitude over the Sudeten question and later to minimize facts about the sufferings of those in territory occupied by Hitler. There are plenty of examples of illogical thinking and misrepresentation in Fascist, Communist and Pacifist journals, but here circulations are negligible, they preach only to be converted, and motives are undisguised.

A few years ago the *Daily Express* ran a campaign against the Co-operative Societies, charging them with dumping Russian wheat, with not paying income tax, aiming at revolution, etc.; on this the *Twentieth Century* for May, 1932, commented: "The Directory of Directors shows that Mr. William May, who is chairman of the Home and Colonial Stores is also a director of the *Daily Express* Building Company Limited, and London Express Newspapers Limited. The Home and Colonial Stores is probably the largest company of its kind in England and an important competitor of the co-operative societies."

A principle we can observe working everywhere is that any news or comment tending to discredit the *status quo* must be eliminated. The newspapers thrive under the present economic system, and however corrupt or inefficient that system is, it must be held up for approval. Unrest in an industrial area, the spread of Communism, sweated labour, the growth of a pacifist body, all will be kept out or minimized. Accordingly anything that tends to glorify the *status quo* is stressed. This has a more immediate connection with a paper's welfare. Advertisement revenue can only be obtained if consumers are spending freely, and they will only do so if they feel cheerful and confident; the Press then cannot afford to be radically disquieting. "The death of His Majesty King George V ... the Abyssinian War... war in Spain . . . the abdication . . . caused in varying degree, depression, uncertainty and unsettlement which had an adverse effect on the business world, and caused in several cases a cancellation of advertising." (Hon. R. E. Beckett, chairman of a company owning the *Yorkshire Post.)* The Press must behave like the multiple grocery shops, where butter is always "down Today." In *Property or Peace* Mr. H. N. Brailsford gives from his own experience as an editor a very revealing account of the pressure brought to bear on newspapers.

News Distortion

I. Inside the citadel, the garrison gallantly awaited its fate, but with nerves at breaking point, knowing that at any moment the mine might be sprung.

Their one hope was that the anti-Red column, under Colonel Tejeiros, which is marching on Toledo, might arrive in time. But it was 14 miles away, held up by the strong Red concentrations this morning.

The Reds made no secret of the time they intended to explode their mine.

All night long sirens sounded, and a few minutes after dawn the final preparations were made.

A last ultimatum was rejected by the garrison, who, it is stated, were invited to evacuate the women and children from the building.

But the defenders under Colonel Moscardun adhered to their declaration of a few days ago that they all preferred "to die inside the Alcazar rather than outside it"—an indication apparently that they mistrusted the intentions of the Reds towards themselves and their families. *Daily paper, 19 September, 1936.*

II. Crazed with the creed of Bolshevism, without pity, without mercy for women and children, the Reds in Spain have blown to fragments the Alcazar at Toledo. This noble building, nobly defended, succumbs at last.

Within the garrison, a remnant of which is still gallantly holding out, there were 400 women and children. Their presence, at least, might have stayed the Red hand. Instead, these outer barbarians gloated over the approaching doom. They counted the hours till Madrid should signal massacre.

Readers of the *Daily Mail* will be sickened, but they cannot be surprised, by this Red war on women. From the first we have told the world the truth about the wolves which tear at the throat of Spain.

Only yesterday we printed more attested records of the deeds which the Moscow-incited rabble have blackened the name of Spain. Their acts are monstrous, demented, the very ecstasy of cruelty.

Another part of same paper, same date.

III. By the capture of Toledo the heroism of the anti-Reds (nightly slandered by the B.B.C. as 'rebels') has struck a decisive blow in the fierce struggle with the dark forces of anti-Christianity and brutal violence. There are few more thrilling episodes in military history than the magnificent defence of the Alcazar in the teeth of every form of attack.

The shambles of the Alcazar will not be in vain. The memory of the women and children and cadets who heroically perished will steel the Patriots in their cleansing task and goad them to sterner endeavours.

Nor will the dreadful message of Toledo be lost if the world at last digests the peril of the Red-manipulated "Popular Front," and the nature of the doctrine that Moscow disseminates.

The feeble moderates who aspired to govern Spain were instantly swept aside when the hour struck for these dastards and assassins trained by Russia.

Inevitably the history of such governments repeats itself. They begin with a slobber of good intentions and end with the overthrow of religion, and the reign of murder, rape, and chaos.

Same paper, 29 September, 1936.

Consistency evidently is not one of this journal's strong points. In I the garrison holds out, in II the building "succumbs at last," in III, ten days later, the garrison is relieved. (It reminds one of the riddle, "Which is the largest city in Europe? Madrid, because it took Franco a year to march through the suburbs." According to newspaper placards it fell thrice in 1936.) Few people have time regularly to test news by comparison; but one can assay reliability on internal evidence, just as to a certain extent one takes into account a speaker's manner in estimating his trustworthiness.

I is written in short paragraphs, in a semi-dramatic style. A plain recital of facts would leave the reader to his own feelings: instead, he must be made to respond with a thrill. (The short paragraphing is also intended to make the matter easily assimilable.) Then there is the mere slovenliness of the writing, shown in the slick alliteration (used also sometimes for emphasis, sometimes to carry the reader along without inspecting the meaning) of "garrison . . . gallantly," "crazed creed," etc., and in the tautology of "last ultimatum." There is a sprinkling of cliches, stock phrases which have lost their edge through being so long in use, and if found in quantity an indication that a writer has nothing fresh to say. Thus garrisons, if they are on the right side, are always gallant (that comes twice), nerves are at breaking point, blows are decisive, and so on.

Again, the terms 'Red' and 'Bolshevik' rouse suspicion. They are applied to the forces of a government of Liberals and Socialists, but these words are of no use to the writer because they are factual, and are not, like 'Red' and 'Bolshevik,' powerfully charged with hatred and fear. Since they are not given the context of the news, the readers cannot be expected to know that the government supporters are no more all Communists after the Russian model than Franco's adherents are Fascists of the German type: but they have been schooled to pop their eyes and run for cover at the mention of 'Red,' so that to use these misnomers for the Spanish is simpler and disposes of them far more effectively than rational argument.

A vicious result of much political propaganda is the simplification of issues. The supporters of the approved side are lily-white in virtue; the others are black with sin. This is clearly sentimental and obscures the truth. In very rare contests is the cause of the one side entirely good and the other bad, and in none are the antagonists angelic and diabolic respectively. In Spanish affairs one set of propagandists presented the forces of freedom and Christianity struggling against atheistical and tyrannical Bolshevism, while some government supporters made the issue one of democracy and enlightenment against Fascist bullies and reactionaries. (This is not to say that both sides were equally wrong, or to suggest that one should have adopted an attitude of indifference. As a contrast to the quotations above, Sr. Semprun Gurrea's *A Catholic Looks at Spain* provides an example of writing which takes sides without losing balance or causing confusion.)

Such distortion, which is not confined to the million-sale dailies, obscures the real issues, and aggravates the passions involved, thus creating an atmosphere which makes any settlement impossible. This labelling habit of mind is often exemplified in conversation. It is evident also in political cartoons; 'capitalists' on the one hand are depicted as potbellied and heartless ogres, while in other papers pacifists and Socialists are lumped together as feckless and inefficient busybodies. In this way is fostered the futile habit of trying to solve problems by finding a scapegoat.

Instead of argument and facts, the papers quoted employed abuse and hysterical appeals to feeling. As for the "war on women and children," that is horrible enough, but is it very much worse than war on men? (One assumes that the Franco forces had a special kind of bomb which hits only men.) Such indiscriminate attacks are part of the theory and practice of modern war, and it is worse than silly to indulge in emotional appeals unless you try to do something to make such warfare less possible. This newspaper's contribution has been for years to agitate for more and faster bombers.

One or two minor examples may be added. Two high-class Sunday papers report a university debating society:

> The motion . . . "That this House would welcome the return of a Labour Government," was carried by 132 votes to 119. The distinguished visitors were Dr. Hugh Dalton and Mr. Geoffrey Shakespeare.

The motion under debate was "That this House would welcome the return of a Labour Government." The visiting speakers were Lieut.Col. R. Fletcher, M.P. for Nuneaton, and Mr. Geoffrey Shakespeare and here are examples of what can be done by newspaper loyalty:

Queen walks five miles at the Fair. *News Chronicle.* The Queen's six-mile tour of B.I.F. *Morning Post.* Queen's seven-mile walk round B.I.F. *North Mail.* The Queen walks eight miles at British Industries Fair. *Yorkshire Herald.*

27 September, 1937, the *Daily Mirror* reported that the Duke and Duchess of Windsor arrived in Paris "without a cheer, without a smile from the dozen curious English and Americans who saw them arrive." The *Daily Express*, on the other hand, said "More than 400 Parisians welcomed their old 'Prince Charming.' With them were groups of British and Americans. . . . An American woman called out 'Long live the American Duchess.' The crowd cheered and the Duke waved." As *World's Press News* pertinently commented, "Maybe somebody was at the wrong station."

But considering the conditions under which newspapers are produced, the standard of accuracy in matters of fact is high, and it would be unreasonable to attach too much importance to the discrepancies quoted. Such mis-statements can often be excused, and are not to be compared with more serious misrepresentation.

News Suppression

The following newspaper reports of the same date are from the *Daily Mail* and the *Eastern Daily Press* respectively:

The Prince of Wales at a Vienna Cabaret

The Prince of Wales (second from right) watching a cabaret performance at the Femina during his stay in Vienna, which he left yesterday for Budapest. He proposes to return to-morrow, and to visit the Semmering Mountains on Saturday. II.

After a visit lasting just two and a half days the Prince of Wales left Vienna this afternoon for Budapest. ... It is reported that he may pay a visit to the winter sports resort of Semmering, near Vienna, on his return journey to London, where he is due on Thursday next week.

The Prince's last morning in Vienna was spent in a visit to the model working-class flats which the city has constructed as its solution for the slum problem. He was especially interested in the "Karl Marx Hof," Vienna's largest municipal building, which on February 12 last year was the headquarters of the Socialist insurgents and was attacked by the Government forces with artillery, resulting in much bloodshed and loss of life.

Today the scene was altogether peaceful, and the Royal visitor was shown the huge wash-house, where a thousand families were doing their washing, and the up-to-date kindergarten, the most modern in Vienna. (Only about half this report is quoted.)

The omission by the more popular paper of the Prince's interest in an apparently successful experiment in rehousing is unlikely to be accidental; it looks as if the aim is to avoid the inference "Why don't we have something of the same kind here?"

The reader is asked to consider a short questionnaire on two newspaper extracts of the same date. The first is slightly curtailed.

1. How do the two passages differ in manner, and is there any reason apparent for the difference?
2. Which report appears to be the more reliable?
3. What can be inferred about the characters of the two papers?

Powers Almost Agreed at Montreux

Agreement on the main points in dispute at the Dardanelles Conference is believed to be imminent following private talks between the delegates to-night. The British point that there should be no mention of mutual assistance pacts in the treaty is understood to have been conceded.

The talks, which threatened deadlock over the weekend, suddenly took a more hopeful turn Today following the arrival of a Foreign Office official with fresh instructions from London. The chief stumbling block was the claim by Soviet Russia, backed by France, Rumania and other Powers, that warships should have free passage through the Dardenelles not only when executing the League covenant against an aggressor but also in defence of mutual assistance pacts.

Britain urged that such a position would increase her commitments to an extent she could not accept. She asked that the reference to mutual assistance pacts should be dropped.

It is understood that this point will be conceded to Britain, and there will be no mention of pacts in the Treaty. Instead, some countries may make separate declarations or enter into special arrangements with Turkey.

The question of maintenance of the Straits Commission, another matter of disagreement, is still in suspense, but it is not likely to wreck the Conference. Other points on which agreement is expected to be reached shortly are. . . .

Dardanelles Deadlock

A complete deadlock has been reached on most of the vital questions before the conference here on the future of the Dardanelles.

A leading delegate told me to-night that, although the draft convention had been read through twice, all the important questions at issue were still referred back for further consideration.

Such procedure, he said, was almost unknown in international meetings of this importance.

Mr. G. Rendel, the British Foreign Office expert, who returned to Montreux Today with fresh instructions from the British Government, had long conversations with several of the delegates, but they do not appear to have brought the many problems before the conference any nearer solution.

It is now recognised that, without Italy, any new arrangement must inevitably be inoperative.

This afternoon the delegates visited the famous Castle of Chillon immortalised by Byron's poem. In the ancient Hall of the Knights, Lord Stanley and other delegates could be seen discussing the problems of the day, while Swiss girls made merry round a maypole.

Some recent and startling instances of suppression are recorded in *The English Press* and *Challenge to Death* (Constable). A pleasing minor example is noted in the PEP *Report on the British Press.*

The modern newspaper might be described as an ingenious device to prevent us receiving and understanding the real news. We have discussed the principle regulating the admission of matter; what it means in practice is not disguised by directors, editors and others. Kennedy Jones, one of the founders of the *Daily Mail,* said that what sold a newspaper was first, War, secondly, a State funeral, and third, a first-class murder. Another journalist wrote that the three guiding principles in journalism were (1) Money; (2) The Stomach; (3) Love; and yet another relates of Northcliffe: "Being so very human himself, he knew what would appeal to men and women. I remember that when I was acting as news editor of the *Daily Mail* he impressed upon me the fact that there were four subjects in which the public were always interested, Crime, Love, Money and Food." (Tom Clarke.) Now that we have schools of journalism the principles are codified and laid out in chart form for the guidance of learners; here are extracts from one:

***News* :** The basis of all that you write must be news—new facts, new points of view—and some of the most readily acceptable articles spring from

Basic Elements

***Money* :** It is our birthright that we must struggle for our existence—fight to make our living—and this heading covers many subjects.

***Food* :** An atmosphere of "Plenty" is good because it is stimulating: an atmosphere of "Want" is bad because it is depressing.

***Sex* :** "People" are always more interesting than "things." Hence the popularity of psychological articles—human subjects with a sex basis.

***Health* :** There is nothing we are so ready to discuss as our ailments, or the physical and mental recreations that keep us well.

In the original chart the headings branch out like a family tree into numerous kindred subjects.

Snobbery

Vienna, Saturday.

King Edward figured in an incident typical of him last night. As he was leaving the opera house a crowd of people greeted him with so much enthusiasm that in the throng a child was knocked down and injured on the knee.

The King saw the incident and had the child picked up and placed in his own car, which was driven off to the hotel where His Majesty is staying. The King had his young guest attended to, and he was later able to leave little the worse.

Vienna, Saturday.

It is officially stated that there is no truth in the report that a boy was injured by the King's car yesterday. No one was injured, and consequently no one was taken to hospital.

Reuter

The King in Vienna Car Accident

Vienna, Friday.

A boy of 13 was pushed by a surging crowd under the wheels of King Edward's car to-night as he was returning from the opera to his hotel.

The King was sitting back saluting the crowd as his car nosed its way carefully along the street. Suddenly there was a cry and the Royal car stopped with a jerk in time to avoid the boy.

The King had seen someone fall beneath the wheels. He jumped to the door and tried to force his way through the crowd. But in the excitement a dense mob had hemmed in the injured boy, and the King struggled in vain for several minutes to get through. He had to return to his car and order it to be driven back to the hotel.

Meanwhile, the boy had been taken to hospital, and the King's first order was for a member of his staff to go there to inquire about the patient.

The King was told that the boy had received cuts on the knee which had been stitched up, and had then been sent home. *The Times* and *Telegraph* had no mention of the incident.

This specimen of the way in which the Press makes copy out of Royalty might have gone under one of the earlier headings, it is so good an instance of invented news. Even without the other extracts one might surmise that the *Express* reporter had been rather too ubiquitous. ("The *Daily Express* aims to give its readers the finest news service in the world. Its reporters are everywhere. Today the *Daily Express* prints news from Madrid, from San Sebastian, from Nuremberg, from Moscow, from Lisbon—all interlocked in the story of these momentous days.") To begin with, the incident is just a little too true to type. The deification of Royalty requires that every action be exalted. If one had to invent a story about a king's stay in Vienna, this is just the kind of thing that could be made up by anyone in a hurry without much imagination. Naturally the crowd "surges," kings always "sit back and salute," royal cars invariably "nose their way." And so with the rest of it. The whole account is trite and obvious; there is not a scrap of convincing or circumstantial detail in it. Whether it happened or not we must say it did because it is the kind of thing people have been trained to expect of Royalty. The King of Sweden appears to be as democratic as any other monarch, and to be as much respected by his subjects; but neither the Swedes nor their papers think such adulation necessary.

In England, however, the Press and cinema invest the Royal Family with semi-divine qualities. When one reads of "royal weather" one is reminded of the savages who make a fetish of their chief, and believe that he can control the climate. The most trivial incident is magnified, the most obvious commonplace action is presented as something nearly superhuman . . . and yet after all so like the rest of us.

The Queen bent to check her daughters' whispers, turned the leaves of their service books and, with gentle touches, restrained the natural curiosity of the two children, as would any ordinary parent. *News-Chronicle.* The Duke of Kent had a thrill last night driving to a dinner at the Salters' Hall, St. Swithin's Lane, E.C. Another car travelling West pulled out from behind a van at the corner of Walbrook and Canon Street, E.C. The Duke applied his brakes hard, and brought the car almost to a standstill.

Daily Mirror.

There are various social, political and economic reasons why flunkeyism is carried to such lengths. One observer will say that Royalty, with its Jubilees and Coronations, is exploited for trade, another (bearing in mind the way in which Royalty is associated with the armed forces in films and pictures) that it is used to propaganda for rearmament, another that Royalty is staged to divert attention from the realities of poverty and unemployment. Whatever the reason, the excess of this servility should disgust anyone who has a serious belief in Royalty as an institution. Snobbery is an important ingredient quite apart from Royalty, but the finding of specimens and the consideration of reasons may be left to the reader.

Epics and Tragedies

Ocean flights, record attempts, feats of endurance are regularly 'splashed' in the Press. The competition for circulation necessitates a daily 'stunt,' something to put on the posters; and if the chief news item of the day is likely to be common to all papers, the one which can get the biggest thrill out of its readers will sell most. It need not of course be the most important item. An economic conference may be in session which may make good deal of difference to the peace and welfare of a continent. But you cannot make much 'copy' out of an economic conference, unless you hit on the idea that it is being manipulated by Reds, or find "human interest" in one of the delegates who has paralysed hands and types with his toes.

Some observers find a reason for the publication of exciting 'stories' in the fact that most readers do not derive much excitement from their lives and compensate for it by reading newspapers and detective fiction. A third reason for some of these record attempts, or at least for 'splashing' them, is commercial. Long-distance fliers need clothes, watches, and food, their planes are made of proprietary materials, and require many specialised parts. The makers of such goods think they are getting publicity if their products are used in such flights, and they are prepared to buy space in the Press. Thirty or more items were advertised a few years ago in connection with the Campbell-Scott flight. Here is a specimen of writing-up:"

"The boom of the starting gun—a roar—a glittering flashing bullet hurtling through space—a flash—and gone!

That is the story of how Britain retained the Schneider Trophy yesterday, when two million people saw three British and three Italian pilots laugh at death in an attempt to cover seven 31-mile laps over the Solent in the quickest time. . . .

That air epic of Today will never be adequately described. While these daredevils of the air crashed past us I heard women scream hysterically, saw them faint—and saw men turn their heads away. . . .

What was the race for the two million people who watched?

This:—

A battery had opened fire in the sky! They are coming! The dainty deadliness of them!

Something silver hurtles by; and loud speakers and half the world shriek: 'Waghorn, Super marine. Waghorn, Super marine!'

We nearly dislocated our necks craning skywards.

The silver something-became a dancing dot on the horizon, while the unbelievable noise of the engines battered at our ear-drums, and we realised that there was an heroic lunatic in the dancing dot.

'Atcherley,' cried the speaker. 'Atcherley is playing pitch and toss with his life!'

'Monti,' howled the wireless. 'Zoom'—he passed while our

hands had only begun to wave. 'This speed is Satanic,' whispered a white-faced official. He clutched my coat and screwed up the clothes in his hand; curious little tremors ran through the spectators' faces as the terrific roar of the engine caught them square in the ear-drum.

Round the course they went. There was a fearful monotony about it. Round and round.

I marked the crowd.

They were white and afraid, but loving it like people on a scenic railway on the brink of a dive.

A gun fired. It was over.

An hysterical woman screamed—shrilly screamed—at steady intervals, but the others drowned her.

Cheers crackled round the coast. Hats flew up like gargantuan confetti; women giggled—some cried. It echoed over from Portsmouth and we in Ryde sent it back across the Solent.

Minutes of terrific cheering, and then the mosaic of white sails broke up on the Solent, and curious sea-gulls ducked and chattered where six men a few moments ago had battled with fate."

This is meant to be very exciting—the breathless manner, the staccato sentences and paragraphs show that. Next it is clear that the excitement was not felt by the writer, nor by the crowd to the extent that the writer would have us believe: it is calculated hysteria, a quite cynical attempt to get a 'kick' out of a reader jaded by daily stunts. (If you read it aloud, in the manner of a news-reel commentator, there is not much need for comment.) The exaggerated phrasing—"laugh at death," "air-epic," "battled with fate"—the glib alliteration, the aposiopesis ("and saw men turn their heads away . . ."), a labour-saving means of stimulating apprehensive shudders—all are familiar devices. Alliteration demands that cheers 'crackle'—an interesting novelty; and exactly why (near the end) are the sea-gulls 'curious'? The crowd was right in drowning the hysterical woman, but they might have found a more deserving victim.

Angle of Humanity

The last example leads naturally to another staple of popular journalism. A death under abnormal circumstances is a tragedy, to be exploited from the Human Interest angle; ghoulish details, and the grief of relatives are exhibited. The *New Statesman and Nation* remarks that "the practice increasingly followed by news-editors of competing popular dailies is to detail reporters to telephone anyone and everyone who is connected or believed to be connected with victims of tragedies. The object of the quest is always the 'human angle on the news'—the first words of a mother who thus learns that her child is dead, the reactions of the wife to the news that her husband is charged with murder. If photographs can be purloined—'snatched' is the technical word—from a bereaved household's mantelpiece, so much the better. A few years ago the Home Secretary referred to a case of a woman who was pestered by a newspaper to ask for the exhumation of the body of her daughter who, as far as anyone knew, had died a perfectly natural death. Instances of this occur daily, but the sufferers' complaints are rarely heard. Some time ago Lady Ellerman wrote in *The Times* that on the day she brought home the body of her husband she was confronted at her home with groups of Press cameramen, who responded with laughter to a request that they should go away. They were there to take pictures of her husband's coffin and of herself in whatever aspect of grief they could surprise her. At the cemetery men with cameras ran beside the mourners, leaping over graves and vying with one another to be first on the scene; and as the coffin was lowered the silence was broken by the clicking of cameras.".

Interviews : In situations such as those just mentioned it is quite common for interviews to be invented. An undergraduate who had not long left school committed suicide at his college. The headmaster of his school and his housemaster were pestered by telephone for information and interviews, which they withheld. But this did not stop 'interviews' and faked portraits appearing in the next day's issues. But when you read the views of such experts as a film star on morality or an airman on international policy, you can be fairly certain that the persons whose signatures are attached have at least seen the articles, though only the signature is their own work.

Murder and Atrocity

Unfortunately for the papers which thrive on it, there are times when no war is in progress, though from a glance at their editorials it must be admitted that it is not their fault. The tendency shown in peace time by the full reporting of murder cases becomes fully developed in times of war and crisis. Atrocity and similar stories are in themselves good copy; they sell a paper. They are a potent means of enlisting support for the party favoured by the paper, and of stirring up hatred against the other side. By this aggravation of hatred they make it unnecessary to disprove the opponents' case by argument, and tend to make a moderate view impossible. During the war an American priest was sentenced to ten years' imprisonment for saying that the existence of such stories was not a good reason for treating the Germans as beasts; and this was not in the U.S. an exceptional case. (Cf. *The Public Mind*)

There are always atrocities in war. That they were invented in addition and circularised to keep up the fighting temper is now well known from Lord Ponsonby's *Falsehood in Wartime.* It makes humiliating and salutory reading; atrocity stories are still being used and will continue to be used on suitable occasions. The brutalities involved in the Nazi seizure of power gave opportunities to the atrocity monger and many of us found that because we detested Fascism we were ready without sufficient corroboration to believe rumours which discredited the regime; and during the Spanish War, when popular papers behaved just as they did during the Great War, some familiar stories appeared. A daily printed the following.

How a young girl Communist jabbed a hatpin into a priest as he lay dying in a Barcelona gutter was told to a *"Daily—"* reporter by Mrs. Pollard, of the Greenways, Hendon, who has just returned from a holiday in Spain.

(The report continues to give harrowing details.)

Another paper affirmed that "Diligent inquiries by a *Daily*— reporter failed to find either 'The Greenways' or 'Mrs. Pollard.' As the London Postal Directory knows of no Greenways at Hendon, he went to the Greenway, only to find that at no house in the street was there anyone called Pollard." But there may well have been a person who did tell the story, as there are people who make them up and believe them in much the same spirit that others read and enjoy them. It is noticeable that such rumours often come by round about ways— "Further Red atrocities in Spain against women and children are revealed in a letter received by Mr. Robert Honlihan of Clare Castle, Co. Clare, from a brother in Spain." (Lurid but antiquated anecdotes followed.) In the same way one quite often meets people who know of others who saw the angels at Mons, but never the person who had the experience. One of Lord Ponsonby's instances shows how this works:

When the fall of Antwerp got known, the church bells were rung (meaning in Germany).

Kolnische Zeitung.

According to the *Kolnische Zeitung,* the clergy of Antwerp were compelled to ring the church bells when the fortress was taken, *he Matin.*

According to what *he Matin* has heard from Cologne, the Belgian priests who refused to ring the church bells when Antwerp was taken have been driven away from their places. *The Times.*

According to what *The Times* heard from Cologne via Paris, the unfortunate Belgian priests who refused to ring the church bells when Antwerp was taken have been sentenced to hard labour. *Corriere della Sera.*

According to information to the *Corriere della Sera* from Cologne via London, it is confirmed that the barbaric conquerors of Antwerp punished the unfortunate Belgian priests for their heroic refusal to ring the church bells by hanging them as living clappers to the bells with their heads upside down. *Le Matin.*

Sentimentality : It is cardinal in newspaper policy that readers should not think. Sympathy for unemployed men might easily prompt doubts about a social system which is complacent about their decay; we must sympathise with them of course but we need not bother to do anything about it, it is not our responsibility. (The way some papers talk about the unemployed gives the impression that they are a special class which the reader is never likley to join.) Unemployment, however, may always be written up from the human interest angle, and the efforts or sufferings of the unemployed may be used to titillate the reader's sympathy (for a moment) or love of sensation. Not that this cynical attitude is confined to newspapers which support the *status quo;* one finds the *Daily Herald* writing up from the human interest angle such a piece of news as the arrival in England of 300 refugees—"I was the first to greet them . . . meet the man whose sense of humour stopped mass hysteria," etc. It is worth considering why news items such as the following receive prominence in our papers:

Buying Old War Horses

There has been such a ready response to the appeal for money with which to buy old war horses in Flanders out of their misery that Our Dumb Friends' League were able two days ago to send agents to Belgium to make further purchases.

Observer.

The Mayor said he was a great animal lover, and he detested people who were cruel to animals. "It is bad enough with children, but when it comes to dumb animals it is terrible," he said. Newspaper report.

Cruelty to animals is detestable enough, but cruelty to men is worse by any rational standards. To say the least of it, the English scale of values is oddly out of proportion here: one often finds that cruelty to animals is punished more severely than manslaughter by car. The results of this are probably far-reaching, but it is not often they are found as clearly illustrated as in this example:

Result of Appeals

	£ S. d.
East Islington Mothers' and Babies' Welfare Centre, Marchioness of Lansdowne..	49 10 8
People's Dispensary for Animals of the Poor, Christopher Stone	11,812 0 9
Promise of a further £7,000.	

The earlier extracts quoted show that by distortion and suppression of the news a dangerously inaccurate world-picture is given to its public by the Press. The later quotations indicate that the reader is not encouraged to attach much weight to politics, economics and international affairs. He might not admit it openly, but gardening, racing, the cinema, etc., are his real interests, and he is usually well informed about them. *The Times* considers a change in the rules of a card game worthy of a column on its central news page; *The Observers* does the same for the arrival in London of a new film star; the B.B.C. announces first the postponement of a boxing match and then the wounding of a British ambassador in the outbreak of war in China. Every few years there is an election when the citizen is supposed to help choosing a government which, if there is any basic difference between the parties, may mean peace or war, will affect educational policy, and alter perhaps the lives of millions of people in India. To this choice he brings a mind nurtured on trivialities; and it is not surprising that he rarely sees the real issues and is easily influenced by emotional appeals. Often he does not trouble to vote; in 1937, at a suburban by-election (when less feeling is aroused) only 37 per cent of the electorate voted, and in the London municipal elections of 1931 the percentage was 31.3.

The mere physical make-up of a paper determines the way people respond to an item of news. One reads in a sober daily that a submarine has shot a torpedo at a British ship, and one forgets the incident: later one picks up a less continent journal and finds the items heavily headlined and accompanied by rather dubious pictures of the vessels concerned—and one produces the required shock, feels that this is a grave incident, a danger to British prestige, and that half a dozen of the weightiest warships should burst their boilers in a dash for the Mediterranean. (This was in 1937.)

In the following additional example, consider which of the reports appears to be the most trustworthy. It may be omitted if necessary.

I. Hendaye is full of rumours as to the fate of the political hostages held in Irun. Many are reported to have been shot. Popular Front leaders assure me,however, that they were all evacuators to San Sebastian yesterday.

II. What of the hostages held there in strict imprisonment? It is impossible to report anything there of them, except that none has yet been seen in France. Men of the Right who were in Fuenterrabia say that the prison doors were opened at dawn and all the men released. Others who were there in the afternoon, report that there were shootings at 1.30, when your Correspondent did, in fact, hear fusillades echo across the Bidassoa Mountains. A conversation between militiamen who linger, clad in blue overalls, on the French side of the international bridge, was heard Today. Said one man: "And the prisoners, they asked to be shot rather than to be kept shut up there and perhaps burned. But the guards refused to shoot them." Said another: "They went up in lorries and shot them all."

III. It is reported that a number of hostages were executed this morning by the Red forces in Irun, who electrocuted them by bringing them into contact with high-tension wires by which they were terribly burned.

The Comments : In nineteenth century journalism the news was kept separate from the articles which commented on it, and this is still true of the best papers. The less scrupulous organs hardly need leading articles to give their views on events, because they are implicit in the selection and presentation of the news.

Even the more reputable papers sometimes fail to maintain their standards of dispassionate reporting:

Ras Mulugeta (is) in full flight. . . retreating troops are being heavily bombed and are reported to be either too weary or too dazed to take proper precautions to save themselves.

It is clear that the taking of Amba Aradam was a magnificent feat of arms. . . . The combined effects of shells and bombs appeared to have crushed even the fanatical courage of the best of the Abyssinian warriors, to whose bravery in the face of heavy losses warm tributes are, however, paid. . . . The task of harassing the fleeing Abyssinians is being left to the air force. A long column of fugitives estimated at 20,000 is said to have kept the Italian armies fully occupied yesterday. It is estimated that during the course of the day 30 tons of high explosives were dropped on the enemy, who at first replied with heavy rifle fire against the low-flying machines, but later appear to have accepted their fate passively and to have abandoned stores, livestock, and even their wounded.

The account is hardly objective. The same newspaper until recently failed to separate news from comment in its reports on Russia—for some years it had no correspondent in that country.

The four extracts from leading articles which follow are from one day's issue of different papers; and the reader can estimate on internal evidence their reliability as guides to public opinion.

Keep Clear of War

By taking Irun, the Patriots have struck a resounding blow for the cause of liberty in Spain and throughout Europe. The beaten Reds, having murdered an Archbishop and a hundred priests held as hostages, are rushing, still armed, into France. It appears that the road lies open to the inevitable capture of San Sebastian, and the miscreants in Madrid begun to feel something of the terror they have visited on thousands of forlorn victims.

Under this hammer-stroke that fiendish arch-Bolshevik, Caballero, has ousted the dummy, Giral, and formed a so-called government of unashamed and violent Communists.

Great Britain, except for that strange minority which is eaten up with admiration for the Bolsheviks, will welcome yesterday's notable victory for Christianity, order and decency. Good wishes and sympathy towards the Patriots in their struggle are legitimate, and cannot, indeed, be repressed; yet this country must rigidly resolve to keep out of all entanglements either in Spain or in other regions of Europe.

The Spanish conflagration may well be followed by crisis elsewhere. Other trouble may be looming on the Continent, but it is none of our business. However loud the din of the pacifists and meddlers at home, it must remain none of our business.

But the resolve to keep out of Europe's broils and snares lays on Great Britain this second duty—intensively to rearm. To remain aloof we must regain strength. Above all, we must achieve real air power.

The Fall of Irun

After ten days' brave defence against what appear to have been heavy odds both in men and in weapons, the Spanish frontier town of Irun has fallen to the Spanish rebels. The defence was warned at the outset that if it did not surrender it would suffer the fate of Badajoz (where 1,500 prisoners were shot in cold blood), and it seems that the men and women of Irun who have not escaped across the frontier are now paying that terrible penalty. The most convenient road whereby supplies could be delivered from France to the isolated Government strongholds in the north-west has thus been closed, and the rebels will now be able once more to besiege San Sebastian, a town which Wellington's forces failed to take in the Peninsular War. It is generally understood that the rebels' plan of campaign is to take San Sebastian before launching their converging attack on Madrid. All the evidence goes to show that not only were the loyalists' guns and ammunition at Irun inferior to those of their enemies but that they did not make the best use of what they had.

Spain's Fratricidal Fanaticism

Irun has fallen to the Spanish insurgents after a desperate and prolonged resistance, and amid incidents on both sides that illuminate the horrors of this fratricidal campaign. To all appearance the way is now open to the capture of San Sebastian, whose defenders have small supplies of ammunition and lack artillery, tanks and aeroplanes. The stories that are told Today of the burning of Irun, of the shooting of prisoners and hostages, and the mowing down of men, women and children who were endeavouring to escape to safety, emphasise the need for haste in every possible effort that can be made to humanise a war in which every principle that governs the fighting of civilised peoples has been ignored by both sides. Should San Sebastian be stormed the insurgents will have established their hold on the north of the country. Whatever the moral effect of their victory in this quarter, and of the smaller successes that the Government claims in other areas, the map of the war is not changed greatly to the advantage of either party, for whatever troops may be released in the north are far from Madrid.

One consequence of the insurgent success is the change in the Spanish Government, which transfers power from a puppet Cabinet into the hands of the men who have really controlled affairs at the centre. With Senor Largo Caballero at the head and Senor Prieto at the Ministries of Air and Marine, the new Administration is dominated by advanced Socialists and Communists, two members of which party occupy the offices of Agriculture and Education—neither of them of much significance in present conditions in Spain.

Irun

After Badajoz, Irun. And what new horrors lie ahead?

The phrases of the correspondents grow terribly familiar. "Men, women and children were massacred." "Every prisoner was shot out of hand." So familiar that realisation of their terrible meaning is blurred.

The mind, indeed, shrinks from imagining what lies behind such words; the tortured agony on the one side, the bestial ferocity on the other. "Children were massacred." Think of that, not as three words, but as a thing happening.

A few weeks ago Irun was a pleasant frontier town, its men going about their business, or chatting cheerfully in its cafes. Women are tending their homes: children playing in its streets.

Today that pleasant town is a smoking ruin. Hundreds of quiet homes are masses of charred wreckage.

And in its streets lie the mangled bodies of men and women and children, shot down, knifed or bayoneted as they stood dazed and frightened, or as they fled.

This is the bestial reality that is called politely "civil war."

A group of generals aim to seize power. They "raise the standard of revolt." They "march on Madrid." They "capture a town." Pretty enough phrases: and there are finer still ready for use by those who see in it all a splendid crusade of patriotism.

But this that has happened in Irun as it happened in Badajoz, is the vile reality of it. And if Mola and Franco have their will, the horror of Badajoz, the horror of Irun, will be repeated in town after town, in village after village.

"War is hell," said Sherman: and it was a civil war of which he spoke. But this hell that has been unloosed in Spain is worse than any Sherman knew.

And the end seems far off. The agony of the Spanish people has only begun.

I is a masterpiece in the art of confusing. "The Patriots, the beaten Reds. . . ." This sharp and unlikely division is a method we recognise. Next the violence of the phrasing might raise suspicion—"miscreants of Madrid," "fiendish arch-Bolshevik Caballero," etc. At this point some external evidence may be added. According to *The Times,* Caballero was a Socialist, and in the cabinet "the moderate wing of Socialism is represented in greater strength than any other Labour group, although the Prime Minister and the Foreign Minister must be counted as sympathisers with Communism. The Cabinet, in sum, is a genuine representation of the Popular Front." The Ministry consisted of six Socialists, three Republicans, two Communists and two others. After abusing those who disagree with it ("No case—abuse plaintiff's attorney"), the leader draws a somewhat inconsequential conclusion.

"The Fall of Irun" is a straightforward resume, only slightly coloured by feeling. (This extract suffers by curtailment; I and IV are reproduced in full.) The manner is cool and deliberate; the length of the paragraph shows that it presumes a reader accustomed to make sustained effort. Short paragraphs suggest that the expected readers have not a great reading capacity.

III is intended for a comparatively intelligent reader; the writing is considered and unexcited. It is a trifle ponderous, compared with II; it runs to polysyllables, and an excess of these sometimes indicates that solemnity of manner covers poverty of matter, and attests the writer's self-satisfaction. The attitude here appears well balanced, though the suggestion that war can be humanised remains a pious aspiration and one unwarranted by the nature of modern warfare. Where chemical and mechanical means preponderate, there is less chance for humanity and bravery. The strategists or politicians in whose scheme of things war is an instrument do not envisage the humanising of war.

Turn the ideas of I upside down, and the result is IV. There is the same jerky paragraphing, a similar attempt to work on the feelings merely. It is not quite as contemptible as I, but it is not much more trustworthy; the recipe for producing the *Daily Herald* closely resembles that of the *Daily Mail.* At this point another extract is added, though not from a newspaper, to show that violent and exaggerated phrasing is not confined to the Right:

The hands of Chamberlain and his Cliveden Set are red with the blood of tens of thousands of the Spanish people. Chamberlain and this Cliveden Set are the same criminals who have starved the unemployed, left the Distressed Area to rot, and cut down the

Social Services while they and their class batten on Government subsidies and armaments profits.

Communists say the time has come to hound these people out of public life. The time has come to end the domination of Britain by a gang of millionaires and their despicable agents. It is time the people took things into their own hands, and set up a People's Government to carry out the policy desired by the people and in the interests of the people—a policy of alliance of the peaceful countries against Fascist aggression, a policy of social progress at home.

Pamphlet, *Hitler's Friends in Britain.*

The next example consists of a number of comments on the Jubilee of 1935, and the object again is to arrange them in order of reliability.

I. "It was a mighty and awakening revelation of what is meant Today by the Monarchy, the nation and the Empire in their political trinity. If the world was thrilled, as we are told, it was because we ourselves were touched to the core. If the world was astonished, it was because we astounded ourselves. Up to a day or two before the event nothing like the magnitude of what hap pened could have been anticipated. In a manner singularly characteristic of our people, who some times give little sign of the depth of their mood before their greatest manifestations of what is in them, the thing rose suddenly, smoothly, with the elemental power of a tidal wave.

Though the possibility would have seemed unbelievable to a former generation, there is no doubt that last week's Great Day surpassed in several respects all that was seen and heard at Queen Victoria's second Jubilee."

II. "The Jubilee celebrations are deliberately designed to divert public opinion—particularly that of the workers—from realities to false issues. They constitute as a whole one elaborate 'circus,' staged expressly to divert attention from the fundamental rottenness of the social structure for which the British monarchy serves as a gilded figure-head, and from the malignant crookedness and self-seeking of thedictatorial gang who really rule and use George Windsor as a lightning conductor.

The Jubilee celebrations are, in fact, part of the class-war preparations of the ruling capitalist gang who know that their evil system is tottering to its collapse. The right way to greet the 'Jubilee' is to make it an occasion for mass demonstrations of loyalty to the Red Flag of Revolutionary Socialism, of loyalty to the fraternal union in struggle of all who are exploited and oppressed. . . ."

III. "The celebration of the Jubilee is in effect a call to the nation to rejoice over the twenty-five years of our history from 1910 to 1935.

It is the opinion of those who sign this paper that the events of the period have been of a character which forbids rejoicing.

These events include a war in which out of the population of Great Britain and Ireland 812,317 men were killed and 1,849,494 were wounded.

It has been a period of growing unemployment. In 1913 when three per cent of the total number of trade unionists were unemployed the problem was thought to be serious. In 1935 when 2,397,000 are unemployed we are bidden to official rejoicings.

Those in Great Britain dependent on Poor Law Relief who already numbered 903,509 in 1915 were 1,498,247 twenty years later.

These are three items among many which might be taken from twenty-five disastrous years.

We consider that rejoicing is out of place, and we protest against the arranged celebrations."

IV. "The doubt has been raised, and in by no means intellectually disreputable quarters, that the present year is not the fittest to be the occasion of national rejoicing. With the world in its present plight, it is said, we should turn rather to fasting than to celebrations; we should apply ourselves to the remedying of our present discontents rather than the elaboration of our gratitude. That would seem to be a one-sided and partisan view, the fruit of warped if honest thinking and ungenerous though genuine feelings. It is in no sentimental or jingo spirit that the nation, irrespective of creed or party, unites to celebrate the twenty-fifth anniversary of the accession of His Majesty George V. That our beloved sovereign has guided his people safely throughout those troubled years is matter for heartfelt congratulation. . . ."

V. "Nobody can study side by side the modern technique of advertising and the stuff with which the Press is being filled on the jubilee without realising that the latter is an example of the former. Just as the public is persuaded that life is not worth living without so-and-so's beer, or somebody's brain food, or so-and-so's soap powder, liver pills, hire purchase, wireless sets, suits, or what-not, so it is being persuaded that but for the King and the Royal Family the world would stop spinning on its axis and the British Empire would, blow up with a bang!

That is why every day some member of the Royal Family must be 'featured' by the Press doing something or other which is *(a)* sample and homely ("Just like us!") and, at the same time *(b)* noble and royal ("More than we could do!")."

Misleading and mischievous comment is not confined to politics. Almost any event of public importance can be made the occasion for fostering what H. G. Wells called a "vast and increasing inattention." This can be seen in the second of the two quotations that follow, a leading article from a popular paper, commenting on the news item of which *The Times* report is here printed:

> I. Mr. F. G. Thomas spoke on "Basic Mental Mechanisms involved in Mass Entertainment" as seen in the organised and commercialised amusement parking pleasure beach. The huge permanent structures of the Blackpool pleasure beach, he said, exploited almost without exception the fear-escape propensity. The most obvious function of the "Big Dipper" and the "Grand National" was to place their patrons in a situation which, if it occurred in a vehicle in ordinary life, would be fraught with extreme danger, but which, in this instance, offered also an infallible means of escape. Fear could also be commercialised on the pleasure beach in the form of fear of the unknown, combined with curiosity to elucidate it—Part of one of several addresses at the meeting of the British Association, reported by *The Times.*

Handling Sources

Twenty years ago the normal source in the average city dealt with maybe a couple of papers, a radio and a TV station. Today news outlets have proliferated to the point where any local official source deals with perhaps two cover-price papers, several freesheets, a specialist local business magazine or two, maybe two radio stations, a TV station, three cable channels and a rapidly rising number of news or community websites.

This growth has hugely accelerated the tendency for official organisations to hand press relations over to dedicated professionals. It has also meant that there are a lot more journalists hunting for information where once only a few roamed. These days you are far more likely to be one of many and will find yourself dealing not with the person with the expertise, but with their mouthpiece. All the more reason, then, to know how to deal professionally with sources and how to make the best of, and occasionally subvert, the channels down which officialdom would prefer you to go. For although most dealings with sources are routine, straightforward transactions where both sides gain, there are times when you are in a highly competitive game of wits with sources to make sure that the strongest and most complete version of the story hits the streets and not the self-serving one they would prefer.

The Guidelines : Before considering the specifics of dealing with official sources, news management techniques, contentious sources and some of the other perils, here are a few key guidelines for dealing with any source:

> To do otherwise is to trick people into giving information, which is not only dishonest but also unsafe. People are often very free with talk until they realise you are a journalist. Then they become a lot more guarded and start to qualify their information. This is because instead of merely shooting the breeze, they now have to take some responsibility for the quality of these facts. Not telling them you are a reporter is a good way to get them to exaggerate in a way people often do in informal conversation. The chapter on investigative journalism deals with the very rare times when concealing your identity is justified.

Believe it or not, journalism is quite a lot like real life. From this flows the devastating truth that if you want sources to help you, then being friendly, honest and treating them fairly works a lot better than bullying, trickery or intimidation. Being fair is especially vital. If they are being criticised or accused of wrongdoing you should not only put these claims to them, but also give them time to reply. Ten minutes before deadline is not good enough.

Copy Approval : Showing a source the finished article before publication is soliciting censorship. The usual reason given is that this is a chance for factual errors to be corrected — and if you believe that is the real motive, you will probably believe anything. Showing someone what will inevitably be described as 'the draft' of a story encourages the idea that it is being given to them for approval and, hence, possible alteration. It is the journalists' job to produce accurate copy, not something that is the basis for negotiations with the subject.

The Retraction : Many times a source or subject will say something to a reporter that they subsequently regret. There is not a lot of point in journalists training themselves to question good information out of people if they then offer them a subsequent opportunity to withdraw it. However, if sources want to correct what they told you, then you must let them, unless you have very good grounds for thinking some subterfuge is afoot — in which case, report both their earlier and later statements. Sources' appeals for a retraction on the grounds that they will be fired are another matter. Handle these by questioning them closely, then passing the matter on to an executive. It is not a reporter's job to play God; leave that to editors.

The Payment : This is another issue reporters can kick upstairs to editors. It is the executives' decision whether they can afford — financially or morally to pay for information. The dangers of the practice are obvious. First, it establishes a market and encourages people caught up in stories to demand payment. Second, paid informants have an unimpressive record of reliability. They know that the stronger the story, the higher the fee and so have a direct inducement to invent or embroider. A few years ago the *Sun*, Britain's most popular newspaper, had to pay out £ l million libel damages to Elton John because they believed, and printed, a fictitious story sold to them by a gay male prostitute. It is not a lone example. Neither, however, are the instances of cheating public figures exposed solely through a paid-for story. If you are a mass-market tabloid, the temptations to pay for stories are understandable.

Government Sources

These are ones authorised to give you information — from the owner of the corner store commenting on how trade is, to the chief press spokes-person for the head of government making a statement about why she has resigned. They span the full range of human helpfulness, cussedness, expertise and idiocy. Most, if approached in the right way, are helpful.

When it comes to dealing with PR and press departments, authorised does not always mean well-informed. Some have good knowledge of their organisations and can answer detailed questions. Others are mere go-betweens, transporting your questions to the official concerned and ferrying back the answers, with an inevitable loss of freshness — and no opportunity to ask follow-up questions. For this reason, try to cultivate officials who will give you information directly, rather than it being filtered through their PR person.

In recent years, there have been big changes in the way large commercial, political and government organisations handle the media. There has been much bleating from journalists about the iniquities of 'news management' and 'spin doctors'. All that has happened is that these bodies have started to employ press spokespersons who are rather more of an intellectual match for journalists than hitherto. The result is a more sophisticated, although rarely subtle, approach to handling the media, the chief feature of which is to be proactive, rather than merely reactive. The following should be borne in mind.

Often applied wrongly to all PR people, this term originally described people working on a political campaign whose job it was to shmooze journalists after new polls, candidate debates, etc. and give an interpretation that was favourable to their party. It has gradually been applied, wrongly, to almost anyone in the PR or image business. A true spin doctor is someone in the political trade who is a chief press spokesman or senior aide. Apart from routine statements and press conferences, they interpret events to the press on behalf of their boss, try to anticipate bad news (and divert attention from it) and also attempt to manage expectations in a way that helps their cause.

This last situation is where most journalists are led astray by spin doctors. Fearing, for instance, that bad news is in the offing, they brief journalists that results verging on the disastrous are expected so that when the real outcome is known they can smilingly report a veritable triumph. The frequency with which this ploy is tried on journalists does not seem to impede its success.

True spin doctors do, however, have one great advantage over lesser fry in their trade. They are close, often very close, to their boss and anything they say on the record has serious authority. They also spend much of their lives dealing fairly staightforwardly with routine questions and the best of them are invaluable sources. Just make sure you protect yourself by constantly asking: why are they telling me this?

News Management : Organisations, be they public or private, commercial or political, routinely have a great many reports and statements that they wish, or are obliged to, release. The idea that they should choose the most advantageous way and time to do this is not particularly shocking. Indeed often this 'news management' is helpful, making sure journalists have enough time to write for their editions, or avoiding a clash between a report's release and a major event.

Skull duggery, however, there is. It comes mainly in three forms and is nearly always connected to information that the organisation fears will play negatively. First is the dodge of timing the release of the information to coincide with the least convenient moment in the news cycle - say late at night, or towards the end of a Friday afternoon. The chances of it being ignored or meekly treated are then fairly high. Second is to leak the main angle of the story to a sympathetic news outlet in the hope that by the time the others have caught up or received the information through the official channels, the story will either be stale or its 'agenda' already set: The third trick is to sugar the pill with some fragment of good news which is then spun as the main angle.

The British government in 1999, for instance, was scheduled to release new hospital waiting list figures. Knowing that these were not good, and seeking to avoid adverse headlines, the figures were released on the same day as the annual school exam results (confident that this rarer story would overshadow the hospital data). The government also tacked news of the hospital figures on to a release about a grant of £30 million to help the situation. It worked. All papers ran the story small, and my paper gave it just three paragraphs in early editions. When we rumbled what was going on (the figures showed waiting lists had risen by 04 per cent in two years) we elevated the story to a page two lead. Your only protection against this and other forms of news management is to use your wits.

Sometimes organisations are so displeased by press coverage that they simply cut off access to their information. Crude, and rare, this practice is generally only seen in arts journalism, where an unfavourable review so irks a theatre or gallery that they simply ban the critic concerned. The film industry seems especially prone to this branch of censorship. In the US, according to a study by the University of Southern California, journalists have been banned from screenings. Judy Gerstel, for instance, wrote a report about poor audience response to *Hook* for the *Detroit Free Press,* was promptly ex-communicated by the studio and soon found that two other studios (Warner and Universal) had dropped her as well. Ultimately there is no solution. It is the studio's information and they have a legal, if not a moral, right to do with it what they want. The response should be to tell readers of the attempted manipulation and to encourage 'if she goes, then so do we' support from other papers. After all, it might be them next time.

Official Sources

These are sources not authorised to give you the information they are passing on. They may be whistleblowers well-placed in an organisation, or someone with no official connection to the information. They could be passing on documents, or a mere suggestion to go digging in a certain area. Invariably their information will be contested, at least initially, and almost always they will not wish to be quoted in the story. It is from such sources that some of the best stories come - and the most trouble if they are wrong. In dealing with these sources, you should bear the following in mind.

People are rarely helpful to newspapers because they are saintly. They want to damage political, commercial or personal opponents, advance some cause (or harm a rival one), take revenge or simply cause trouble. While someone else's revenge mission can be useful, it is best to know what they are about from the start. So ask yourself (and occasionally them) what their motives might be. Their unattractive calculations may not disqualify the story, but they are a good reason to tread carefully.

The stories given to you by contentious sources are rarely as black and white as they would have you believe. Save time by asking them if there is another side to the story, or if there is any qualifying information you should know. Crazy, horrendous, absurd things do happen; but not as often as most sources claim. Under the front-page headline 'Shame On The City-Shocking Story of New York At Its Worst', The *New York Post* once carried a story of a man who raped a three-year-old girl on a grass verge by a busy Manhattan highway while passing motorists parked and watched. Does that sound likely? What actually happened was that three motorists saw a man attacking a girl, leapt from their cars to give chase and other drivers were then caught in the resulting jam. A clear case of a single-source story that was not checked.

A lot of named sources frequently claim to be 'in the know' when they are in fact only marginally so. The classic case of this is the coverage by the Western press of the Soviet Union in the two years following the 1917 revolution. Western correspondents were barred from Russian soil and so papers sent them to Riga where, 300 miles from Petrograd, their only sources were former Czarist generals and officials and deposed politicians. All claimed to be 'in the know'. Virtually none of them was. The results for the *New York Times* were, according to the famous study conducted by Walter Lippmann and Charles Merz, surreal. Between 1917 and 1919 the paper reported: the Bolshevik government had fallen or was about to fall (91 times); Lenin and Trotsky were preparing to flee (four times); Lenin and Trotsky had fled Russia (three times); Lenin had been imprisoned (three times); Lenin had been killed (once).

Always ask sources if there is any documentation to support what they are telling you. If they will not let you have it, ask for a photocopy; if they refuse that then ask if you can at least read it in their presence. If they still refuse, forget the story. And if you do get documents, be suspicious until you are satisfied they are genuine. Sometimes even photographs are suspect. Ed Behr tells a cautionary tale in his book *Anyone Here Been Raped and Speaks English* of the agency given photographic evidence of atrocities by one side in an African civil war. The pictures are of a woman being raped by soldiers. All very convincing until the local bureau chief had the sense to ask for the contact strip. They showed the harrowing rape scenes and then, in the final frame, the 'victim' with her arms round her 'attackers', smiling and posing for a group photograph.

Passion does not guarantee unreliability, but it helps. The more strongly someone feels about something, the less good they tend to be as a witness. Question such sources very carefully. They often fit facts to their theories and are blinded by those attitudes into ignoring key information. Beware especially the committed activist, fired employee, ex-wife, former husband and spurned lover. Ask them if anyone can confirm what they are telling you. An instant modification of their original account will often follow.

Unattributable Sources : The sensible motto is: use 'off the record' as sparingly as you can. If you don't, you will end up with a lot of sources you cannot name. And if you are discussing some species of unattributable information, get it absolutely clear with your source what you have agreed. That way there will be no subsequent argument. Are they, for instance, giving you material which you will have to confirm and source with another party (background)? Or are they giving you the information on an unattributable basis, in which case you can use it, but not their name? Make sure that when an interview subject uses a phrase like 'off the record' it means the same to them as it does to you.

Above all, do not accept their reluctance to be quoted without a fight. Keep on at them to go on the record. Argue that the importance of the story depends on verification from named sources. If they persist in wanting to talk 'on background', continue the interview and then, at the end, try to find something they might be happy to be quoted on and then edge them towards attribution. Negotiate. And do not let people say to you at the end of the interview: 'Oh, by the way, that was all off the record.' The rule is: it is only off the record if you have both agreed that. And once you have an agreement, don't go back on your word. Do not name them in the story and, if they wish to be on deep background, tell no one except your editor who they are.

One of the main problems with 'off the record' is the way it has been picked up by politicians and their advisers and used for their own, sometimes shady, purposes. To illustrate this, here is an example given at a Harvard University seminar on journalism in Moscow:

> You have been called in for a rare personal interview with a senior government adviser. He tells you that everything he will say is off the record. During the interview he tells you about a major change in economic policy. You are excited by the story and rush back to your office and write it, quoting 'well-placed government sources'.

Well, it turns out that the government intends no such change, that the adviser knew that when he spoke to you and was feeding you the story to deflect attention from some other problems the government had. More common is for politicians to use off-the-record briefings to float an idea, which, if attacked, will be denied. In both cases you look a fool. If you suspect you are being set up, get a second source.

Getting too Close to Sources : Finally, here is a story that illustrates the dangers - to reporter and paper - of a specialist getting too closely involved with sources. It concerns one Alfred 'Jake' Lingle, who was a police reporter for the *Chicago Tribune* in the 1920s. Lingle was highly regarded at his paper. A lot of well-informed stories about organised crime in that city came from him and his contacts and he built a legendary reputation with readers and colleagues. Lingle prospered and, thanks to what he said was a bequest of $50,000 from his father, the $ 65-a-week reporter dressed well and maintained several homes. His fertile supply of crime stories, however, was suddenly stopped on 9 June 1930. As he entered a train station on Randolph Avenue, Lingle was gunned down in the street in broad daylight by a man dressed as a priest.

The killing had all the marks of a gangland professional hit. Lingle's paper was outraged.

> The meaning of the murder is plain. It was committed in reprisal and in an attempt at intimidation. Mr Lingle was a police reporter and an exceptionally well-informed one. ... To the list of those who were killed in the St Valentine's Day Massacre [when seven died in a gangland feud], the name is added of a man whose business was to expose the work of the killers. *The Tribune* accepts this challenge. It is war.

The *Tribune* backed these fine words with a $25,000 reward for information about the killers, other papers followed suit and Lingle was accorded a civic funeral, complete with military bands and guards of honour. Tens of thousands of Chicago citizens lined the streets and bowed their heads in respect as the cortege passed.

But not long afterwards, some hitherto unknown details of Lingle began to emerge. It turned out his father only left him a few hundred dollars, not $50,000. When Lingle was shot he had over $1,000 in cash in his wallet and was wearing a belt-buckle encrusted with diamonds. It was, apparently, a gift from Al Capone, the most notorious of the city's organised crime bosses. Moreover, his bank account showed deposits of more than $60,000 in the previous 18 months.

One of his joint accounts was with City Police Commissioner, William F. Russell, who resigned in disgrace immediately. He and Lingle had been friends since their youth and the crime reporter had been selling his influence over Russell to other policemen wanting transfers and promotion, to politicians, hoodlums and major gangsters like Capone. He was a frequent guest at Capone's retreat on Palm Island, Florida, and had day and night access to this, the most feared man in the United States at that time.

But Lingle liked to gamble and gambled heavily. Despite several successful attempts to fix dog races, he was soon losing $1,000 a week at the tracks and at Capone's illicit casinos. By the summer of 1930, his gambling debts with the organised crime boss totalled more than $100,000 - worth more than $1 million at current values. His attempt to extort money from members of Capone's own gang was, for the crime boss, the final liberty that Jake Lingle was ever going to take. The killer in priest's clothing was hired.

Three weeks to the day after Lingle was shot, his paper was forced to admit:

> Alfred Lingle now takes on a different character, one in which he was unknown to the management of the *Tribune* when he was alive ... He was not and could not have been a great reporter.

4

Significance of News

A newspaper's role is to find out fresh information on matters of public interest and to relay it as quickly and as accurately as possible to readers in an honest and balanced way. That's it. It may do lots of other things, like telling them what it thinks about the latest movies, how to plant potatoes, what kind of day Taureans might have or why the government should resign. But without fresh information it will be merely a commentary on things already known. Interesting, perhaps, stimulating even; but comment is not news.

The oft-quoted dictum on this issue was written by C.P. Scott, the editor of the then *Manchester Guardian*, in a signed editorial on 5 May 1921. He wrote that the newspaper's:

> ...primary office is the gathering of news. At the peril of its soul it must see that the supply is not tainted. Neither in what it gives, nor in what it does not give, nor in the mode of presentation, must the unclouded face of truth suffer wrong.

This is a tall, if not impossible, order. But then he added, and this is the bit that has since been trotted out a million times, 'Comment is free but facts are sacred'.

The real point of this statement is what it says about the comparative values of facts and comment. If you take a room full of journalists and ask them who has got an opinion on an important topical news event, every hand will go up. Ask who has some fresh, unpublished information on this event and almost every hand will go down. The fact is that almost everyone has a comment, be it interesting or not, and very few have new information. The one is a common place, the other is a thing of scarcity and hence value.

The Perception

There are almost as many definitions of news as there are stories. The most common hackneyed definition is that it is not news if a dog bites a man, but it is news if a man bites a dog. This reminds us that news is the unusual. But there is more to news than that. It is also something fresh, something that people have not heard before and, crucially, is of interest to readers. That means not just matters which affect the public or have an impact on public life, but also what is *of* interest to the public. News of a divorce between two well-known actors is not a matter that is *in* the public's interest, but it is of interest to the public. The best illustration of this is still the old *New Yorker* cartoon of two men on a train. One holds a paper headlined 'Lots of Important Stuff You Have to Know' and the other has a paper headlined 'Rumors, Gossip and Wacky Stunts'. The joke is that the one with 'Lots of Important Stuff Can't Keep his Eyes off 'Rumors, Gossip and Wacky Stunts'. .

Importance

News then is the fresh, unpublished, unusual and generally interesting. The first three elements can nearly always be objectively established; it is the last part — what is generally interesting? — that causes all the arguments every day in newsrooms around the world.

There is not generally a problem at the two extremes. If 450 people are killed when a plane carrrying the President crashes onto a city-centre department store, that is plainly very big news, guaranteed to make anyone who reads say 'Wow!', even if only to themselves. On the other hand, I have just bought a new car. Is that news? It is fresh, unpublished and it is certainly unusual. But it's not news because it is only of interest to my family, bank manager and car dealer.

It is all the stories in between these two extremes that journalists argue about, trying to decide if a story is strong or 'sexy', worth 200 words or 700, a news brief or a splash lead on page one. To the novice it is, along with intros, one of the great mysteries of their working lives, made all the more impenetrable by the ease with which experienced hands pass swift and seemingly sure judgement on a story. Fortunately, there is some detailed and practical help available.

Salient Features

Let's get one thing established at the outset: there is no escaping subjectivity in judging news stories. It pervades the whole process of journalism and no reporter or news editor, try as they might professionally to suppress their own prejudices, will ever be able to do so completely. This is most obvious when they judge the basic story subject. I think homelessness is interesting and important, you think it is inevitable and boring. Such subjectivity, although unavoidable, is an ever-present danger, especially when journalists (often news editors) try to pass off their personal prejudices as objectivity. Awareness of the tendency is, however, some protection against its worst excesses.

Subjectivity is not what a lot of young journalists see when they first step into a newsroom. Nor, sometimes to their amazement, do they often witness lengthy debates on a story's virtues. Instead they see a lot of news judgements being made swiftly and surely and seemingly based on nothing more scientific than gut feeling. The process is, however, a lot more measured than that. It just appears to be instinctive because a lot of the calculations that go into deciding a story's strength have been learnt to the point where they are made very rapidly — sometimes too rapidly.

The following is an attempt to identify what is — or should be — whirring around inside journalists' heads when they judge a news story. For want of a better phrase, we can call them news value factors. There are eight of them. Five are concerned with the story (subject, news fashion, development, source, knowledge and timing); one with audience (the readers); and another with the world that the audience and paper inhabit (context).

Subject : This is the broad category that the story falls under — crime, environment, health, diplomacy, economy, consumer, military, politics and so forth. All subjects are in theory equal, but some are more equal than others. Crime, for instance, has a higher value than fashion because it is patently of broader interest. Each of these categories then breaks down into sub-divisions, for example, crime breaks down into murder, fraud, abduction, racketeering, drugs, robbery, blackmail, rape, assault, etc. For the general audience, each of these has its own rough value which is normally based on its rarity in a given society or area. This is where 'context' (see below) comes in. For instance, abductions generally have more news value than assaults because they are rarer.

News Fashion : There is also such a factor as news fashion — subjects which suddenly swim into the news consciousness and are, for a time, flavour of the month. This is seen at its most glaring in activities which have perhaps been around for a long time in a fairly unobtrusive way, but which suddenly acquire a phrase or word to describe them. Under the new catchy title they then get reported out of all proportion. 'New crimes', such as air rage are a classic example. Robbing people in the street, bustups between motorists and using cars to break into premises have been around for as long as there have been streets and cars. But given the names 'mugging', 'road rage' and 'ram raiding' they acquire an extra frisson and have all been the news fashion for a period.

The history of this phenomena goes back a long way. In 1862, *The Times* whipped up a fair old panic over the sudden outbreak of what the paper called 'garotting' — attacks from behind. In some areas, when the stories were at their height, people refused to leave their homes. The panic, however, soon subsided. Since then, news fashions have included the Great Cyclist Terror of 1890s, when the *Daily Graphic* set middle-class hearts aflutter with reports of hordes of cyclists who 'rang their bells and expected people to get out of the way while pedalling as fast as eight to ten miles an hour.' In the 1950s every working class male youth was a Teddy Boy, in the 1960s every biker a rocker, in the 1970s every long-haired youth was a drug-crazed hippie, in the 1980s every large gathering of the young was an acid house party and in the 1990s every minor contretemps between motorists was 'road rage'. Easy to sneer now, but hard to resist when everyone is talking about the latest scare. Some stories coolly examining the data on the phenomena are usually the antidote.

Development : This is the specific event within the subject and sub-division which is the point of the story. Its rarity is the main part of its value and this exists without any reference to the audience. It is the straightforward assessment of how uncommon this particular development is. As an example, take the long-running dispute between Britain and France over the latter's refusal to allow UK beef to be sold because of possible BSE contamination. A development which involved plans to hold talks would be a minor development (unless one side had previously declined to meet). Talks on issues are, after all, held all the time. But a development which consisted of one side or the other walking out of the talks would be a lot rarer and thus a bigger development. A low rarity value is the chief cause, along with a lack of timeliness, for a story being disregarded or downgraded. The development has three other elements:

Source : The value of the development depends in part on the source from which it was obtained. An opposition politician might tell you that the president is about to resign, but if the president, or one of his close aides, tells you this then it is clearly a stronger story. It will be an even better story if you discover that he is about to resign, but also that he does not want the real reason known — and you know it and pass it on to your readers.

Knowledge : This is a question of how many people know about the development. The highest value attaches to stories which are the first report of a development unknown to all but the source(s), including perhaps their colleagues and private circle. The story's value is lowered if it is already in the public arena because it has already been reported by another newspaper. Stories that have already been broadcast on TV or radio may have their value lowered, but not to the same extent. You frequently hear people in national newspaper newsrooms say of a story: 'I thought we knew that', meaning that this angle may already have been reported. If a search of the cuttings turns up a prior example then out of the paper goes the story. The statement is, however, frequently an excuse for news executives to down-play a story they otherwise don't like. If you hear it spoken frequently without good reason, your prejudice alarm should ring.

Timing : News, unlike wine, does not improve with keeping. Elapsed time, however, is not the most important of factors in itself. If you learn of a major development three weeks after it has occurred, the crucial factor is not the delay, but how many people have learnt of this development in the meantime. If the story is still not public knowledge, the three-week interval will not significantly reduce the news value. It may, depending on the reason, even increase it. While shortness of time elapsing between the development happening and your report of it can add value, timing is more often a negative factor, subtracting value when there are delays which allow the story to become widely known.

Readers : This is the first of the factors that does not relate directly to the specifics of the story. The importance of the audience in judging news stories is why you should make every effort to learn as much as you can about readers. Unless you do, you cannot possibly judge their interests and tastes and so properly weigh the value of the subject and development. It would be like lecturing in a dark room to an unknown audience.

But you should use your knowledge of readers to inform your judgements in general and not to influence them incessantly in a detailed way. The day you see news reporting as a commodity to be marketed is the day you cease to be a journalist. There is a point where pandering too avidly to what you think are the readers' preferences also becomes filtering to remove stories which do not fit readers' known prejudices or omitting inconvenient parts of them such as context, explanations and qualification. This is important. It is part of the journalists' mission to debunk popular myths and to challenge comfortable assumptions. You cannot do that if you are too conscious of readers' reactions and too anxious to placate them. You will end up being about as reliable as some eager-to-please lover who speaks only the words he thinks want to be heard.

The English satirist Michael Frayn had this in mind when he wrote in *The Tin Men* of a computer being programmed to produce daily newspapers according to the results of mass surveys. People were asked what stories they liked best, how often they wanted them to recur and which details they enjoyed. Should there be an air-crash story every month or more frequently? Is it preferred, or not, that children's toys should be found among the wreckage? If a murder is reported, should the victim be a small girl, an old lady or an unmarried pregnant woman? And should the corpse be naked, or 'partially clothed'?

There are a lot of mass-market journalists around the world who, equipped with their own assumptions about readers' appetites rather than any survey results, approach reporting in much the same way as Frayn's imaginary computer.

Context : This is the situation in any given circulation area (society, town, city or region) that relates to the subject and development and helps you to judge rarity. This is why the news value of a story will vary depending on where it happens. It explains why a rural Danish weekly will rate the story of a shooting far higher than a New York tabloid would. In one place it is the exception, in the other it is an event that happens many times a day.

Sometimes this works in what appears-to be reverse, when many instances of a particular development accumulate. For instance, it may not be thought to be news if a dog bites a man. But if a certain breed of dog repeatedly bites people — and badly — then it will become news. Every single event adds to the rarity of the accumulation of cases. This is a reminder of why context should always be reported, sometimes in substantial detail.

Occasionally the context is generally known, but more often it has to be researched and so becomes inseparable from the development in the story. It should always then be reported.

Context is also important for defending journalism against the allegation that it is negative, sensationalist or only interested in bad things. For instance, if you live in a place where people entering hospital are routinely cured and cared for, then it will be news if someone is suddenly neglected and dies. To report that is often condemned as negativist. Apart from the fact that it is not the job of journalists to be either negative or positive, those who make that allegation should ask themselves what atrocious standards of medical care it would take to produce headlines like 'Man Enters Hospital and Lives'.

General Factors

Once you are aware of these general factors, judging the strength of news values can really only be done on a story-by-story basis. So here are some:

- A new UN peace initiative in an African state torn by civil war.
- Government ban on the import of all foreign-made cars.
- Famous soap opera actress to divorce.
- Opposition politician calls press conference to condemn government finance policy.
- Another opposition politician calls press conference to announce he will probably stand for leader.
- Four young girls murdered in small area of your city within three days by sex maniac.
- Government announces major new initiative to clean up dirty restaurants.

So which story do you think is the best? What would you put on the top of the front page? Well, of course, it is an impossible exercise unless you know what paper we are talking about and who its readers are. So try it first with your capital city's biggest-selling paper in mind and then again with a leading paper for the businessman.

My choices would be the murdered girls for the popular and the ban on foreign car imports for the businessman's paper. To reach those decisions I tested the stories against a kind of scale of story strength I have used over the years. Never committed to paper until now, it has largely been automatic and unconscious, as these things often are. Here it is;

Bottom End of the Scale : These are stories about conflicts of ideas or new ideas. These are 'say stories'- nothing has happened, someone has just said something. A classic giveaway of this kind of story is the word 'warns', 'urges' or 'calls' in the headline. A May 1994 issue of the Moscow *Times,* an otherwise excellent English-language paper, once had nine out of 13 news stories which were say stories. Were they really saying that in a huge country covering eight time zones only four newsworthy things actually happened over a weekend %

There are two common traps for the journalist here. First is the assumption that because a politician says something, we ought to record it. Not true. Every journalist should have the motto on his or her desk: 'They are only politicians'. Just because some middle-aged man in a grey suit has chosen to make a speech or a statement does not make it news. Most speeches and statements are expressions of the entirely expected. It is only when they say something surprising that it becomes news. A leading reformist, liberal politician condemning the slow pace of change in a society is nothing new. But if he announces his conversion to communism, then it is news.

The second trap is what has been called the pseudo-event: press conferences, interviews and the like. Press conferences are not, as some journalists seem to think, news in themselves. Nothing has actually happened. The world has not been changed one bit. All that has happened is that some politician or celebrity has wanted to make a statement, usually for their own motives, the prime one of which is publicity. The only thing that matters is the content of their message. Treat all such pseudo-events with scepticism.

What People Say would Happen : These are stories about threats or demands for action. Such exhortations are over-used by politicians, aided and abetted by lazy journalists who find attendance at press conferences so much more congenial than scuffling around looking for genuine stories. But at least such events sometimes have the virtue of having good, hard information about a situation imparted along with the hot air and waffle.

What People Say is or was Happening : These are stories about research, about people passing on to you what they have found out. Something concrete will have occurred.

Top End are Stories : These are about developments, events, accidents, disasters, court hearings and many other hard, real, provable occurrences.

The more people affected by an event, the stronger the story about it will be. If the readers are affected directly, then so much the better.

Effect of Reporting : Something which affects people only for a day or so is clearly weaker than that which affects them permanently.

As with all such rules of thumb, there will always be occasional exceptions to this scale. News fashion can often be responsible for these. Stories which a week before would have hardly merited a small inside piece are suddenly transported to the front page because they have caught the present news wave. Other developments, an incident, accident or disaster, means that suddenly the story's subject is news flavour of the week. It can also work in reverse and often explains why being first to publish on an issue does not bring the kudos that it ought. In news, timing is often everything.

Finally, reporters should always remember that the fact that they have found something out does not make it news. The 'story' they are trying to sell to their editor may have taken days and even weeks to research, they may have had to brave all kinds of difficulties and overcome all kinds of obstacles — but that does not make the story stronger. Only in very exceptional circumstances does the reader care how the reporter came by the story.

Electronic Media Support

Every few weeks the Gallup organization poses the following question to a sample of the American public: "Do you approve or disapprove of the way (name of the incumbent) is handling his job as president?" The percentage of 'yes' responses makes up what is called the president's approval rating. This approval score matters: It is crucial determinate of presidential effectiveness. President who have high public support scores have an easier lime getting their programmes passed by the Congress and implemented by the Bureaucracy. Presidents who are high in the polls have a much better chance of influencing domestic elites and foreign leaders. In addition, the Gallup index has been found to be a good predictor of the vote share Congressmen and Senators from the president's party receive during mid-term elections, and a very good predictor of how well a first term president will do in the general election.

Because presidents need public support to govern effectively, political analysts are disturbed by an unmistakable pattern in these evaluations. With the exception of the Eisenhower Administration, and for the time being the Regan Administration, public support has; declined systematically over the course, of a presidential term. Many analysts have argued that in terms of the (president' ability to get things done—that we are moving from an eight years presidency to a six month presidency, and that presidents and their aids are forced to push untested legislative programmes, programmes whose consequences have not been well thought out, through the Congress, for fear that they will not have the support necessary to do so later in the term. The question arises, then, why do presidents lose support?

The Explanations

Several explanations have been offered by scholars: Some suggest that the men we elect are at fault, that they lack the ethical, intellectual, or political attributes—In Tom Wolf's words, "The Right Stuff"—that the presidency requires. Other have argued that presidents have lost support because their policy initiatives have not been successful, due to the complexity of the modern world and the intractable nature of modern social and economic problems, solution to which require sacrifices by large sectors of society. The Office of the Presidency is simply too much for any one mortal: the psychological and physical demands of the job invariably wear presidents down to the point where they are no longer effective, and in some cases "self-destruct" either politically or emotionally, or both.

The declining support trend is a complex phenomenon that has no one single cause, but instead many factors are involved. In this paper, I would like to highlight one of those factors: the television networks and their nightly news programmes.

The Thesis : The Television networks are not provided for in the U.S. Constitution. Nevertheless they are major actors in American politics. They are the primary source from which the public gains its information both about the state of the nation and the conduct of the nation's public officials in promoting its general welfare.

The great power of the network news programmes, and their special attention to the presidency, enable them to play a major role in determining the fate of modern presidents. I believe, in fact, that the networks, seeking to realize their own goals, set in motion a dynamic pattern that can unravel the career of individual presidents and the public's support for the office of the Presidency.

Thus, the era of televised news coverage has produced a tendency for the modern presidency to be defined by, and systematically destroyed by, the image of presidential performances presented on the evening news.

In the same way that a roulette wheel slanted in a certain direction produces unfair results, regardless of the honesty and integrity of the croupier, I believe the television networks are organizationally "slanted" against the office of the Presidency, and that a negative image of the president is the result, regardless of the political ideology of the incumbent or his performance in office, call this phenomenon the "Six O'Glock Presidency" because its origins are the needs of the commercial networks rather than the values implict in the Constitution.

In-depth Interviews

This research is based on in-depth interviews with executives, correspondents, and technicians who work for the three major networks and observations made as a participant observer in the White House, in addition to the coding and analysis of over 5,500 news stories which appeared in the CBS Evening News from 1969 through 1985.

Two core assumption lie at the heart of the Six O' Clock Presidency thesis. The first assumption is that commercial and logistical concerns contribute to policies which favour extensive coverage of the president.

News Coverage

The second assumption is that news judgement decisions, the needs of the technology of television, and the work routines of White House reporters contribute over time to a negative portrayal. Let's examine these assumptions in turn:

Extensive Coverage : Virtually one-fifth of a typical evening news broadcast concern presidential activities and policies. The White. House is the only beat in Washington to which reporters, crew, and equipment are permanently assigned because the presidency is the single biggest continuing news story that the network news presents. As a matter of fact/ since the assassination of John F. Kennedy, a crew referred to as the "death watch," made up of technicians and correspondents from the three networks record every step the president takes that can be recorded. The "networks have several important economic and political incentives for covering the president extensively; *First,* by focusing on the president the network is able to deliver to its affiliates a news programme which focuses on national news and therefore does not compete with local news'programmes. Second, extensive coverage of the president allows affiliates to meet the Federal Communication Commission's requirement to serve the public interest. Third, news coverage of the president legitimates the networks's role in American politics and elevates network prestige, thus offsetting criticism of prime time programming.

Most importantly, though the news division focuses intensely on the activities of the president because doing so is logistically easy and inexpensive. Direct communication between the bureau and the White House is possible virtually 24 hours a day. No advance ordering of satellites or coaxial lines is necessary, nor is the transmission of Washington news stories to New York charged against a producer's budget. Finally, yards, perhaps miles of videotape collected by the "death watch" pool are readily available. These are strong incentives for a cost conscious producer to use Washington stories. The point here is that because news coverage of the president is comparatively inexpensive and convenient to produce, the evening news has a major organizational incentive to broadcast news stories about the president other than the fact that the president may inherently be deserving of that coverage. Former White House correspondent Robert Pierpoint put it this way to me.

When you are a producer putting together a new show for 15 million Americans every night, you want to be sure that you are going to have stories that look and sound like news. But if you are facing court decisions that may not come down in time or satellites that aren't working or available, or if your correspondent trying to get from the Beirut airport to the transmission point doesn't make it, you are in deep trouble. But you can always count on a piece from the White House that looks and sounds like news.

The Negative Bias of Washington News Extensive coverage is not by itself detrimental to the presidency. I believe that a further examination of the way the news is collected reveals a built-in bias towards the incumbent. Here are a few of those built in biases:

Unlike a newspaper whose number of pages can be increased or decreased depending on the amount of news to be covered, the time limit of the evening news programme is fixed—22 minutes, without commercials. This means that the actual amount of news delivered in a typical evening news programme is relatively small when compared to the amount of news which appears in a typical newspaper. For example, the entire transcript of an evening news programme would barely fill the front page of the *Loss Angeles Times.* This means the individual reports must be short and therefore uncomplicated, producing in Walter Cronkite's words, "inadvertent and perhaps inevitable distortion." This also means that the complexity of the presidency is rarely captured in news reports.

Dan rather put it this way:

> There is no way a White House correspondent can come put therein a minute and 15 seconds, and give the viewer even the essence, never mind the details or the substances [of a president's policies]... One of the great difficulties of television is that it has a great deal of trouble dealing with any subject in depth.

Need for Pictures : Television news uses its technology ("picture") to compete "with other news media; The need for picture affects news coverage of the president in three ways. *First,* it makes the reporting of complicated stories that focus on complex issues more difficult. *Second,* it highlights those aspects of the office that are amenable to pictures and ignores those that are not. Finally, the need for "interesting" pictures reinforces journalism's penchant for the novel and the unusual (e.g. presidential faux pas).

The need for pictures contributes to the distortion of the presidency because pictures capture, condense, simplify and exaggerate complex political phenomena. Pictures often portray politics in "black" and "white", "good" or "evil" terms. The "grays" the qualifications, the nuances, are often lost. News pictures, like political cartoons, are effective devices for symbolic communication (which is why television is ideally suited to political campaigning). When presidents or candidates control media access, they have a formidable political tool at their disposal. But because pictures present complex political phenomena in symbolic terms reality is often exaggerated. This is how a producer for ABC's "World News Tonight," who was a deputy White house press secretary during the Carter Administration, explained it to me. Basically, when things aren't going well at the White House, the evening new's portrayal is worse than in fact the reality is. And then when things are going well for an Administration the stories suggest that things are far better than they are. There is a tendency to extremes because television is so dependent on pictures. The Camp David peace agreement between Israel and Egypt is a good example. Those pictures of Carter and Begin and Sadat embracing are just wonderful visuals. The impression they leave is that what occurred was 100 per cent positive. A newspaper reporter, however, might go on for two-thirds of his story about what a great achievement it was. But might for the last third talk about the history of the problem and certainly how insurmountable it has been up to this point. He might also add that this achievement hasn't been as great as it may appear. A negative example would be hecklers at an event who threw tomatoes at the president. This is so visually compelling that the resulting story will be a one minute spot that says, yes, the president spoke, but he was heckled throughout, and following his speech the crowd threw three tomatoes. The visuals of the tomatoes splattering on the secret service agent would be the lasting impression that you would come away with. It would have to be, arguably, ten times more dramatic to come across in print. So in print you would talk about what was said in the speech and so forth, that he was heckled throughout, and then three tomatoes were thrown.

The need for pictures also biases news coverage towards those aspects of the presidency that are amenable to visual portrayal. Many times this is due to White House restrictions. For example, President Carter's efforts to get the hostages released could not be shown in pictures. Instead description of the president's actions had to compete with visually and emotionally engrossing pictures of angry Iranian students burning the American flag. Presidential action such as the ordering of troops on a mission to free the hostages will receive more coverage then stories concerning the evolution of that policy decision, or, more important, the constraints which inhibit the exercise of presidential power. Because actions (e.g. ceremonies, bill signing, a firing of air traffic controllers, a presidential tour of a disabled nuclear power plant) receive more attention and have greater impact than "processes" (such as the development of policy options, negotiations, the evolution of ideas, the structure and functioning of the office, the constraints on presidential power) the power, purpose, and functioning of the office is systematically exaggerated and distorted. This is a direct consequence of the environmental constraints affecting television coverage of the president.

Finally, the need for interesting pictures reinforces journalism's penchant for the unusual, the departure from the norm. Thus, network news coverage of presidential faux pas and clumsiness (e.g., presidents falling down stairs, dropping their election ballot, bumping their head on a helicopter door) and visually compelling but often gratuitous, trivial, and unrepresentative stories containing compelling visuals receive more coverage than they might otherwise merit solely because of their value in pictures.

Does it matter? Former President Gerald Ford think so:

> *Every-time* I stumbled or bumped my head or fell in the snow, reporters zeroed in on that to the exclusion of almost everything else. The news coverage was harmful.. .[This] helped create the impression of me as a stumbler. And that wasn't funny. In addition, the need for pictures encourages coverage of conflict and controversy and other melodramatic events rather than the plain, routine functioning of government, which is not amenable to interesting pictures. This is how one producer for the CBS Evening News explained it to me:

There is a real big mandate for pieces to not be boring; no stand-up, no bland looking stuff. [CBS News] wants it to be more visually enticing. So you try to be more creative. People are not going to watch if it is just a stand-up. And audience polls show that they like what we are doing, which is pepping up the news. I covered President Reagan when he went to Pittsburgh. There were the angriest demonstrators in the two years that I have been travelling with him. However, If I just had the two crews that was the normal standard on the road I couldn't have gotten good pictures of those demonstrators. I had another crew sent in from New York just to cover them, and that became the main focus of the story.

Recapitulation : On the one hand, we have a complex and multifaceted Office that is based on persuasion and the subtle exercise of power and influence, an office in which most significant activities are conducted in private; an institution with limited formal power that must struggle to reach and maintain consensus; an institution in which the execution of routine governing chores is offered as one measure of competence; and an institution that depends on public support for success.

Yet, on the other hand, we have a medium which requires simplistic, visible indicators of presidential performance, a medium which is ideally suited to the portrayal of conflict; and a medium whose stated purpose is to report, interpret, as well as critically analyze the news.

Extensive Coverage

The extensiveness of television's commitment as well as the factors which contribute to negative portrayal produce a dynamic which has contributed to an increase in negative coverage of the modern presidency, and the erosion of public support. This coverage is not due to evil or disloyal persons politically opposed to the president occupying positions of power within the broadcasting industry; instead, it is simply a natural function of the nature of television news and its needs. Though some Administrations may transcend the dire consequences of the Six O'Clock Presidency, each Administration must contend with them.

Because the dynamic results lost public support, I shall first consider its effect on the standards used to judge presidents. I will then consider how modern presidents have responded to this erosion of public support and how they have attempted to manipulate network news to serve their own ends.

Effect on the Public Opinion : I believe that Six O'Clock Presidency phenomenon has led to the cumulative erosion of the standards used by the public to judge presidents and, for this reason, recent presidents have been judged more harshly and more quickly. Because citizens rely almost exclusively on network news for information about national affairs, they are inclined to judge the president on the basis of his portrayal on the evening news. Network needs, we have seen, lead to a premature evaluation of the president. Thus, the erosion of public support for presidents would not take place as quickly if television news did not cover the president extensively. Repeated disillusionment with successive regimes also leads to the decline in residual public support for the Office and the political system.

Effect on the Presidency : The Six O'Clock Presidency impacts on the presidency in three ways, along the''lines'of the three sets of value clusters Bruce Buchanan says are used to Judge presidents.

The value first cluster can be termed' ectiveness values.' By this is meant the expectation 'that' presidents will devise pragmatic ways to solve any and all problems that confront the nation. The premium from this perspective is on getting the job done, with questions of the appropriateness of means and methods distinctly in second place. The *second* cluster, 'moral values' combines precepts of democracy, and constitutional propriety. Presidents have been expected to implement 'and' embody such virtues as respect for the constitutional order, for the rights and liberties of individual citizens, and increasingly for maintenance of the international moral order. ..The *third* cluster, 'survival values' involves the preservation and ultimately the very survival of the social and political order in more-or-less recognizable form.

Buchanan believes that these values can be reduced to a single judgmental query, "Is the presidential action in question effective? Is it morally right? Is it dangerous?" Let's examine how the Six O'Clock Presidency influence each of these value clusters.

Effectiveness Values : The Six O'Clock Presidency obviously makes the president's job more difficult. Recent administrations have devoted increasing resources to public relations efforts. High level aides and the president himself also appear to spend an inordinate, amount of time on image making and image enhancing activities with the result being less time spent on substantive issues. In the beginning of a president's term, the White House attempts to use the media to marshall support for its legislative programme. Later, however, these efforts are much more defensive in nature, and are aimed primarily at keeping the level of negative news coverage to a minimum.

Most important, the erosion of support has made it mote difficult for the president to govern—to get his programmes through the congress, to bargain effectively with foreign and domestic leaders, and to mediate conflicts among conflicting social, economic and political interests. Because presidents lose support so quickly, new Administrations have only a few short months to devise and implement their legislative agenda. This has led presidents and their staffs to grasp at often ill-conceived but broadly based policies (e.g., "supply-side economics"). An all-out effort is then exerted to drive these policies through the congress. Such efforts invariably antagonize Members of Congress who believe that the legislature's role in the policy process has been preempted, and who become bent on retaliation.

Moral Values : In an effort to recapture lost support, however, presidents often abuse their office, engage in covert activities, disregard the rights and liberties of individuals, and trample on the roles of other Constitutional actors, most notably the Congress. In recent years the presidency has been at the centre of national scandal and national disgrace. Many of the abuses which originated here, however, can be attributed partly to a belief by presidents and their staffs that they could not maintain enough support to achieve their goals through legal channels.

In recent years we have seen how well-intentioned reforms have contributed to the weakening of the House of Representatives. Ironically, just when younger and less parochial members were moving to positions of power within the Chamber, those positions were considerably weakened in response to the abuses of an entrenched elite. A weakened chamber has not facilitated the attainment of social and economic justice. In a similar vein, those who look to the presidency for widescale social change have an interest in maintaining an effective and strong institution—one which, however, adheres to and promotes democratic values.

Survival Values : It is the psychological effect brought on by lost public support, however, that is of the greatest concern. The erosion of public support arguably places additional psychological pressure on the president. Four psychological exposures have been associated with the presidency—frustration, dissonance, deference, and stress. The Six O'Clock Presidency exacerbates each of these debilitating psychological experiences. Presidents become increasingly frustrated because they are unable to get the "real" story of their administration to the American people. Because presidents may come to believe that their administration, their family, as well as themselves, have been falsely and unfairly portrayed on the evening news, the internal moral barriers which may have prevented them from being less than truthful with the media (and therefore with the public) become lowered. Thus, the temptation to justify deceptive and illegal activities and outright lies is increased. All of these factors invariably increase the stress the president experiences. In response to this stress, and in an often futile effort to secure their' place in history, presidents have taken unnecessary and unwise policy risk which have not been successful (e.g. the failed hostage rescue mission). When they do so, especially in the nuclear age, they jeopardize the security, safety, and ultimately the survival of the nation.

Possible Solution

What can be done? Potential solution to the problems posed by the Six' O'Clock Presidency must address the internal logic of the argument. This means altering one or both of the assumptions which drive the dynamic. Thus) possible reforms are of two kinds: One set of reforms would address the extensiveness of news coverage of the president. The second set of reforms would address the way in which news about the president is gathered and produced. I shall address these possible reforms in reverse order.

Change the Nature of News Coverage : One way altering the cycle of news coverage is to change the way their presidential news is gathered, produced and reported. For example, if more resources were to be assigned to news coverage of the president and the format of the 'evening news programme was changed (lengthened, with longer reports), reporters could be given more lead time for the preparation of reports and more time in the programme in which to air them. News stories about the president could be longer and more complex, detailing the nuances and subtleties that get lost when reports are limited to less than two minutes of air time; This courses of action would also involve a redefinition of news and the altering of assumption about the nature of the viewing audience (thus reducing the need for conflict, drama, simplicity and pictures). Consistent with the stories of reforms would be the re-education of White House reporters with more formal training in history and political science.

Such a wholesale restructuring of the history is highly unlikely and impractical given the fact that a much simpler and direct solution that would achieve the same result is at hand.

Turn the Cameras Off : The pattern of news coverage of the president that I have presented in this paper is partly a function of the scope of the network's commitment to news coverage of the president. Thus, covering the president less, according to the logic of the argument, would defuse the impact of the negative nature of presidential news. This reform would involve changes in network policies concerning the reliance on Washington news and the Washington bureau's reliance on presidential news. Covering the president less would involve some hard-headed thinking by the networks about the consequences of their coverage of the president, and the examination of some firmly entrenched assumption about the inherent news value of the president. (Does he really warrant that much coverage?) Thus, it may be necessary to resign, or assign on a temporary basis, one or both of the network news crews permanently stationed at the White House, and instead rely more on network pools. This would undercut the incentive to use White House news. White House reporters would not push for airtime (a minimum level of which is guaranteed to some in their contracts with network); the network would not be collecting news it didn't use. If the resources were re-directed to other areas (e.g. coverage of the regulatory agencies) the incentive would be further reduced because stories from other sources would be available.

I believe the time has come for a serious examination of this proposal.

5

Readers' Angle

What are the psychological processes that determine the news reading choices of the individual readers? One of the best explanations we have, that of Wilbur Schramm, is reproduced in part, below. You should read it carefully, for you will be asked some questions based upon it.

I think it is self-evident that a person selects news in expectation of a reward.

The Reward

This reward may be either of two kinds. One is related to what Freud call the Pleasure Principle, the other to what he calls the Reality Principle. For want of better names, we shall call these two classes *immediate reward and delayed reward.*

In general, the kinds of news which may be expected to furnish immediate reward are news of crime and corruption, accidents and disasters, sports and recreation, social events, and human interest.

Delayed reward may be expected from news of public affairs, economic matters, social problem, science, education, and health.

News of the first kind pays its rewards at once. A reader can enjoy a vicarious experience without any of the dangers or stresses involved. He can shiver luxuriously at an, axe-murder, shake his head sympathetically and safely at a tornado, identify himself with the winning team or (herself) with the society lady who wore a well-described gown at the reception for Lady Morganbilt, laugh understandingly (and from superior knowledge) at a warm little story of children or dogs. News of the second kind, however, pays its rewards later. It sometimes requires the reader to endure unpleasantness or annoyances — as, for example, when he reads of the ominous foreign situation, the mounting national debt, rising taxes, falling market, scarce housing, cancer, epidemics, farm blights. It has a kind of "threat value." It is read so that the reader may be informed and prepared. When a reader selects delayed reward news, he jerks himself into the world of surrounding reality to which he can adapt himself only by hard work. When he selects news of the other kind, he retreats usually from the world of threatening reality toward the dream world.

For any individual, of course, the boundaries of these two classes are not stable. For example, a sociologist may read news of crime as a social problem, rather than for its immediate reward. A coach may read a sports story for its threat value; he may have to play that team next week. A politician may read an account of his latest successful rally, not for its delayed reward, but very much as his wife reads an account of a party. In any given story of corruption or disaster, a thoughtful reader receives not only the immediate reward of vicarious experience, but also the delayed reward of information and preparedness. Therefore, while the division of categories holds in general, the predispositions of the individual may transfer any story from one kind of reading to another, or divide the experience between the two kinds of reward.

But what is going on psychologically beneath these two kinds of choice of news?

The kind of choice which we have called immediate reward is simple associational learning, or problem solving. A stimulus is presented; a response is made; the response is rewarded. When the stimulus is again presented, there is a tendency to make the same response. If it is again rewarded, the tendency to make that same response is progressively reinforced. If it is not rewarded, the tendency is progressively extinguished. The stimulus in this case, of course, is the news item. The response is the decision to read or listen to the item. The reward maybe either a reduction of tension or discomfort (e.g. curiosity, worry) or an increase in satisfaction (e.g., from a vicarious enjoyment of the achievements of the winning team).

But what is the process which leads a reader or listener to select a news item even though he knows it may not reduce tension, but actually *increase* tension; not relieve discomfort, but actually *increase discomfort;* not bring satisfaction, but actually bring dissatisfaction and worry? We have already suggested that these two kinds of reading are related to what Fraud called the two principles of mental functioning, the Pleasure Principle and the Reality Principle. That is, the immediate reward choice is learned through trial and error because it succeeds in reducing drives and tensions. The delayed reward choice, on the other hand, is made not because it is pleasant, but because sit is realistic. It is not pleasant to be afraid or to anticipate danger; but it is necessary, if one is to avert harm and avoid danger.

O.H. Mowrer, in his reinterpretation of conditioning and problem solving, has advanced a concept of learning which is extremely suggestive to any student of the process of communication. He points out that there are really two aspects of learning, related respectively to the two nervous systems. The central nervous system is the one chiefly through which we affect society, the autonomic nervous system is the one chiefly through which society affects us. The Central system is the one through which habits — that is, learned responses of the skeletal musculature — are formed. The autonomous system is the one through which attitudes or emotions — that is, learned responses of glands, smooth muscle, and vasomotor tissue — are formed.

Habits, of course come into being to reduce drives and solve problems. Attitudes and emotions, on the other hand, are themselves drives or problems, and call forth skeletal reactions on the basis of which the central nervous system may go into action and develop habits.

Therefore, responses to the two kinds of news corresponds to what Sherrington calls *anticipatory* and *consummatory* responses. One is made as the consummation of a drive and with the expectation of immediate reward. The other is made to set up a drive, and in expectation of danger or delayed reward. One reduces a drive and is therefore pleasant; the other sets up a drive and may be painful. The two responses are not always cleanly differentiated. For example, the dramatic quality in a foreign news story may give an immediate reward, while the content arouses only fear or anticipation of danger. But learning may take place through either method. Gordon Allport gives an example of learning through the anticipatory response; "Suppose I mispronounce a word in a public speech... and suffer mounting shame and discomfort. Tension has been created, not reduced; dissatisfaction and not satisfaction has resulted; but in this sequence of events I shall surely learn."

When a child starts to read a newspaper he usually begins with the comics and the pictures. He proceeds to the sports news, the human interest stories, and sensational stories of crime and disaster, all before he makes much use of public affairs news. It is interesting to conjecture how a child begins to read public affairs news. Perhaps he has an experience in which he is able to make not-too-long-delayed use of something he has read in the paper. Perhaps it helps him to answer a question at school, or to take his raincoat and avoid a soaking, or to avoid a street which is closed for repairs—in other words, to avoid trouble by being informed. He looks at the paper with respect. It reading the particular item was of benefit to him would it not be well for him to read other items also? As his understanding broadens, he perceives more of the causative and repetitive relation of events in society. And thus he substitute other stimuli for the stimulus which has had a proved reward and as his horizon broadens comes to see more and more reasons for reading news of public affairs.

Thus the time when he comes to read public affairs news is an important point in his socialization. Most of the news in the immediate reward group is important to him individually because of the individual satisfaction and drive-reduction it accomplishes. But the news in the delayed group is important to him because it arouses the tensions and anticipation that are necessary for survival and development, that help him to be more effective, better prepared, socially. ...

General Classes

If we accept tentatively the theory that there are two general classes of news, two patterns of reading, and two aspects of the learning process involved, then another variable important. Within each kind of news, what determines the likelihood that a given item will be selected? What determines the attractiveness of a given item to the reader?

Leaving out chance, conflicting mental sets, and the qualities of presentation which call attention to one item over others or make one item easier to read than others, we can hypothesize that a person chooses the items which he thinks are likely to give him the greatest reward. The exact yard-stick by which he measures this predictive value is an individual matter based on experience and personality structure, and powerfully influenced by the momentary situation. But in general there seems to be greater expectation of reward when there appears to be greater possibility of the reader identifying himself with the news.

The Proximity

This may be what the textbooks mean by proximity as a news value, but is not to be interpreted as mere physical proximity. For example: fight in an American city may be physically nearer than a battle in the South Pacific, but if a mother has a son in the battle then how much more easily can she identified herself with the distant battle than with the nearer fight. On the other hand, the American scrap is likely to seem closer to the average reader than a Dutch coup in Indonesia, although one may ultimately have large repercussions for the colonial system and for international trade, whereas the other will doubtless pass out of the realm of important affairs as soon as the participants sober up. Similarly, it is a greater reward to identify oneself with the local team which is winning a championship than with a far away team that is equally good. One of the startling accomplishments of mass communications has been to bring far corners and faraway people almost next door, so that it becomes relatively easy for a reader to identify himself with the personal affairs of movie stars in Hollywood, and for thousand of sports fans who have never been in South Bend to feel like alumni of Notre Dame. It is also easier to identify oneself with an event which is vividly described and which has a minimum of indirection. But it is safe to say that the individual world of the reader will for the most part determine the ease with which he can identify himself with the given team, and this in turn will powerfully affect the probability of the item being read.

Exercise: 1. In which of the following news stories (synopses) would you have a high interest? A low interest?

(a) A prominent club woman was beaten and choked to death today by her 15-year-old son, who said she had engaged him ever since he was arrested for trying to chloroform and photograph a girl friend.

(b) The erstwhile Soviet Union threatened to resume testing atomic and hydrogen bombs unless France stops nuclear tests in the Sahara.

(c) An 18-year-old youth was executed today for a murder shot he did not fire-despite a dramatic appeal for his life to the governor.

(d) There's a farmer near here who makes more money selling water than he makes from the eleven oil wells on his farm.

2. Below is a list of twenty reasons that people have assigned for their choosing to read a particular news story. For each of the four news stories above check as many of the reasons as you would apply to the choices you made of the stories you would read (if any) and of the stories you would reject (if any).

(a) This might be amusing.

(b) Somebody should do something about this matter.

(c) This needs explaining.

(d) I know someone who'll want to hear about this.

(e) I dislike such stories.

(f) I'm tired of reading about this.

(g) I know something about this that's not in the papers.

(h) This makes me feel sad.

(i) This will help me keep up with what's going on.

(j) This may affect me personally.

(k) This is disturbing.

(l) I can imagine this happening.

(m) This might be exciting.

(n) This might give me something to talk about.

(o) This is something I should be concerned about.

(p) I always read stories like this, but I don't know why ?

(q) This information might be useful to me.

(r) This looks like good news.

(s) I'd like to find out how this happened.

(t) I know how that person must feel.

Kinds of Readers

Merrill Samuelson presented sixteen synopses of news stories to a sample of readers and asked them (1) to rank the stories in an order of interest (i.e. preference) and (2) to apply to each story one or more of the reasons for reading that are listed in Exercise (above). By factor analyzing these data, he was able to differentiate five different types of readers.

One type (D) had high interest scores on such stories as the Soviet Union's threat to renew bomb testing and very low interest scores on crime stories and the trivia-puzzle type of story such as the one about a farmer making more money selling water than from his eleven oil wells. Moreover, the reasons assigned for the preferences were mainly "The needs explaining" "This may affect me personally," and " This is something I should be concerned about," On the basis of the interest scores and the reasons given, he categorized this type of reader as one who reads mainly for delayed reward.

A second type (A) had high interest scores on many of the same news stories on which Type D readers had high interest scores, but they did not give as many of the same reasons as did the Type D readers. This type of reader, who was more highly educated than the other types, was less involved in the events he preferred to read about than were Type D readers.

The interest scores of a third type (B) and the reasons they assigned enabled the experimenter to categorize them as an immediate reward type of reader. This type preferred the stories that were puzzles and which supplied a complete and early solution, such as how a youth could be executed for a shot he did not fire and how a farmer could make more money from selling water than from the eleven oil wells. The main reasons to this type were "This needs explaining," "I 'd like to find out how this happened," and "This gives me something to talk about." This type of reader is less concerned with the environment he lives in than are Types D and A, and is less interested in the deferred solutions to the long span problems that are inherent in international politics and social problems.

Readers of a fourth type (E) selected both immediate reward and delayed reward kinds of stories, although they had a low preference for crime stories. The main reasons they gave were "This will help me keep up with what's going on," This needs explaining," and "I'd like to find out how this happened," The main reasons given for rejecting stories (mostly about crime) were "This is disturbing" and "This is something I should be concerned about."

The preferences, rejections, and reasons of a fifth type (C) did not form a pattern that could be explained by the experimenter.

As research into news reading behaviour continues we may learn more about the motivation of different types of readers. As the studies presented in this chapter suggest, the explanations are in the personality structure of the individual reader. Researchers need to develop better personality measures that would be appropriate in this area and to include in their studies more questions than have so far been asked.

Exercise

1. How would you categorize each of the stories in Exercise given above as immediate reward or as delayed reward?
2. An editor to whom you have applied for a job asks you to write an explanation of not more than 150 words on why people choose to read a particular news story and reject a particular news story. Write your explanation.

Personal Choice

Although the news that one selects to read is determined by his basic personality needs and drives and his life history, it is also related to one or more of his roles in society. As a voter and a taxpayer, the reader is interested in some of the news about government, and newspapers accept an obligation to inform him in that area. As a housewife, a reader is interested in news about prices of consumers' goods. As a parent, a reader is interested in news about education and juvenile delinquency. As an investor, a reader is interested in some of the news about business; most investors are forty or more years old and most are men, although an increasing number of women read business news. As a member of some group, a reader is interested in news about that group and about the matters with which the group is concerned— for example, religion. Most readers have one or more hobbies — for example, sports and bridge — and the newspaper caters to their interests. So many people have some community of interest that specialized magazines are published about the interests; the amount of space that a newspaper can devote to each of these special interests, however, is limited.

The same news story is sometimes read by some persons in one role and by other persons in a different role. An example of such a story: "The United States Supreme Court ruled yesterday that natural gas pipeline companies may use a "short cut" procedure to increase gas rates without consent of their customers. The decision brought a surge in the price of major natural gas stocks on the New York Stock Exchange." Some readers were interested in this story as consumers of natural gas and some as investors in a natural gas pipeline or local gas distributing company. A wire service which reported this decision tied into the decision the effect on the stock market, and a local newspaper tied in an interview with the local gas distributing company which purchased its gas from a pipeline company. The competent newspaper and wire service editor analyzes every event with the view to supplying answers to questions which will come to the mind of readers who will read in different roles.

There have been many definitions of news, but none is quite satisfactory- Perhaps as good a definition as any is that of Turner Catledge, executive editor of the *New York Times*: "News is anything you find out today that you didn't know before."

Since, however, a newspaper's capacity for printing news compels it to be selective, an editor needs some kind of guideline or benchmark for estimating what will interest his readers. What he does, therefore, is to look for the presence in each event of certain elements which he believes to be interesting. Although he thinks of a story as being about some subject matter, such as crime, labour, or death, he also looks for an additional dimension which makes the event different from similar events of its class. Sometimes this element is odd, eccentric, or bizarre, but most often it is merely unusual. Some examples:

> A St. Paul man today shot and killed his second wife, 12 years after he killed his first wife.
>
> Cancer killed bandleader Jimmy Dorsey, today, less than seven months after the death of his brother Tommy [also a bandleader].

The first story was a crime story about an obscure retired postal employee. The second story not only had a similar unusual element, but it concerned two persons who were well known. Thus, if we were designing some calculus of reader interest, we would say that the second story has three interest elements: (1) death, (2) well-known person, and (3) singularity.

Newsworthy

When a participant in an event is well known, the event is more news-worthy than when the participant is not well known. Some persons are prominent because of their high status in society and others because of the frequent exposure of their name or face or voice to newspaper readers or television viewers. Personalities on the television screen, for example, become so familiar to the viewers that the viewers come to feel they know them well. The following Associated Press story was well displayed in San Francisco newspaper:

> LAKE SUCCESS, N.Y. — Television personality Arlene Francis suffered a brain concussion yesterday when her convertible went out of control on the Northern State Parkway and collided headon with another car. A woman in the second auto was killed.
>
> Authorities at Harkness Pavilion said she was being treated for a minor concussion, a fracture of the collar bone, a cut on the scalp and bruises.

Miss Francis is a regular panelist on the TV show, "What's Myline?"

The points to be noted in the foregoing story are that injuries to the women were of two different orders but that the orders of prominence were reversed. If neither woman had been prominent, regardless of the order of the injuries, the event would have been a "constant."

Easy Identity

Readers identify easier when events are near to them. Schramm's defines the nature of news proximity as being psychological, not merely physical. An event that happens in our own community has higher news value than an event that happens a considerable distance away. But, as Schramm said, a mother whose son was in military service in the South Pacific would be more interested in a battle in that area than in a fight in an American city. Readers are also interested in events that happen in places in which they have formerly lived or have visited.

An editor whose newspaper is read by most of the people in his community always assumes that the presence of a local element in any story makes it more interesting than a story in which the local element is absent. Thus, a news story about a fatal automobile accident in another community has a higher news value when one of the persons killed was a resident of the editor's community.

Editors also are alert to "local angles" in wire service stories. An example; a wire service reported the explosion in Berlin, New York, of a propane gas tank truck which killed two persons and injured fifteen others. This despatch generated a "could-this-happen-here?" story in a California sub-urban newspaper in which local fire marshals and highway patrolmen were quoted as to the California laws which regulate the transportation of propane on highways.

If you should ever work for a wire service, you would learn early in your employment about the importance of the "points" on a wire; a "point" is one of the cities in which a newspaper receives the wire report. Thus, you would include in a story a reference to any person living in any of the communities and any reference to any of the communities. Whenever a wire service correspondent in World War II wrote about some soldier or sailor involved in a military action, he included the name of his city and, when available, his street address.

News Dimensions : Our knowledge of the news value of the two dimensions of interest we have just discussed — well-known persons and proximity - is soundly based in psychological theory. Perhaps psychological theory also tells us some-thing about the interest value of certain other kinds of news, such as news about cute children, animals, and money, but we have little objective evidence to support some of the dicta that have been mentioned by textbook writers. Below, however, is a list of about fifty mutually exclusive categories of news elements that were developed for a content analysis, and it might be interesting to speculate about the degrees of interest readers would have in some of them. Only a few are defined here. Keep in mind that each news story is likely to have *two or more* of these elements. Thus, a particular news story might be classified as "Our Community Crime" or "Persons Well Known/Labour." These categories fit only the content of the particular issues of the newspapers which were studied. For an analysis of other newspapers at other times a few of these categories would be dropped and perhaps certain new categories would have to be developed.

Persons Well Known : Persons presumed to be well known to most readers of the particular newspaper because of their fame or notoriety or particular accomplishment.

Persons Not Well Known : Persons in the news because of their particular accomplishments or activities or position, but not well known to the usual reader of the particular newspaper.

People in Groups : Persons in the news because they are officers or committee members of their clubs, lodges, societies, fraternal organizations, Boy Scouts, and other non-governmental groups; pallbearers, etc.

Hollywood : Persons not otherwise well known who are associated with the Hollywood entertainment industries. Excluded: activities of those persons classified as "Persons Well Known."

Our Community, Our Region : An element with which all members of the newspapers community (or region) identify themselves because of the place of the community in the news item or the effect this news may have on the community.

Our Nation : An element with which almost all readers of United States newspapers might identify themselves as members of this nation.

This does not imply that all events happening within the boundaries of the United States have this element; nor does this element apply only to stories taking place within these boundaries.

Our Allies : During a "cold war" period, some political and economic events in a country formally and informally allied to the United States have a peculiar meaning to an American reader because they are or seem to be related to the security or welfare of the United States. Excluded: news in which American men or equipment are directly involved or in which the United States interest is directly stated.

Our Enemies : Most political and economic events in the Communist controlled nations affect the American reader in a different way than do events in other foreign countries. Such events may be threatening or reassuring.

Other Nations : (a) News about happenings in foreign countries other than those mentioned in "Our Nation," "Our Allies," and "Our Enemies." (b) Also those happenings in the countries included in ' 'Our Allies" and "Our Enemies" which do not directly or indirectly affect the welfare of the United States.

Governmental Acts

Politics

Rebellion

War

Defense

Atomic Bomb-Atomic Energy

Diplomacy and Foreign Relations

Economic Activity

Prices

Taxes

Labour, Major

Labour, Minor

Agriculture

Judicial proceedings, Civil

Crime

Communism in the U.S.A.

Sex

Relations

Accidents, Disasters

First Order

Second Order

Third Order

Social and Safety Measures

Race Relations

Alcohol

Money

Health, Personal

Health, Public

Science and Invention

Religion

Philanthropy

Weather

Natural Deaths

Transportation

Education

Children, Welfare of

Children, Cute

Animals

Marriage and Marital

Amusements

The Arts, Culture

Human Interest

For Class discussion

1. Which combinations of two or more elements in a news story would speculate would generate the highest interest? The lowest?
2. These news stories evoked tremendous reader interest at the time they were published: Lindbergh's flight across the Atlantic, Gertrude Ederle's successful swimming of the English Channel, and Floyd Collins' entrapment in a Kentucky cave. What common element did they have that evoked so much interest.

Various News Items

News may be classified in various ways as to origin, subject matter ,and treatment. Here are a few kinds of news that get published, this list of categories, however, is not exhaustive.

Chronicle : Much of the news is taken from records in public offices and from reports by police and other officials. It is a kind of news that is easy to get: a newspaper just assigns a reporter to the police station, courthouse, city hall, and federal building.

In small cities, nearly all of this kind of news that is available is published, but in large cities only the news that is important or interesting is selected by editors. Much of this kind of news could be called a "constant" because it relates to something the reader has often read before with only the names of the participants being different. Most accidents and crimes are constants. The reaction of readers is often "I'm tired of reading about this " or " I always read stories like this, but I don't know why." Some newspapers publish this kind of news only as a record.

Editors would like to cover a wider range of readers' interests than they do but have not developed an adequate technique for finding out about a different kind of news. It is the practice of London popular newspapers to pay informants for tips about news, but few American newspapers have done that. The Council Blufts (Iowa) *Nonpareil* however, developed a list of persons who often supply tips on "off-beat" news sources. Reporters contact them daily, weekly, or monthly. One example : a story that the federal building was tilting and was scheduled to be demolished; the tip came from an architect.

Sometimes it is possible for the news writer to organize the facts in a chronicle type of news story so that reading the story is emotionally rewarding. One way is to organize the facts in a climatic order when the facts justify that form of news story. Some chronicle type items are highly read.

In 1922, Walter Lippmann said it was the nature of news to signalize an event; that is, to report (only) some overt act. News, he said, is "but the report of an aspect that has obtruded itself. The news does not tell you how the seed is germinating in the ground, but it may tell you when the first sprout breaks through the surface. Thus, a labour dispute doesn't get reported until there is an overt act, such as a strike, and most white readers could not have been aware of the frustrations and aspirations of Negroes until the Negroes had conducted public demonstrations of protest.

Since Lippmann wrote in 1922, however, newspapers and wire services have been perceiving news as more than just "spot" news. They are reporting facts that may indicate what is going to happen. They are trying to supply more background about over events and the people who participate in some of the events, and they try to report change in society. As students of history know, social change is brought about by new technology and new ideas. Editors are now more habituated to perceiving change and the causes of change as something to be reported — what JamesB. Rest on has called the reporting of "quiet revolutions". Newspapers also are reporting changes in manners and morals.

For Class Discussion

1. What is your evaluation of this statement: "Because of the excellence of our newspapers and magazine Americans are the best informed people in the world"?
2. A competent foreign correspondent who is a Latin America specialist has said that most American editors were surprised by the success of the Castro revolution in Cuba because, instead of publishing the "what's behind the news" kind of news they had been receiving from Cuba, they substituted the more dramatic " spot" stories received from Cuba and other parts of the world. If this is true, whose fault was it?

"Give Lift" News : Since newspapers report so much news about conflict, most editors would like to report more news about people who exhibit courage, sacrifice, and compassion — news (to paraphrase William Faulkner) which suggests to readers that man's

spirit will endure and prevail over the: basic animal drives. Such news gives the reader a "lift" spiritually and suggests to him that we do not live in a jungle world. Here are two examples of such local news stories that the Associated Press thought were worthy of being included in its daily report; the stories were widely used by newspapers.

Christians Help to

> LAWRENCE, KAN. — Somewhat to the surprise of the 35 Jewish families in Lawrence and about 80 Jewish students at the University of Kansas, a quiet campaign is going on to raise funds for remodeling the Jewish community center into a synagogue.

"We did not know about it; we did to organize it," said Herman Cohen, president of the community center.

Who did? Some Christians, One of them, O.O. Ringler, explained the project was started because the Jews are the only religious group in Lawrence with no place to worship. The closest synagogues are in Kansas City and Topeka.

"It gives a person a wonderful feeling to have something like this happen, "said Cohen. "It is a fine thing to have others trying to help us."

Know Anybody Salvation Army Has Helped? : KINGSPORT, TENN. -The newsboy kept walking past the Salvation Army Christmas collection kettle. Each trip he dropped in two cents.

An Exchange Club member, helping man the kettle station, finally figured it out. The 9-year old lad was donating his two cents profit from each paper sale.

Just to be sure, the clubman went up and purchased a paper and gave the boy a nickel tip. A few minutes later the lad was back at the kettle. This time he dropped in seven cents.

" Do you know anybody the Salvation Army has helped?" a club member asked the newsboy.

''Yes, sir. We got a Christmas basket last year,'' the boy replied.

Wednesday, the Exchange Club had the newsboy as its special guest at a luncheon. He left with a new bicycle, wearing a new jacket, and with a savings account book showing more than $60 on deposit for his future education.

He was introduced only as Gary. The club said it wanted to publicize the deed rather than the boy and his family.

Salvation Army records showed that Gary is one of five children, aged 2 to 13. The parents have worked irregularly this year with the top income for one month about $57.

Gary's third-grade teacher said he almost never misses a day of school and often shares what he has with some youngster less fortunate than he.

How When, and Where the Newspaper is Read : The newspaper, like the telephone and the automatic washer, is a utility. How, when, and where is it used? A 1961 study has supplied some answers to these questions. The study revealed that readers use their newspapers in these ways:

50.4% Proceed through most of the paper one page after another and read whatever is interesting.

14.2% Proceed through the paper page by page, but scanning quickly:

20.0% Turn first to some specific item (e.g. the stock market tables or a particular column) and then proceed through the paper one page after another;

12.6% Turn first to some specific item and then proceed page by page, but scanning quickly;

2.8% Turn to a specific item but do not look at or read anything else.

These findings indicate not only that the newspaper is read rather thoroughly but also that a large majority of readers expose themselves to a synopsis, at least, of everything in the newspaper. This fact explains why some readership studies have turned up news stories on the inside pages which have had higher readership than any story on the front page. The findings are confirmed by the "reader traffic" data obtained from several hundred readership studies: a large majority of readers go clear through the paper; whether they read or do not read something on each page depends upon what is on the pages and the interests of the individual readers. Some readers scan but do not read anything on some pages; for example, some men are not interested in the content of women's pages. The amount of newspaper content that each reader reads is determined by (1) his needs and interests and (2) the amount of time available to him.

Readers' Mind

The reader has a different mental set when he reads a newspaper and when he reads a book or magazine. "Reading a book," says Irving Kristol, 'is quite a different experience from reading a magazine. The original commitment by the reader is much more substantial. Picking up a book is an affirmation of more serious purposes.' 'There is also some difference in original commitment in reading a newspaper and reading a news magazine because they are read under different conditions.

For class discussion : Considering the fact (a) that the newspaper reader has a different original commitment when he reads opinion and when he reads news and (b) that most readers go through the newspaper page by page selecting to read those items that interest them, what is the proper location in the newspaper for the editorial-opinion page?

Ninety percent of readers of a weekday newspaper read it at home, 6 per cent at work, 3 per cent when visiting, and about 2 per cent on their way to or from work. This is a national average; it would not apply, for example, in New York city, where fewer newspapers are home delivered.

The average weekday newspaper is read at different times of the day. It is picked up and looked at 2.4 different times by each individual reader.

The study which reported this finding also reported that the average reader spent 3 6 minutes a day reading his newspaper; this is a self-estimate and is about the same self-estimate reported in previous studies.

The editor tries to produce a newspaper that will maximize the time a reader will devote to it. Nevertheless, the amount of time that a reader allocates to newspaper reading is determined, to some extent, by the readers individual living habits, such as the time he or she gets up in the morning, the time the children leave for school, the time the housewife does her marketing, and several other reasons.

The following table shows when people read a newspaper, listen to news or the radio, and watch television news:

	Read Newspaper	**Listen to Radio News**	**Watch TV News**
Early morning..................	16%	25%	3%
Late morning....................	12	8	1
Midday..............................	1	18	1
Early afternoon............	7	5	3
Late afternoon........................	21	9	3
Early evening........................	20	12	17
Late evening..........................	20	12	17
Other, not specified..............	2	3	0
	87%	85%	45%

The table indicates that more people listen to news on the radio before nine o'clock in the morning than read a newspaper before that time. It also indicates that fewer people get their news from television than from the newspaper or radio. When respondents in this sample were asked, 'Where do you usually get the news of the day first?" their answers were: radio, 52 percent; newspapers, 28 per cent; television, 17 per cent; "can't say," 3 per cent.

The Lead : The beginning of the news story is called the lead or *intro.* For many years the beginning was a formless, rambling sentence or combination of sentences that led up to the account of the event. Here is an example from the report of a national political convention:

This, the last day of the Republican jubilee, dawned as bright as the prospects of the great party of freedom, and remained throughout one of those days of brilliant sunshine which are set a long intervals as are the diadems in the early Summer. As on the previous day, the streets were crowded at an early hour with surging crowds....

Summary Lead : Some time after the Civil War a definite from developed which summarized the what, who, when and where of the reported event.

It has been stated that the summary form of lead originated during the Civil War; that, because of the unreliability of the telegraphic services, some war reporters adopted the procedure of reporting a battle by sending a brief summary followed by a detailed Labouration. Their reasoning was that the summary would reach the newspaper speedily even though the more lengthy "body" of the story might be delayed.

We find the summary lead being used in the eighteen-eighties, first by wire services and later by local reporters. This way of reporting news had a particular advantage, in the opinion of Melville E. Stone, the first general manager of the Associated Press: it virtually assured objectivity in reporting because it restricted the writer to the what-who-when-where formula. Since the Associated Press supplied news reports to newspapers supporting both political parties, Mr. Stone believed the Associated Press should establish a reputation for reliable factual reporting even though some inherently interesting events had to be reported in a colourless manner. This form also permitted a newspaper to eliminate all or a part of the body of an Associated Press dispatch.

The advent of the spoken radio newscast influenced newspapers to abandon the practice of having a summary lead for all news stories. Summary lead are still used for most routine news stories, but news writers now often write in the way that people talk. If a person talked in the way that some summary leads are written, he would sound as if he was out of breath. The comprehension of the reader of a long lead is about the same as the comprehension of a listener to such a lead. A listener, in most circumstances, has the opportunity of interrupting a speaker with questions and of asking him to repeat all or a part of his narrative. Since a newspaper reader cannot employ this "feedback" he must regress in his reading. This is frustrating, and it sometimes causes the reader to abandon his reading of a news story just as he would turn the dial on his radio. His reward from reading under such conditions does not justify his effort.

Length of the Lead Sentence : It is important for comprehension that the first sentence of the news story be fairly short. An easily comprehensible sentence has the effect of drawing the reader into the story—of inducing him to continue reading. The average number of words in the first sentence of the Associated Press A-wire report is 23 words. Since the Associated Press makes a strong effort to achieve ease of reading, this score may be regarded as a suitable par for the local news writer.

The writer should summarize as much as possible in the first sentence without letting it be too long. In some instances he has to sacrifice brevity to include a key fact, but he should try for brevity. The way he achieves this goal is by distributing some of the *Ws* in the first two or three sentences instead of including all of them in the first sentence. Here are two ways of reporting the filing of a damage suit:

> Irving Loring, 40, of 268 Brucker street, a passenger in a sports convertible that toppled off a Shoreline

> highway cliff last March 24, filed a $200,000 damage suit in superior court yesterday against the driver, Walter Patterson.
>
> Loring, a credit manager for a wholesale liquor company, alleges that Patterson, 22, of Piedmont, drove the car at a "wanton and reckless rate of speed" and was under the influence of intoxicants at the time the car went off the cliff.

Loring says he suffered severe face and skull injuries that required 140 stitches.

As Rewritten:

What A passenger in a car that toppled of a Shoreline highway cliff last March 24 sued the driveryester day for $200,000 damages.

Who Irving Loring of 268 Brucker street, a credit manager for a wholesale liquor company, alleged his facial and skull injuries required 140 stitches.

Where In a complaint filed in superior court, he charged that the driver, Walter Patterson, 22 of Piedmont, was under the influence of intoxicants.

Why He also alleged that Patterson was driving at "Wanton and reckless rate of speed."

The second version of this report is more easily comprehended because (1) the number of words in the first sentence is only 19 instead of the 33 words in the first version, and (2) most of the *Ws* are distributed through the first three paragraphs. Since the names of the principals are not well-known, they are referred to as "passenger" and "driver" in the first sentence so that the reader understands the "what" without having to think about who they are while he is reading the first sentence. He may continue reading to find out whether or not the principals are persons he knows or has heard about. The first sentence in the second version also corresponds more closely to the way one person would tell another person about the event.

Exercise: Rewrite this lead: "An early transfer of between 200 and 3 00 flights daily from the traffic jam at Chicago's O' Hare International Airport to Midway Airport on the southside was recommended yesterday by John E. Egan, former alderman from the Midway ward [3th] and for 17 years chairman of the city council aviation committee. Egan now is a sanitary district trustee."

Purposes of the Lead : The lead has three objectives. Whether a writer tries too achieve all three of them door only one or two depends upon the character of the event. The objectives are (1) to tell the gist, or substance, of the event, (2) to draw the reader into the story, and (3) to cause the reader to see the event.

Stating the Substance of the event : Before a reporter or dictates a story he decides which aspect of the event to put in the lead. This decision is sometimes called "playing the feature " or "playing up the angle."

When the action reported has been completed it is often possible for the lead to be a single sentence.

Ajuror in aburglary trial was himself arrested yesterday.

A new way of producing atomic energy without either uranium or million-degree heat was announced today.

"Go ahead and smoke-moderately", is the recommendation of Dr. William A Reinhoff, noted Baltimore surgeon, who discounts the idea that smoking causes lung cancer.

Multiple "Whats": In some events the news writer perceives two aspects to feature. The second of these is an aspect that adds interest to the report.

A labourer was sentenced yesterday to pay a $ 150 fine for stealing three chunks of copper worth $65 from a University Labouratory.

The Stale of New Jersey, which spent $1,200,000 to capture and convict Bruno Richard Hauptmann, executed him tonight with a penny's worth of electricity.

Some "whats" are so routine that they are barely newsworthy, but some circumstance, when added, may enhance interest in the report. An example: a woman sued an automobile driver for injuries she received when she dashed into the street to rescue her small son from the path of the car. She lost her suit for damages. One reporter wrote the lead this way:

A verdict in favour of Samuel Howell, charged with negligence when his automobile struck Mrs. Nancy Farlow, was brought in by a circuit court jury yesterday.

Another Reporter's Lead was : A mother, who was injured while trying to save her 4-year old son from the path of an automobile, was denied damages by a circuit court jury yesterday.

Not a great many readers of the first version would continue after reading the lead sentence unless they knew one of the principals. But a very large number of readers would continue reading the second version to get an answer to the" why".

Here is an example of a news story that left out of the lead an essential part of the "what":

> A Jonesboro man today sued the Universal Oil Co. and its employee, Ira Thompson, for injuries received in an automobile accident last November 6.
>
> The complaint, asking $10,000 damages, was filed in circuit çourt by Madison Wilson. He alleges Thompson was driving the company's car.

What is the "what"? Was this an accident in which two cars collided? Since it was not that kind of accident, the writer had to write a third paragraph to tell all of the "what." A better lead would have been :

> A Jonesboro *pedestrian* sued the Universal Oil Co. and its employee, Ira Thompson, today for $10,000.
>
> Madison Wilson filed the complaint in circuit court alleging he was struck by a company car driven by Thompson last November.
>
> The second version is seven lines shorter than the first version. Since the key word "pedestrian" was the second word in the lead sentence the reader knew at once the nature of the event.
>
> The effect of an action or an event is sometimes the principal "what" in a lead.

Pedro Lopez, alias Peter De Lucci, age 34, entered the home of J.F. Foderer, 1548 Howard street, on January 19 (according to his own testimony) at about 5:20 p.m., and stole a radio and some jewelry. He aided the police in recovering the loot. His attorney was Percy Jackson and the assistant district attorney was I.D. Matteis. Lopez was born in Puer to Rico. He had served two terms in San Quentin reformatory.

Burglary after sunset constitutes first degree burglary. Second degree burglary is burglary during daylight. Lopez was tried yesterday in superior court presided over by Judge Aylett Cotton. If he had been convicted of first degree burglary, he would automatically, under the statutes, have been a third offender and his sentence would have been 12 years to life. Second degree burglary carries a sentence of one to five years. Judge Cotton ruled that Lopez committed the burglary in daylight although the prosecutor conjectured that Lopez would certainly have been seen carrying away property in daylight. Sunset, it was stipulated in the evidence was 5:42 o'clock. The defendant was convicted of second degree burglary and sentenced to San Quentin for one to five years.

In the type of news story which reports changes, innovations, and developments in society, industry, education and other spheres of life, the best lead is often one of the concrete instances or examples of the matter being reported. The beginning of such a news story also, as a rule, presents a scene or a person doing some act or talking.

LUBBOCK. Texas - Thousands of white-faced cattle with round, sad eyes and unsophisticated tastes nose about in long troughs filled with a green, flaky concoction.

Nearby, workmen are finishing off a new 25,000 square-foot meat-packing plant scheduled to begin handling 400 head of cattle a day next month.

"We can do as good a cattle feeding job here as anybody in the Corn Belt— and do it cheaper," boasts sport-shirted Durward W. Lewter, part owner of Lewter, Inc.'s feed lot and packing plant here."

"We have our choice of the best cattle here. We're in the heart of the grain sorghum area with its cheap feed. And right at hand is the cotton that supplies us with the meal and hulls for feed supplements."

A Change on the Range Mr. Lewter's words sum up:

some of the reasons for a quiet but significant change taking place today on the western range lands — a change that already is having an economic impact in these parts and one that's likely to have increasingly-wide repercussions on traditional patterns of raising and marketing beef cattle.

Historically, cattlemen in the range lands stretching through New Mexico, west Texas, Oklahoma, western Kansas and Colorado have shipped most of their herds to other areas, principally the Midwest, for fattening on corn before they were sent to market. (*Wall Street Journal.*)

Drawing the Reader into the Story : There are several ways of writing the lead sentence that induce the reader to continue his reading. One of them was mentioned before, viz., generating surprise by adding an antithetic element to cause the reader to learn the ' 'why." A somewhat similar device is the *question* lead. It prepares the reader to make a response in somewhat the way he is prepared to respond when personally addressed in a face-to-face relationship.

Who should pay for the proposed addition to the Community Hospital—patients who would pay higher room charges or city taxpayers?

The City Council will discuss this question tonight after it has received a report from a citizens' committee.

A lead which is a *direct addressed* the reader—a "you" lead - is also calculated to induce the reader to continue reading because it involves him to some degree.

If you've recently had a baby, bought a car, or moved, chances are your name is for sale.

It's worth from a penny to a dollar in the expanding market for mailing lists of people with special interests or needs.

Such lists are purchased by advertisers from firms that cull names and addresses of potential customers from public records, newspapers, subscription rolls and other sources.

The quote lead. Beginning the story with a quotation is, in most instances, disapproved. The reason is that readers are mainly interested in action, not talk. Quotation may repel the reader instead of drawing him into the story. In some circumstances, however, a quotation can draw the reader into the story when the question is very brief. One instance is when it is a part of the gist of the story.

"Under no conditions."

That was Governor Cox's answer yesterday when asked whether he might change his mind and accept the Republican nomination for Vice President.

A quote lead is sometimes a good way to introduce a personal experience story.

"My fingers were raw. We figured that it we could hang on by morning, someone would find us."

"I kept hold trigger till no noise. Then saw blood."

So Takao Phillyaw, Japanese-born widow, explained how she killed her husband's cousin at her east side apartment last night.

When there is no other way to put people into a dull story a quote lead may draw the reader into the story. Reports of meetings of the city council, the planning commission, and the school board are often reported without a single name's being mentioned. The news story reports only the actions taken, and the action relate only to inanimate objects and abstract matters such as proposals, plans, and taxes. The reader is not able to visualize the proceedings. Here are two versions of a report of a planning commission meeting; the main difference is that a single quotation in the body of the first story has been transposed to the lead in the second.

80-Foot Dome Shopping Centre Plan Put Off **:** Action on a proposed hemispherical, 80-foot high, $550,000 shopping centre for Alto was postponed yesterday by the Country Planning Commission pending notification of nearby residents of the height of the building.

Samuel Nelder, Tiburon Peninsula property owner, had requested a use permit and architectural supervision for the shopping center on eight acres on both sides of Belvedere drive between Reed boulevard and Highway 101.

Architect John S. Bolles has planned an 80-foot high "geodesic dome" of aluminium.

"Isn't anyone objecting to the height of the building?" asked Commissioner Felix M. Warburg.

R.D. Dobbs, principal planner, explained that the height was not mentioned in the notice to property owners.

Planning Director Mary Summers' pointed out that a country ordinance limits buildings to 45 feet in height unless a variance is granted.

"Isn't anyone objecting to the height of the building?" asked Country Planning Commissioner Felix M. Warburg yesterday.

The commission was considering Samuel Nelder's application for a use permit and architectural supervision for construction of a 80-foot high "geodesic dome of aluminium for his $550,000 eight-acre shopping center.

The commission decided to postpone action pending notification of nearby residents about the proposed height.

The dome was recommended by architect John S. Boles. The property is on both sides of Belvedere drive between Reed boulevard and Highway 101.

R.D. Dobbs, principal planner, explained that the height was not mentioned in the notice to property owners.

Planning Director, Mary Summers pointed out that a county ordinance limits build dings to 45 feet in height unless a variance is granted.

For class discussion; Which version of the foregoing news story do you prefer, considering that the action taken by the commission was reported in the third paragraph of the second version?

There tends to be an overuse of quotation margin both the lead and the body of news stories. Words and expressions carry unnecessary quotation marks.

The Governor today characterized as "inaccurate" the legislative counsel's report on dividend tax with holding.

The main purposes of quotation marks in the lead are to indicate exact language, to set off an obvious error, a nickname, and a slang expression.

Conversion of a lengthy quotation in the lead to indirect quotation often facilitates comprehension.

This lead was written from a" handout":

> DETROIT — The United Auto Workers Union today announced a new collective bargaining programme for next year, which, it said, "features a division of profits above ten per cent on net capital before taxes between the corporate executives and the stock-holders; the workers and consumers."

As Rewritten : DETROIT — The United Auto Workers Union today called for a profit-sharing plan in next year's wage contracts, and postponed demands for a shorter work week.

Some Pitfalls : A few statements may be made about what do avoid in writing the lead.

Avoid the Say-nothing Lead

Stanford University research scientists announced today they have uncovered surprising new information about the neutron, one of the small particles which make up the atom.

As Rewritten : Stanford University scientists plucked a secret from the heart of the atom today. They found a way to measure the size of neutrons— a key that may open doors to other mysteries of the atom age.

An empty lead sometimes results from the writer's abortive effort to introduce some kind of image into his reporting of a fact.

With aplomb despite a hair disarranging wind, Mrs. Lyndon B. Johnson christened an 11,000 ton ship today. But because of the weather, the big cargoliner had to stay where it was.

A former editor of the London *Daily* Express wrote in his memoirs:

I saw the MS. of a reporter's story about Mr. Churchill's meeting at Wood ford last night. It opened with an amusing incident about the electric lights failing. But, of course, it was a most important speech and the introductory angle was wrong. In fact, it sacrificed the substance for the shadow. It was rather like saying "Nibbling an olive and holding a glass of vodka in his hand, Stalin declared war on Britain last night."

Avoid the Cluttered Lead

Too many names and too many facts are sometimes crammed into the lead sentence. This can be avoided by distributing some of the names and some of the modifiers of the essential elements in succeeding sentences and paragraphs. One idea in the lead sentence is about all the reader can comprehend easily. Nevertheless, necessary qualifications that are omitted result in an over generalization that can mislead the reader.

Charles F. Noyes Co., Inc., through Herbert C. Born, vice president, in a $350,000 transaction, has leased for Emily S. Geyer to Ninth Federal Savings and Loan Assn. of New York City, one of the largest in the nation with its main offices at Broadway and 42nd street, the property at the north-west corner of First avenue and 45th street, directly opposite the United Nations development a plot of 4,800 square feet, fronting 40 feet on First avenue, and 100 feet on 45th street, for a long term of years with options of renewal, on which the buildings are being demolished, as a location for its first branch office.

Exercise : The foregoing news story is an unedited handout that was published in the real estate section of a New York newspaper. Rewrite it for an average sentence length of 21-25 words.

A second example which was not a handout:

The Bridges trial jury was excused over the Thanks giving week-end to day as defense counsel Vincent Hallinan, supposedly chastised by a six month's contempt sentence, nevertheless raised a dispute over prior Communist hearings that provoked a day of argument.

Overstuffing the lead sentence may often be avoided by making two sentences of the lead paragraph.

A 21 -year old reformatory parolee, who said he wanted to" point up in equalities of the parole system," set fire to a newspaper pressroom and fired a shotgun blast in a radio station last night.

As Rewritten : A youth on parole from a reformatory set fire to a newspaper pressroom and invaded a radio station with a shotgun lastnight.

He said he wanted to ' 'point up in equalities in the parole system."

The Lead Sentence should not Present a False Tone for the News Story : The lead sentence is a lens through which the reader looks at the rest of the story. A frivolous lead sentence, for example, is inappropriate to serious subject matter. The following sentence began a story for which the lead was appropriate; it signals the reader that the event is humorous.

An optimist attempted to cram himself and a tuba he was carrying abroad one of New York's jammed subway trains today. He didn't make it. He should have taken up the piccolo.

If the man with the tuba had been killed or injured, the lead would have been inappropriate.

Helping the Reader to See the Event : The reader of a news report, unlike viewing some television news shows, is often two or three degrees removed from reality. The police reporter, for example, gets most of his facts from policemen who have gotten them from eyewitnesses and participants. The reporter translates the words he has heard into written words. The written words are symbols of spoken words. The reader, in consequence, reads only the symbols.

An appropriate choice of words can enhance vividness. But the news writer, with respect to some events, may also enhance vividness by reconstructing the event for the reader in one or more sentences in the lead. He adds the dimension of visualization.

A school bus carrying as estimated 38 children struck a wrecker, sideswiped an automobile, then plunged into the Levisa fork of the Big Sandy river today.

A construction dredge, under tow in wind-whipped Lake Michigan, early today dipped under high waves and plunged to the bottom, taking the lives of eight of the 18 men abroad.

A driverless butane gas truck, belching flame, struck a mailbox Friday and headed straight down a sidewalk into the front door of the Hillcrest Haven rest home, killing three elderly patients.

NEW YORK - The crowded Lock-heed Electra crashed into a dike, flipped on its back and plunged, blazing, 500 feet along a swamp. Seventy-six passengers and crewmen hung head downward, pinned in their upside-down seats by safety belts as flames closed in on the cabin.

But not a life was lost today when American Airlines' Electra Flight 361 crashed at the end of a runway to New York's LaGuardia airport.

In some instances, it is better to make the lead sentence longer by adding a few words than to strive merely for brevity. This is justifiable because the headline has already reported the substance of the event and that information has been stored in the mind of the reader before he started to read the lead. In the fourth lead quoted above one newspaper's headline was "AIRLINER CRASHES, BURNS; ALL 76 ABROAD SAFE" and a four-column picture showed the upside-down plane. Another example:

FORT WORTH, Texas—An angry mob yelling "get those niggers" tonight hung an effigy of a Negro from a tree in the front yard of a Negro barricaded in his home.

Here are two ways of reporting a certain kind of event. The writer of one of the stories, however, has an advantage over the second writer because he wrote the story for the succeeding news cycle and had more time for both writing and for obtaining one or two additional facts.

Syntax of the Lead Sentence : The lead sentence, generally, should be in the *normal sentence order*. The normal sentence order is (1) the subject, (2) the finite verb, and (3 or 4) indirect object or direct object. Thus: (1) Stanford University scientists (2) plucked (3) a secret (4) from the heart of the atom.

Of the sixty lead sentences quoted in this chapter, all but four are written in the normal sentence order. One sentence begins with a conditional clause ("If you've recently had a baby....," p. 51); one is an interrogatory sentence (p. 51); one is in ellipsis with the normal sentence order implied ("Under no conditions....," p.52); and one begins with an adverbial clause modifier ("With aplomb ....,"p.54).

The subject of the lead sentence is usually the " who"(" A passenger inacar....," p. 45) or the "what" ("Averdict in favour of Samuel Howell....," p.47). It is nearly always easier to write a lead sentence in the normal places automatically. Moreover, since the normal sentence order is *fixed* in the English language by our habits of speech, a sentence in the normal order facilitates the reader's comprehension.

The writer should deviate from the normal sentence order only when he wishes to *emphasize* a sentence element other than the subject. The beginning of the sentence and the end of the sentence are the emphatic parts. When, therefore, the writer wishes to emphasize the time aspect of the event—the "when" he begins with the time.

Five minutes before the legal deadline, Mayor George Wilson today filed for reelection.

Six days before he was scheduled to retire on a pension, an Air Force officer was given a dishonourable discharge from the service today.

There is no justification, however, for this kind of lead:

> Meeting at noon today, the Rotary Club heard Governor Morris defend his tax programme.

> You may already have noticed in the leads that have been quoted in this chapter that "today" and "yesterday" were nearly always "buried" inside the sentence. The "when" aspect of the event is seldom important or interesting. In some news stories the "when" is reported as far down in the story as the fourth or fifth paragraph, so that the reader can concentrate on the more important or more interesting aspects.

To stress immediacy, newspapers and wire services "update" the lead of a news story for the succeeding news cycle (called a *second-day lead);* for example, they change the lead in an afternoon newspaper of a news story that was first written for a morning newspaper. Believing that readers are more interested in fresh news, they rewrite the lead to give the story that appearance. Because this effort has sometimes led to absurdity, now there is less stress on the ' 'when" in the second-day lead. Here is an approved example of "updating" in the afternoon news cycle:

> NEW YORK-Novelist Virgil Payson was in Bellevue hospital today for psychiatric observation.
>
> City Magistrate Joseph Martin ordered Payson committed after the author was arraigned *yesterday on* a charge of simple assault brought by his wife, singer Margaret Newsom.
>
> Obituaries often are" updated" for the second-day lead in this form "Funeral services will be held today for..., who died yesterday."

The "where" element of an event is sometimes worthy of emphasis:

> Within 100 yards of the road intersection at which his wife met death in an auto accident last year, a Jonesboro man was killed in the same way last night.
>
> Also sometimes worthy of emphasis are the "why" element ("Because he was discharged, a Labourer

yesterday shot,..") and the "how" element ("Caught in a collapsing slag pile,.... was crushed to death yesterday").

To emphasize some unusual aspect of the event or to hedge a prediction, the writer begins the lead sentence with a modifier.

Barring unforeseen developments, the local baseball club will be sold to Kansas City interests.

Even though he killed his wife for their joint insurance, the policy of William and Henrietta Fleming is valid, a pleading filed in circuit court today avers.

Alive but incoherent, a wrong-way turnpile driver was the only survivor of a head-on collision that killed seven persons last night.

Exercises

1. Below are several leads containing one or more of the following errors: *(a)* main feature buried under unimportant details; *(b)* sentences overloaded with details; *(c) when* or *where put* before the *who* or *what* when unjustified by relative importance; *(d)* editorial comment introduced; *(e)* style used too rambling; *(f)* wordy phrases used at start.

Rewrite each of these leads in a clearer, more effective and concise form.

(a) In a survey to learn something about the effects of television on the American home conducted by the Business Administration students at Wester State University, using 1,000 local television fans as "guinea pigs," it was found that the average televiewer spends three and one-half hours per day at his television set on the occasions when he stays home.

(b) Disclosure that local post officials are conducting a drive to discover the identity of the largest distributors behind the Irish Sweepstakes ticket-selling in this vicinity, plus the revelation that last May's winners have not been paid off have already resulted in blocking the sale of at least $250,000 in tickets and the disposal of 575,000 worth may be prevented.

(c) During a meeting recently of Phi Pho Nu, national social sorority, elections were held for the coming year. After counting of ballots by election officers, it was discovered that the new secretary will be Hermina Knox. Other officers include Donna Snell, first vice-president; I llene Kennedy, second vice-president; and social activities directory, Gwen Scheively. Alice Niffern will serve the group as president again, having held that post last year.

(d) Among the many fine firms exhibiting in this year's county fair, which continues through Sunday, March 28 in Woodland Park Auditorium with admission free to all, is the Wiere Jewelry Company, which is displaying 250 antique and unusual watches and clocks, many of which date back 200 years or more.

(e) At a meeting of the Greene County election commissioners held last Tuesday, the recent school trustee election was held null and void, due to a technicality in the manner of conducting the balloting. As a result, Ivar Petrone, Leslie Siedbe, and Frank Malligan now find themselves no longer newly elected members to the trustee board.

2. Rewrite this cluttered lead to facilitate the reader's comprehension:

Robert Rogers, Fremton police officer, testified in superior court today that Philip Snead, plaintiff in an assault and battery suit against Sam Vossler, bartender, was drunk and disorderly at the time of the alleged assault.

Rogers charges came under the direct examination of Paul Ghezzi, attorney for the defendant. Rogers asserted that Snead was.. . .

For class discussion: *1.* Why was this lead written this way?

AMES, Iowa (AP)—A rule of the college at Iowa State University requires that administrative officials retire on the July 1 after they reach 65 years of age. Dr. Charles E. Friley has bowed to the rule and quit office as president of Iowa State.

The rule doesn't apply to teachers. Dr. Friley will, accordingly, join Iowa State's faculty as a teacher and researcher.

3. Which of these leads is better calculated to educe an image?

   Dr. Otis Barton, 48-year-old-undersea explorer, went farther under the ocean today than man had ever gone before when he dived 4,500 feet into the dark Pacific in a five-foot round steel ball.

   A man in a steel ball saw weird and wondrous marine life 4500 feet down in the Pacific Ocean today, the deepest descent in history.

6

News Coverage

A publisher, editor, reporter, or other person connected with or employed upon a newspaper, or by a press association or wire service, or any person who has been so connected or employed, cannot be adjudged in contempt by a judicial, legislative, administrative body, or any other body having the power to issue subpoenas, for refusing to disclose, in any proceeding the source of any information procured while so connected or employed for publication in a newspaper.

Nor can a radio or television news reporter or other person connected with or employed by a radio or television station, or any person who has been so connected or employed, be so adjudged in contempt for refusing to disclose the source of any information procured while so connected or employed for news or news commentary purposes on radio or television. (Evidence Code, Section 1010, California Code of Civil Procedure).

Although observers have considered it an absolute shield law, this law has not always proven so in 1971 in Farrvs, Superior Court, an appeals court questioned the law's constitutionality. Los Angeles Herald-Examiner reporter William Farr at the outset of the trial of the Charles Manson "family" on multiple murder charges wrote an account of a prospective witness who said the Manson gang also intended to murder show business personalities. The judge wanted to know where Farr had gotten the information. Farr simply said he had received information from two of the six attorneys in the case and from another source. However, under oath, all six attorneys denied having given this information. Experts saw Farr's case as constituting an exception to the privilege law. His refusal to divulge his sources specifically led to a contempt of court citation, and he was jailed.

In Minnesota, which has a qualified shield law, a judge can still force a disclosure of sources when all three of these conditions are met:

1. That there is probable cause to believe that the source has information clearly relevant to a specific violation of the law other than a misdemeanor.
2. That the information cannot be obtained from any alternative means or remedy less destructive of first amendment rights, and
3. That there is a compelling and overriding interest requiring the disclosure of the information where the disclosure is necessary to preserve justice.

Whether qualified privilege shield laws are really desirable is debatable. With such limitations with good reasons given, a reporter is in danger of being asked to be an arm of the law in turning over material that might be used in the defense or prosecution. Also such shield laws, some believe, define the rights of the reporter too closely, treading on the spirit of the First Amendment.

A set of "pros and cons" for shield laws appear in a booklet, *The Courts and the News Media*, by Albert G. Kerell and Michel Lipman. Among the arguments opponents of shield laws use, they say:

> A shield law could conceivably be a step leading to further governmental encroachment on the press. The news media should not be in a position of petitioning

> Congress for their rights since Congress would be placed in the role of defining *who* is protected by the status — or *who* is a newsman. The next step could be a licensing process, since the news media have asked to be placed in the same Category as the licensed, screened professions receiving such privilege — for example, attorneys, doctors and priests.

News Sources

Press Releases **:** Announcement stories that companies or individuals send out often plague the newspaper office. As one editor put it, these announcements or press releases arrive as a giant snowstorm each day. Obviously, a newspaper can use very little information that comes into the office this way—even if is high quality—because of space limitations. But most releases that come by mail are worthless, especially for the bigger paper which cannot publish information on ever activity of a company and its personnel. While most releases are self-serving, telling the general public what the person or company wants the public to know, nevertheless, sometimes releases can provide sources and ideas for news.

Reference Material **:** However, releases are valuable for setting up a directory of potential sources. The professional release has the name and address of the PR officer and the company which can be contacts, as can the names of new heads of divisions and other personnel mentioned in releases. For example, if a scientific researcher is the subject of a release—may be he or she is just back from a trip—the information on the trip is probably not of general interest, but basic information on the person may be useful as he or she may later be able to supply information for a scientific article. An educator may be useful for an education article or a theater director for a future piece on the arts.

The reporter should not throw too much away without at least an evaluative glance.

Some small weeklies without adequate staff use releases directly. Most newspapers rewrite any releases they decide to use, for several reasons. First, an editor can never be sure of the veracity of all releases; often the lowest person on the totem pole, a trainee in the company, has worded the release. Certainly many releases are incomplete, and the newspaper person must make a call to flesh out or verify information. For instance, a good writer or editor will want the reader to know where an event will take place, a point that a release may overlook. An announcement of a campus event by a university may make sense to campus readers, but the general readers will need to know the address of the lecture hall!

Most standard releases have a release date, or "embargo" line, which tells the paper when to release or print. Editors should respect these restrictions, but they do pose a problem.

Embargo comes from *embargar,* Spanish for "to arrest," "to seize" (and Latin, in, "in" or "on," and barra, "bar"). In commerce, embargo has meant a restraint of ships. In journalism, embargo means that a hold or restraint is to be put on the use of information until a specified time indicated on the release. For example, a major corporation is calling a press conference which will likely say the company is expanding or going out of business, but the company is not to make the announcement until 9 a.m. on a certain day.

For the newspaper which may be on a different schedule, this is bad timing. A 9 a.m. time favours the wire services and afternoon newspapers. A morning paper's main deadline is likely to be 5 p.m. the day before. The morning paper reporter, what do you do when the biggest industry in town says it will have an extremely important announcement the next day at 9 a.m. at a press conference in the ballroom of a local hotel? At this point all you have is an announcement of time and place and no content. Some purists would argue that all you can do is sit back and wait. Others would tell you to get on the phone, call anyone you know or can find out about at offices in other branches of the company across the United States. With a general hint about the topic, a skilled reporter may be able to zero in on specifics.

Conventional newsrooms almost always put embargoes on stories until the time of the speech or event. For example, a national non-profit agency had prepared grandiose plans for reorganization—board officers had heard that much about the plans in a general meeting two days before the scheduled announcement in Detroit. Reporters from New York, Washington, and the wire services gathered for the 7 a.m. announcement breakfast. But to their amazement, the local morning paper was already on the street with a banner headline on the story. The other reporters were all very bitter toward the local reporter who had secured the story and who even developed it with reaction from other sources. The reporters argued: "You broke the embargo!"

The energetic reporter countered: "What embargo?"

"It's in your box in the press room!"

"You may be right: But I haven't been in the press room or looked in my box. I have not seen any embargo."

Of course, the energetic reporter, suspecting that there would be an embargo on the story, had avoided formal press room arrangements, sought out the document from a delegate who had a copy of the reorganization plan in his packet without any embargo restriction.

Investigative Sources : One of the best examples of the importance of reporters developing sources is the classical Watergate case back in the 1970s. How far would Carl Bernstein and Bob Woodword have gotten in the Watergate investigation without a basic source—"Deep Throat," the insider—who whetted their appetite for information and supplied enough to keep them going? They also had a myriad of other sources:

Telephone Books : They were able to make a profile of James McCord, one of the people arrested at the Watergate headquarters, who was at the Watergate complex after the break-in at Democratic headquarters-without talking to him. The reporters followed up on as Associated Press report that McCord worked with the

Committee for the Re-Election of the President (CRP). In the telephone book they found the number of the private security consulting firm McCord ran. When they called, no one answered. They then checked the criss-cross telephone directories which listed phone numbers by addresses. Here they called these people, some were able to supply information, others were not. Eventually a profile of McCord emerged.

Washington Post Police Reporter : A Post police reporter had information of a Howard Hunt connection with the White House from one of his sources and passed it along. Address books of two of the men the police arrested had the same name and number: Howard E. Hunt with White House identification.

Library of Congress : Here Bernstein and Woodward were able to find a cooperative clerk who showed them everything that Hunt had read. Included was material on the Kennedy Chappaquiddick incident, when a young lady with Edward (Ted) Kennedy had drowned and which Kennedy did not report for several hours. Contacts in the White House had said that Hunt conducted an investigation of Democrat Kennedy because the White House feared a Kennedy presidential campaign.

Personal Telephone Sources : Persons provided information on calls and directed Bernstein to Miami for telephone listings subpoenaed by a district attorney. Bernstein was able to confirm a New York *Times* story about money being laudered through Mexico.

Post Researcher : The CRP guarded a list of the 100 people who worked at the national headquarters as if it were a classified document. The *Post* obtained a copy through a researcher for the paper who had a friend at CRP. From this, Bernstein and Woodward were able to make their nightly visits to people by using their addresses and knocking on doors. The most valuable information came from a bookkeeper who told about a slush fund and said that the FBI investigation had not asked the right questions and had, therefore, ignored some things.

FBI and Justice Department Sources : "... the reporters checked regularly with a half-dozen persons in the justice Department and the FBI who were sometimes willing to confirm information that had been obtained elsewhere. The sources rarely went further, often not that far.':

Call from an Unknown Lawyer : The lawyer had nothings to do with the Watergate investigation. But he told Bernstein that Donald Segretti (a political trickster) had a friend, Alex Shipley, who had been approached by an Army friend about doing some "political work" for the Nixon campaign. Bernstein eventually called Shipley in Tennessee and Shipley told Bernstein about Segretti. Bernstein was given names of other Army friends and eventually tracked Segretti down.

Court Records : Bernstein called District Attorney Earl Silbert who was handling the Watergate grand jury investigation and asked him if he could have the jury roster: Silbert refused and rejected Bernstein's argument that the list was public record. Woodward asked a friend in the clerk's office about the list and the friend told him the same thing. Woodward identified himself as a reporter. The clerk said that he could look at the list but that he could not copy any names or take notes. Woodward found the Watergate grand jury list, memorized four or five names and addresses at a time, and slipped off to the washroom and wrote the information. They held back after Judge John Sirica warned against contacting grand jurors.

Federal Courthouse Reporter : Lawrence Meyer on the *Post came* across a confidential copy of a routine legal agreement of prospectors and attorneys for the Watergate break-n defendants. Although it contained little new information, one thing stood out. A phone in the White House with the billing address of a Kathleen Chenow had been disconnected. Looking through the crisscross directory, Bernstein located a former roommate of Chenow. Through the roommate, Bernstein traced Chenow to Milwaukee where she had moved. It turned out that she had been a secretary to the secret White House group known as the" plumbers" which was investigating leaks to the medial.

Address on Envelope : When Bernstein was in District Attorney Earl Silbert's office, Bernstein saw a letter on the desk which proved to be from a company where McCord had bought the bugging equipment. Bernstein made a mental note of the address and proceeded to contact the company. He wrote a story on hcw much money McCord paid the company—$3,500 in thirty-five $100 bills.

Plaint Sleuthing : Most of Woodward and Bernstein's information came from digging. The reporters continued to expand a list of names which they kept checking. These included people who were working in or had worked in the White House, the Justice Department, and the FBI. By checking out even- lead, the reporters found new leads which resulted in new connections.

Many a Record

Transactions between people are recorded many ways. And various kind of records, although they may not always appear to be interesting, can communicate fascinating information—and proof or evidence—about what people do. Studying records can add depth and conviction to a story but you can also find many ideas for new stories by looking through records for unusual facts and matching these facts against other information. Besides police court, and sources you may want to check out follow here. (Be sure to check your state open record laws concerning access).

I irth Records : The court clerk or health department (or a bureau of vital statistics) keeps birth records. If you suspect that people are lying about their ages, checking records can help set things straight. Such research can also help in identifying who parents are-information which you may want to report in some stories.

Death Records : The country medical examiner can supply information on the location, time, and cause of death.

Marriage : The clerk in the marriage licensing bureau can tell you who has applied for licenses.

Divorce : The start of a suit is public. The name and action are available from the court clerk. You can find information about subsequent developments—except for grounds—in the prothonotary, or chief clerk's office, indexed by the party's name, alphabetically by month or year. You will usually need some idea of when the action started.

Wills : You can read the books of copies of wills as well as the original documents from a register of will kept by clerks of specific courts (in Philadelphia, the clerk of the Orphans Court) or by a prothonotary. Wills are filed by year and number.

Real Estate : The registry of deeds or the registry unit of the department of records keeps information which allows you to trace the ownership of a piece of land all the way back to the first owner. You need to know the address so that you can consult the special map which gives a plan number. You can look at the plan which pictures the address you are interested in. Such plans may have more than one file number on them because lots or tracts are sometimes realigned over the years. With these numbers in hand, you can obtain the abstracts, which are usually on microfilm. An abstract will contain the date of sale, the seller's and the buyer's names, and the size and location of the lot or parcels. A special section in a deed, called a" recital," traces the owners and means of sale or transaction. These can include public grant (patient), foreclosure (sheriff sale), will, private grant (deed), or condemnation.

State tax stamps affixed to the deed can give you an indication of the sale price of the property.

Property Tax Records : The assessor's office has legal descriptions of land tracts and records of assessment.

Neighbours on a City Block : Crisscross phone directories (your newspaper and public library have these) list streets alphabetically, with street addresses and residents. You can use these to identify people living on each block. Also, city directories list people alphabetically and by street and telephone numbers, and include information about employment and spouses' names.

Building Permits : On the surface, such permits may not appear to tell you very much, but they include information on renovations and additions and on contracting firms; they also provide you with a master plan of the property. By studying such permits, Jack Tobin identified a number of persons working with the contractors or sub contractors at Richard Nixon's house at San Clemente, Calif. By talking with these workers, Tobin learned that they were being paid with a government check from the National Park Service.

Bankruptcies : The clerk of the U.S. district court has papers on bankruptcy cases filed in that particular district. Such papers give a total look at the assets and debts of a person. In the bankruptcy procedure, the creditor may have in sugated a "205 A examination in which the creditor's lawyer questions the debtor. The title of the investigation comes from the part of the bankruptcy code directing the procedure. If the clerk does not want to make additional material available, you can remind the clerk about the ruling supporting access (Winton Shirt Corp. vs. Elizabeth Truct Co., 104 Fed Reporter, 2nd Series, 777, 3rd Circuit, 1939).

Judgements : County clerks' offices keep records of persons collecting a debt through the judgement of the court. Such records reveal the debtor's credit standing.

Corporations : Businesses file incorporation papers first with the secretary of state in the state capital. Eventually these papers go in the country clerk's office in the county where the new company is located. These files give the company's purpose, its board of directors, its address, and a record of stock issued. *Moody's Industrial Manual* names U.S. corporations, with staff members, history, officials, and budget.

Voter Registration : In the register of voters you can find a person's address, birth date, profession at the time of registration, voting record, and physical appearance.

Auto Records : The secretary of state keeps vehicle records, including information from license applications.

Payroll Records : If the person is working for the state, the payroll record is public. Check with the civil service department.

Professional Records : Regulatory boards in a state keep public records available on the professional groups they control, such as doctors, lawyers, nurses, funeral directors, realtors, hairdressers, and technicians.

Permits and Inspections Reports : The department of licenses and inspections has public records of citations against any licensed establishment. The health department can make available weekly food inspection reports of area restaurants, schools, and other institutions. The fire department should provide you with reports of inspections at public places.

Traffic Accident Reports : In the records department of some cities, you can get a copy of an accident report for a modest fee if you provide the driver's name and the place and date of the accident.

Military Records : The Pentagon can supply you with names of men and women on active duty. The *Army Register, Navy Register,* and Register of Commissioned and Warrant Officers of the *Navy and Marine Corp list* the names of officers.

Income Tax Records : You may see the tax forms of non-profit corporations by filing Form 990 with the Internal Revenue Service, but this can take several months. Members of religious and cull groups, for tax-free status, must fill out a form under Section 501 (c)(3) of the Internal Revenue Code.

Telephone Records : For billing purposes, the telephone company keeps lists of long distance telephone calls. Some times a personal acquaintance in the company can supply these, some government agencies with special powers can also subpoena them. In their investigative Reporting book, David Anderson and Peter Benjamin son add:

> It is also possible to obtain these records by trickey. At least one reporter we know would stoop so low as to call the telephone company business office, and, posing on the person being investigated claim that he didn't recall mailing certain long-distance calls that had been charged to him. He would then ask the phone company to check the numbers and dates of the calls and report back. The same gambit is

> sometimes used by reporters who wish to check on the money a person has borrowed. They simply call the credit company to "recon firm" the loan. A similar technique can be used to check on someone's airplane reservations. Obtaining such information from the phone company, however, works both ways. So, if an experienced investigator is intent on protecting a source's identity, he or she may call from a remote pay phone or from the paper's subscription department rather than from a home or desk phone."

A useful book for more detail on using records is John Ultman and Steve Honeymari's. *Reporter's Handbook: An Investigator's Guide to Documents and Techniques,* a project of the Investigative Reporters & Editors, Inc. (New York: St. Martin's Press, 1983). The book, for instance, includes names and address of places to write in all 50 states for birth, marriage, divorce, and death records.

Many out-of-the-way and little-known sources from groups may be very useful to you. The annual minutes of the United Methodists in one area in Illinois proved to be important information in profiling the Democratic Candidate for the presidency in 1972. A tip that candidate George McGovern had been a seminarian (a fact which he did not include in his fact sheets) led a reporter to interview his former instructors. They in turn pointed to recorded minutes that identified the candidate as a clergyman in his early years. Further sources included interviews done with people in the town where he had been the pastor, yellowed newspaper clips, and reminiscences that a reporter traced down from old-timers across the country.

At the Shreveport (La.) Times, an article series using a wide range of personal and record sources led to then resignation and indictment of the city commissioner of public safety. One of the writers of the series, Lynn Stewarat, recalls: "Our initial confidential source was a high-ranking police department official. Using the background information he gave us, we went to records at city hall to prove our case. Later we studied payroll records, purchase orders, telephone bills, and other internal records."

The series, which printed a ledger of the checks issued to the commissioner, began:

Large sums of taxpayers' money are being spent by some city officials who give no public accounting of those expenditure, a Times survey of records has revealed.

The funds are being obtained by officials with only a vague indications of their eventual use. In each case they are requested by a commissioner and approved without question by Finance Commissioner George Burton.

They include 43 payments totalling $ 17,300 paid in the last 15 months' to Commissioner of Public Safety George W. D'Artois personally.

Each payment was for $400, with the exception of one $500 check, and, since Jan. 1, 1975, these have been issued on an average of twice a month.

The only information on file in the Finance Department to indicate what the funds are being used for are brief letters from D' Artois. In most cases, the letters state that the funds were being requested for obtaining evidence and information from informants on organized crime cases.

D'Artois was asked by the Times for records concerning those expenditures. He produced only a manila folders filled with miscellaneous pieces of paper that included various copies of offense reports, torn scraps of papers and some receipts.

Unlike other divisions of his department, he could produce no tabulated list reflecting date, payment, and case, and said the amount he had received during 1975 was "whatever the finance department says it is."

An unusual turn of events occurred during the Times study when Police Chief T.P. Kelley said he did not know that D'Artois was drawing any funds for such investigations or conducting investigations requiring the use of such funds.

A second article went further back in the records and studied the pattern of the check payments:

Monies paid to Commissioner of Public Safety George W. D'Artois personally by the City of Shreveport increased dramatically the same month that George Burton was first sworn in as Shreveport finance commissioner, a Times study has revealed.

Up until December, 1971 city funds to D'Artois, other than his paycheck, averaged about $600 a year. In the portion of 1971, prior to Burton's election. D'Artois had received only $420. But in December of 1971— the month that Burton was elected and sworn in-D' Artois drew $600, bringing the total for 1971 to $1,020. His payments since then have never dropped below $5,100 a year and in 1975 they soared above $13,000....

When questioned by the Times enterprise team about the increasing number of payments to Commissioner D'Artois since his selection, Burton replied" "He requested funds to purchase information and I honoured his request."

Asked about the markedly lower payments to D'Artois in prior years, Burton answered, "I didn't bother to check. I don't have any idea of what he got before. I don't see the significance of it.

" I don't know his sources of information. I do not have personal knowledge of his sources of information," the finance commissioner said, and, referring to informants, Burton added, "I don't want to be responsible for someone's safety. Who is designated is not my business."

During the period in which the large payments on a regular basis to D'Artois began, there was neither an experienced finance commissioner nor an auditing firm familiar with the city's past financial practices....

Finance department records show that from 1963-1969, checks issued to D'Artois' averaged about four payments a year, and most were in the $ 100 to $200 range. There were no checks— other than pay checks — to D'Artois recorded in 1970.

Access to Public Records : The right to inspect government records does not exist by itself by natural, moral, or common law, but is defined and limited by statutes of the state and federal government.

In many states, groups or committees — often connected with Sigma Delta Chi, Society of Professional Journalists — have published guidebooks on what is available from various branches of government and agencies and how to go about obtaining it. In Pennsylvania there is the Pennsylvania First Amendment Coalition which has put out a booklet, the *Media Survival Kit.* It offers the following advice on what to do when you are denied access to the records of any court, agency, board, commission, or department of the executive branch.

1. Make a written request for access to the documents. If the records were sealed by a judge, make the request to that judge. If access to the documents was denied by the Prothonotary or Clerk of Court, the request should be presented to the Chief or President Judge.
2. The request should identify the documents which you seek to inspect as narrowly and with as much details as possible.
3. Do not state the reason why you want to inspect the documents.
4. If the written request is denied, ask that the denial be placed in writing together with a statement of reasons for the denial.
5. There is no statute covering the right to inspect court records. You may petition the court to open the records, following the same procedure as with closed courtrooms.
6. If you lawfully obtain access to a document which was ordered sealed by the court, you may publish it; however, the court may initiate proceedings to determine who provided you with the document.

The *Media Survival Kit* outlines what records fall under the Pennsylvania Open Records Law (you will need to check your own state). In Pennsylvania the following records are available; they have been held subject to the Open Records Law:

1. Examination papers and scores of all applicants for Civil Service jobs.
2. Records of retired state employees.
3. Attendance record cards of professional employees of school district.
4. Building record side of property records maintained by county board for assessment and revision of taxes, containing information as to construction specifications.
5. Individual salary records of community college employees.
6. Accident reports prepared by accident investigation division of police department.
7. Completed reports prepared by Department of Labour and Industry pertaining to safety and health in industrial plants.
8. Review and refund docket of Board of Finance and Revenue.
9. List of names and addresses of kindergarten children in school district.
10. Police payroll records.
11. List of persons taking CPA examination given by Commissioner of Professional and Occupational Affairs.
12. Address to which a school district forwarded the scholastic record of a former pupil.
13. List of delinquent taxpayers.

The following records have been held *exempt* from the Open Records Law:

1. Field investigation notes made by a staff member of city planning department for purpose of a report to a city council member.

2. Departmental budget reports required to be provided to the budget secretary (held to be a statement of facts and events and not an "account," which consists of debit and credit entries).
3. Names, addresses, and amounts received by welfare recipients.
4. Contents of teacher's personnel file maintained by school district.
5. Financial disclosure statements voluntarily submitted in response to executive order requesting such statements from members of the governor's cabinet and members of certain agencies.
6. Financial information regarding the operation of state-related university.
7. Physical fitness reports and promotional evaluation reports of police department.

In Pennsylvania, if you are denied permission to inspect and copy documents of any agency, board, commission, or department of the executive branch, the Media *Survival Kit* also suggests that you appeal the denial of access under the "Right To Know" Act. A sample form of appeal is available from the Coalition.

On the federal scene, the Freedom of Information Act of 1966 provide access to many documents, and almost every week you read of some disclosure from the past revealed for the first time because an enterprising reporter decided to check on certain documents. In general, the Act provides that all records in the hands of agencies of the executive branch of the federal government can be inspected, unless the documents are covered by one of nine exceptions.

Excepted are classified national defense and foreign policy items; internal personnel matters; items prohibited from disclosure by a statue; privileged and confidential trade and commercial information obtained from an individual; information which would be privileged in a civil lawsuit; "unwarranted invasion of personal privacy," such as medical documents; investigation files where one of a half dozen special bad effects would occur; specified bank records; and oil well information.

To obtain records from a federal agency, write a letter to the agency, being specific and describing in detail the document sought. This request must be answered in 10 working days. If there is no answer, or the request is denied; you can write a letter to the head of the agency. Some suggest you include a legal reason for your appeal, although this is not necessary. Having it sent by an attorney might give it more serious consideration, but not necessarily so. Groups such as the Pennsylvania First Amendment Coalition provide sample appeal letters. This appeal must be answered in 20 working days. If denied, then the next recourse is to file a complaint in the federal district court. The Coalition (headed by Sandy Oppenheimer, Bucks County *Courier Times,* Route 13, Levittown, PA 19057) has sample complaint forms.

Utility of Library

Time spent browsing in libraries can turn up prospective story ideas. You may find an overlooked author in your area. You will find consumer reports which you can localize. Glance through magazine articles. They deal with the relevant themes in contemporary life, many of which you can adapt and discuss for reader in your locality. You can also pick up a few ideas from out-of-town newspapers. Libraries not only contain resources for story research, they can also be the source of new ideas, background information, and fact verification.

Libraries also have books about reference books and materials. Among them are *The New York Times Guide to Reference Materials* (New York: Popular Library, c. New York *Times Co.,* 1971) and Rivers, William L., *Finding Facts (Englewood* Cliffs, N.J.: Prentice Hall, 1975). The *Writer's Resource Guide,* edited by William Brohaugh (Cincinnati, Ohio: Writer's Digest Books, 1979), has listings with addresses for various information services, including consumer topics, sports information, offices, museums, archives, embassies, community services, finance and banking.

7

News from Parliament

Parliament and State legislatures become major news centres when in session. The Government is bound to make all announcements in the house. Political news also comes from in and around the house in session as political parties express their views on various issues and the relative strength of various parties is tested in the house. There are moves and counter-moves by ruling and Opposition parties which find place in news columns.

A reporter should know the rules and procedures of Parliament. State legislatures follow similar rules and procedures with a slight difference here and there. During inter-session periods there are conferences of Presiding Officers of all the houses presided over by the Speaker of the Lok Sabha. This makes rules and procedures more or less uniform.

The Constitution provides for a bicameral Parliament, consisting of the President and two Houses, known as the Council of States (Rajya Sabha) and the House of the People (Lok Sabha).

Rajya Sabha

The Rajya Sabha consists of not more than 250 members. Of these, twelve are nominated by the President for their special knowledge or practical experience in such matters as literature, science, art and social service. The remaining seats are allocated to the various States and Union Territories, roughly in proportion to their population. Each State is, however, represented by at least one member. The representatives of each State are elected by the elected members of the Legislative Assembly of the State in accordance with the system of proportional representation by means of a single transferable vote. The minimum age for membership of the House is 30 years.

The Rajya Sabha was constituted for the first time on April 3, 1952. It is a permanent body not subject to dissolution, but one-third of the members retire every second year by rotation and are replaced by newly elected members. The Rajya Sabha at present has 244 members.

Lok Sabha

The Lok Sabha is composed of representatives of the people chosen by direct election on the basis of adult suffrage. The maximum strength of the House envisaged by the Constitution is now 547—up to 525 members to represent the States, up to 20 members to represent the Union Territories and not more than two members of the Anglo-Indian community to be nominated by the President if in his opinion that community, is not adequately represented in the House. The Total elective membership is distributed among the States in such a way that the ratio between the number of seats allotted to each State and the population of the State is, so far as practicable, the same for all states. The qualifying age for membership of the Lok Sabha is 25 years.

The Lok Sabha, unless dissolved sooner, continues for five years from the date appointed for its first meeting and expiry of the period of five years operates till dissolution of the House. However, while a proclamation of emergency is in operation this period may be extended by Parliament by law for a period not exceeding one year at a time and not extending in any case beyond a period of six months after the proclamation has ceased to operate.

Following the first general election held in the country in 1952, the First Lok Sabha met in May 1952. Thereafter, nine general elections have been held. Elections were last held in December 1989 to constitute the Ninth Lok Sabha. The strength of the Lok Sabha is 544 (525 elected representatives of States and 17 elected representatives of Union Territories) and two representatives of the Anglo-Indian community nominated by the President.

Functions : As in other parliamentary democracies, Parliament in India has the cardinal functions of legislation, over-seeing of administration, passing of budget and ventilation of public grievances.

The scheme of distribution of powers between the Centre and the Sates, followed in the Constitution of India, emphasises in many ways the general predominance of Parliament in the legilative field. Apart from the wide range of subjects allotted to it in the Seventh Schedule of the Constitution, even in normal times Parliament can, under certain circumstances, assume legislative power over a subject falling within the sphere exclusively reserved for the State.

Further, in times of grave emergency when the security of India or any part thereof is threatened by war or external aggression or armed rebellion and a proclamation of emergency is made by the President, Parliament acquires the power to make laws for the whole or any part of the territory of India with respect to any of the matters enumerated in the States List. Similarly, in the event of the failure of the constitutional machinery in a State, the powers of the legislature of that State become exercisable by or under the authority of Parliament.

Besides the power to legislate on a very wide field, the Constitution vests in the Union Parliament the constituent power or the power to initiate amendment of the Constitution.

Under the Constitution, the Council of Ministers at the Centre is collectively responsible to the Lok Sabha. One of the effective methods by which Parliament exercises check over the executive is through its control over finance. This financial power in the hands of Parliament helps in securing executive accountability. Besides, the procedures of Parliament in India afford ample opportunities for the enforcement of ministerial responsibility, for assessing and influencing governmental policies as well as for ventilating public grievances. The procedure of questions (with possibilities of supplementaries and, in the case of inconclusive or unsatisfactory answer half-an-hour discussions, calling attention, short duration discussion), enable information to be elicited and attention focussed on various aspects of governmental activities.

The more significant occasions for review of administration are provided by the discussions on the motion of thanks on the President's address, the budget, including demands for grants of various ministries, and departments and proposals to raise funds to meet the expenditure. These apart, specific matters may be discussed through motions on matters of urgent public importance, private members' resolutions and other substantive motions. In extreme cases, government can be censured or a motion of no-confidence moved against it. Along with these, a close and continuous check on governmental activities is exercised through a comprehensive system of parliamentary committees.

***Relative Role* of *the Two Houses* :** As between the two Houses, the Lok Sabha has supremacy in financial matters. It is also the House to which the council of ministers, drawn from both the Houses, is collectively responsible. On the other hand, the Rajya Sabha has a special role in enabling Parliament to legislate on a State subject if it is necessary in the national interest: It has a similar power in regard to the creation of an All-India Service common to the Union and the States. In other respects the Constitution proceeds on a theory of equality of status of the two Houses.

Disagreement between the two Houses on amendments to a bill is resolved by both the Houses meeting in a joint sitting where questions are decided by majority vote. However, this provision of joint sitting does not apply to money bills and constitution amendment bills.

***The Presiding Officers* :** In the Lok Sabha, both the presiding officers—the Speaker and the Deputy Speaker—are elected, by the House. In the Rajya Sabha, the Vice-President of India is the ex-officio Chairman of the House. He is elected by the members of an electoral college, consisting of the members of both the Houses of Parliament in accordance with the system of proportional representation by means of the single transferable vote. The Deputy Chairman of the Rajya Sabha is, however, elected by the members of the Rajya Sabha from amongst themselves.

The Constitution of India makes certain specific provisions in regard to the office of the Speaker, Lok Sabha, laying particular emphasis on the importance and the independent character of the office in the context of a parliamentary polity. His salary and allowances are charged on the consolidated fund of India.

The Speaker of the Lok Sabha enjoys vast authority and powers both under the Constitution and the rules as well as inherently. As the conventional head of the Lok Sabha and, as its principal spokesman, the Speaker represents its collective voice. He is guardian of the rights and privileges of the House, its committees and members. It is through the Speaker that the decisions of the House are communicated to outside individuals and authorities; he issues warrants to execute the orders of the House wherever necessary, and delivers reprimands on behalf of the House. Within the precincts of the House, his authority is supreme. His conduct cannot be discussed except on a substantive motion.

The committees of the House function under his overall supervision and control. The chairman of any parliamentary committee is nominated by him. Any procedural problem in the functioning of committees is referred to him for directions. Committees like the business advisory committee, the general purpose committee and the rules committee, however, work directly under his chairmanship.

He enjoys a special position in so far as the relations between the two Houses of Parliament in certain matters are concerned. He certifies money bills and decides finally what are "money" matters by reason of the Lok Sabha's overriding powers in financial matters. It is the Speaker of the Lok Sabha who presides over joint sittings called in the event of a disagreement between the two Houses on a legislative measure.

In his over riding concern to see that the Lok Sabha fulfils its rightful role as the prime centre for decision-making and policy formulation, and a major mediating force in the country's democratic policy, the Speaker has to strive to reach a position of dynamic balance in which the forum and the needs of orderly debate and efficient dispatch of the ever-growing volume of public business are harmonized.

Sessions : Normally three sessions are held in a year:

(i) Budget Session (February-May);

(ii) Autumn Session (July-August); and

(iii) Winter Session (November-December).

In the case of the Rajya Sabha, however, the Budget Session is split up in two sessions and so the Rajya Sabha has four sessions.

President's Address : The Constitution enjoins that the President shall address both the Houses of Parliament assembled together, at the commencement of the first session after each general election of the Lok Sabha and also at the commencement of the first session of each year and inform Parliament of the causes of its summons. The address contains a review of the activities and achievements of the government during the previous year and their policy with regard to important internal and current international problems, besides a brief account of the programme of government business for the session.

The President's address is a solemn occasion. The President arrives at the Parliament House where he is received at the gate by the presiding officers and secretaries-general of both Houses and conducted in a formal procession to the high-domed Central Hall of Parliament. As the procession enters the Hall, the Marshal announces the arrival of the President, and the members rise in their places. With the President reaching his seat on the dais, a band positioned in the lobby of the Central Hall to the right of the President, plays the national anthem. During this time everyone keeps standing. Thereafter, as the President takes his seat, the presiding officers occupy and members resume their seats. The

President then addresses the members. After the conclusion of the address, the President rises from his seat followed by the members when the national anthem is played again, whereafter the President leaves the Hall in a procession in the same way as he arrived. The entire ceremony is marked by utmost decorum and dignity befitting the occasion.

Break for Questions

The first hour of every sitting is normally devoted to questions. Questions are of three types. A starred question is the one to which a member desires an oral answer in the House. Any member may ask a supplementary question germane to the main one, while it is being answered. In the case of an unstarred question, a written answer is laid on the table by the concerned minister. A short notice question is the one which relates to a matter of urgent public importance and can be asked with shorter notice than the normal period prescribed for a question. For questions other than short notice questions, the period of notice prescribed is not less than ten and not more than twenty-one clear days.

Closely connected with questions procedure is the provision or half-an-hour discussion. Under this procedure a member may give notice for raising a discussion on a matter of sufficient public importance which has been the subject of a recent question, oral or written, and the answer to which needs elucidation on a matter of fact. Such discussions are held during the last half an hour of the sitting on specified days of the week.

Besides questions, there are various other means by which members may bring up matters of urgent and current public importance before Parliament.

Call Attention Notices : Calling attention notices, essentially and Indian procedural innovation, enable a member to draw the attention of the government to an important development of public interest and to elicit government's views or stand thereon. A calling attention notice may be admitted straightaway by the Speaker at his discretion and the government have to come forward with a statement. The matter is normally raised after the question hour.

Although there can be no debate at the time the statement is made, the members concerned may raise points for clarification and elucidation by the minister. There is no bar also to a notice being given for a debate on a subsequent date on a matter contained in the statement. This procedural device, without the implied censure of the treasury benches normally associated with an adjustment motion, is popular with members on all sides of the House.

Raising of Matter Under Rule 377 : A member who wishes to bring to the notice of the House any matter, which is not a point of order and cannot otherwise be raised through any other procedural device, can do so by giving a notice for the same with a full text thereof. On permission being granted by the Speaker for raising the matter under Rule 377, the member concerned may make a brief and specific statement in the House relating to one matter only without any allegations of a defamatory or incriminatory nature. The Speaker in such cases does not direct the minister to make a statement in response to a matter concerned. The minister may, if he so desires, make a statement on the subject with the permission of the Speaker.

Motions for Discussion, No-day-yet-named and for Short Duration : Members may raise discussion on a specific matter of public importance by giving a notice of a motion popularly termed as No-day-yet-named motion. It is so worded as to record the decision of the House on the subject. A short duration discussion provides an opportunity for discussion of a situation or a statement, but there is no question of putting it to the vote of the House.

After admission of notices by the Speaker, any one of these motions may be selected by the business advisory committee for discussion in the House and thereafter, it is included in the list of business. The mover of the motion in the case of a no-day-yetnamed motion has the right to reply in addition to the privilege of initiating the discussion; no such right of reply is available to the member raising a discussion for short duration. The minister intervenes towards the end to clarify the government's stand. Experience has shown that the members make full use of these alternative procedures for raising discussion on matters of current public importance.

Adjournment Motion : The primary object of adjournment motion is to set aside the normal business of the House and take up for discussion an urgent matter of public importance. A motion for an adjournment of the business of the House for the purpose of discussing a definite matter of urgent public importance can be moved with the consent of the Speaker and leave of the House. Normally, no business not included in the list of business can be taken up in the House. The adjournment motion is an extraordinary procedure.

The Speaker may, give his consent for moving an adjournment motion if he is satisfied that the matter sought to be raised is definite, urgent and of public importance and there is a failure on the part of the central government to perform the duties enjoined on it by the Constitution and the law.

The question of public importance is decided on merits in each individual case. The refusal to give consent is at the absolute discretion of the Speaker and he is not bound to give reasons.

After leave of the House to the moving of an adjournment motion has been granted and time fixed for its discussion, the Speaker allows the motion to be moved at the appointed hour which is normally at 1600 hours. The time allotted for discussion is two and a half hours unless the debate concludes earlier. *Private members' resolutions:* Specific matter may be discussed also through private members' resolutions and other substantive motions. In an extreme case, the government can be censured on a motion of no-confidence moved against it.

A bill, that is draft of a legislative proposal, has to pass through the following stages before it becomes an Act of Parliament.

First Reading : A bill can be introduced in either House by a minister or by a private member, depending upon whether it is a government bill or a private member's bill. Money bills, or financial bills attracting the provisions of article 117(1) of the Constitution can be introduced in the Lok Sabha only.

On the day appointed for introduction of a bill, the minister (or member) in charge of the bill moves for leave of the House to introduce the bill. On leave being granted by the House, the bill is introduced. If the motion is opposed, after brief statements by the member who opposes the motion and the member who moved the motion, the question is put to the vote of the House.

Second Reading : The second reading consists of consideration of the bill, which is in two stages. First, a general discussion on the bill as a whole takes place, when the principles underlying the bill are discussed. At this stage it is open to the House to decide to refer the bill to a select committee of the House or a joint committee of the two Houses or to circulate the bill for the purpose of eliciting opinion thereon or straight away take it into consideration.

When a bill is referred to a select or joint committee, the committee gives it a close and detailed scrutiny clause-by-clause and makes such amendments therein as it deems necessary. Where necessary, the committee may also take evidence of associations and public bodies representing the affected interests or of experts who have special knowledge of matters having a bearing on the measure before it. Thereafter, the committee submits its report to the House, which considers the bill as reported by the committee.

The second stage of the second reading consists of clause by clause consideration of the bill as introduced, or as reported by select/joint committee, as the case may be.

Third Reading : When all the clauses and schedules, if any, of the bill have been considered and voted upon by the House, the member-in-charge moves that the bill be passed. At this stage, debate is confined to arguments either in support of the bill or its rejection, without referring to the details thereof further than is absolutely necessary. Only formal, verbal or consequential amendments are allowed at this stage.

Bill in the other House : After the bill is passed by one House, it is sent to the other House where again it passes through similar stages.

In the case of a money bill, the Rajya Sabha can only recommend amendments therein and return the bill to the Lok Sabha within fourteen days of its receiving the bill. The Lok Sabha may accept or reject any or all of the recommendations of the Rajya Sabha. If the Lok Sabha rejects any of the recommendations of the bill, it is deemed to have been passed by both the Houses. If the Rajya Sabha does not return the bill within fourteen days it is deemed to have been passed by both Houses in the form in which it was passed by the Lok Sabha.

Joint Sitting : In the event of final disagreement between the two Houses on a bill other than a money bill and a constitution amendment bill, or if more than six months elapse from the date of receipt of the bill by the other house without the bill being passed by it, the President may call a joint sitting of the two Houses to resolve the deadlock. At the joint sitting the bill may be passed by a majority of the total number of members of both the Houses present and voting.

Assent of the President : When a bill is passed by both Houses, it is presented to the President for assent. The President may give his assent or withhold his assent to a bill, or he can return the bill (provided it is not a money bill) with his recommendations for reconsideration. If the Houses pass the bill again with or without amendments, the bill has to be assented to by the President. In the case of a constitution amendment bill, the President is, however, bound to give his assent.

Any matter requiring the decision of the House is decided by means of a question put by the Chair on a motion made by a member. At the conclusion of a debate, the Chair puts the question to the House. Those in favour of the motion are invited to say 'Aye' and those against to say 'No'; and then the Chair says 'I think the Ayes (or the Noes, as the case may be) have it'. If the opinion of the Chair as to the decision goes unchallenged, he repeats twice; "The Ayes (or the Noes, as the case may be) have it"; and the question before the House is determined accordingly. If the opinion of the Chair is challenged by any member or member exclaiming 'The Noes (Or Ayes) have it', the Chair directs that the lobbies be cleared.

On the Chair directing that the lobbies be cleared, the division bells are rung. When bells ring continuously, it indicates that a division is to take place in the Lok Sabha. (When bells ring intermittently, it indicates that a division is to take place in the Rajya Sabha. After three and a half minutes the Chair puts the question a second time and declares whether in his opinion, the 'Ayes' or the 'Noes' have it. In case opinion so declared is again challenged he shall direct that the votes be recorded by division.

Divisions : There are three methods of holding a division that is, by operating the automatic vote recorder, by distributing 'Aye' and 'No' slips in the House or by members going into the lobbies.

In the case of recording of vote through the automatic vote recorder, members cast their votes from their seats, respectively allotted to them, by pressing according to their choice 'Aye'/'No'/ 'Abstain' push buttons provided for the purpose. After the result of the voting appears on the indicator boards any member who may not have been able to cast his vote by pressing the button on account of any reason considered sufficient by the Chair, may with the Chair's permission, have his vote recorded. Similarly, any member having by mistake pressed the wrong button, may also be allowed by the Chair to correct his mistake. The result of automatic voting is thereafter declared by the Chair.

When the Chair directs that votes would be recorded on slips, each member is supplied by the division clerks, at his seat, an 'Aye' or 'No' or 'abstain' slip according to the choice indicated by him. On these slips, members are required to record their votes by writing their division numbers and signing them at the appropriate place. After the members have recorded their votes these are counted by the officers at the table and the totals of 'Ayes', 'Noes' and 'Abstentions' are presented to the Chair. The result of the division is then announced by the Chair.

Another alternative procedure for division is that members may be asked, to record their votes by going into the lobbies. This procedure is not much in vogue now.

Constitution Amendment

A bill seeking to amend the Constitution may be brought forward by a minister or a private member. Where the bill is from a private member, the bill, apart from being subject to the normal rules applicable to private members' bills, has also to be examined and recommended by the committee on private members' bills and resolutions, before a motion for leave to introduce it is included in the list of business.

Barring the requirement of a special majority (majority of the total membership of the House and a majority of not less than two-thirds of the members of the House present and voting) for its adoption, and in certain cases, of ratification by the legislatures of not less than one-half of the States, a bill for amendment of the Constitution follows practically the same legislative process as any ordinary legislation.

The Budget : The annual financial statement laid before both the Houses of Parliament embodies the estimated receipts and expenditure of the Government of India in respect of the ensuing financial year. In India the "financial year" commences on the first of April.

The estimates of expenditure are split up into what are called "demands for grants". These demands are arranged ministry-wise and they generally cover the requirements of each administrative service. Under each demand the estimates are sub-divided according to the categories of expenditure included in the demand.

In India, the budget is presented to Parliament in two parts: the general budget and the railway budget. The general budget is presented to the Lok Sabha by the finance minister usually at 5 p. m. on the last working day in February, that is, about a month before the commencement of the budget year. The budget speech of the finance minister is in two parts. One part deals with general economic and financial situation in the country and the other part relates to taxation proposals. A copy of the budget is laid on the table of the Rajya Sabha. The railway budget is presented by the railway minister about a week or ten days earlier.

The budget is discussed in two stages in the Lok Sabha. First, there is the general discussion when only the broad outlines of the budget and the principles and policies underlying it are discussed. Discussion and voting on the demands for grants of each ministry is taken up thereafter.

The Lok Sabha has the power to assent to, or refuse to give assent to any demand or even to reduce the amount of any grant sought by government. In the Rajya Sabha there is only a general discussion on the budget. It does not vote on the demands for grants.

Vote on Account : Before the budget for the whole year is passed, a special provision is made, by which the government is enabled by Parliament to have finances, sufficient for running the administration for part of the year. This provision is called 'vote on account'.

The Finance Bill : The finance bill, which seeks to give effect to the government's taxation proposals is introduced in the Lok Sabha immediately after the presentation of the budget. The provisions in the bill relating to duties of customs or excise, etc., come into effect immediately with the introduction of the bill by virtue of a declaration under the provisional Collection of Taxes Act, usually included in the bill.

The Appropriation Bill : After the voting on the demands for grants has been completed the appropriation bill is introduced. The appropriation bill seeks to authorise the government to draw monies from the "consolidated fund of India" to the extent shown in the budget passed by Parliament.

Supplementary/exeess Grants : No expenditure in excess of the sums authorised in the budget by Parliament can be incurred without the sanction of Parliament. Whenever a need arises to incur extra expenditure, a supplementary estimate is presented to Parliament. If any money has been spent on any service during a financial year in excess of the amounts granted for that service and for that year, the minister of finance/railways presents a demand for excess grant. The procedure followed in Parliament in regard to supplementary/excess grants is more or less the same as is adopted in the case of the expenditure estimates included in the general budget.

Parliamentary Committees : In India as elsewhere, the work done by Parliament is not only varied in nature, but considerable in volume. The time at its disposal is limited. It cannot, therefore, give close consideration to all the legislative and other matters that come up before it. A good deal of its business is, therefore, transacted in the committees.

Both Houses of Parliament have a similar committee structure, with a few exceptions. Their appointment, terms of office, functions and procedure for conducting their business, are also more or less similar and are regulated under the provisions of the rules made by the two Houses under article 118(1) of the Constitution.

Broadly, parliamentary committees are of two kinds—Standing Committees and Ad hoc Committees. The former are elected or appointed every year or periodically and their work goes on, more or less, on a continuous basis. The latter are appointed on an ad hoc basis as need arises, and they cease to exist, as soon as they complete the task assigned to them and have submitted their reports.

Standing Committees : Among the standing committees, the three financial committees—committee on estimates, public accounts and public undertakings—constitute a distinct group a and they keep an unremitting vigil over governmental spending and performance. (While members of the Rajya Sabha are associated with the committees on public accounts and public undertakings, the members of the committee on estimates are drawn entirely from the Lok Sabha). The control exercised by these committees is of a continuous nature. They gather information through questionnaires, memoranda from representative non-official organisations and knowledgeable individuals, on-the-spot studies of organisations, oral examination of non-official and official witnesses. Between them the financial committees examine and report on a fairly large area of the multifarious governmental activities at the Centre.

These committees have adequate procedures to ensure that their recommendations are given due consideration by the government. The progress in the implementation of the recommendations as well as any unresolved differences between the committees and the government are set out in 'action taken reports' which are presented to the House from time to time.

Other standing committees, in each House, divided in terms of their functions, are:

(i) Committees to Inquire:

(a) the committee on petitions examines petitions on bills and on matters of general public interest, also entertains representations on matters concerning central subjects; and

(b) The committee of privileges examines any question of privilege referred to it by the House or the Speaker/ Chairman.

(ii) Committees to Scrutinise:

(a) The committee on government assurances keeps track of all the assurances, promises, undertakings, etc., given by ministers in the House and pursues them till they are implemented;

(b) The committee on subordinate legislation scrutinises and reports to the House whether the power to make regulations, rules, sub-rules, bye-laws, etc., conferred by the Constitution or statutes are being properly exercised by the authorities so authorized; and

(c) The committee on papers laid on the table examines all the papers laid on the table of the House by ministers, other than statutory notifications and orders which come within the purview of the committee on subordinate legislation, to see whether there has been compliance with the provisions of the Constitution, Act, rule or regulation under which the paper has been laid.

(iii) Committees Relating to the day-to-day Business of the House:

(a) The business advisory committee recommends the allocation of time for all items of government and other business to be brought before the House.

(b) The committee on private members' bills and resolutions of the Lok Sabha classifies and allocates time to bills introduced by private members, recommends allocation of time for discussion of private member's resolutions and examines Constitution amendment bills before their introduction by private members in the Lok Sabha. The Rajya Sabha does not have such a committee. It is the business advisory committee of that House which recommends the allocation of time for the discussion of stage or stages of private members' bills and resolutions.

(c) The rules committee considers matters of procedure and conduct of business in the House and recommends amendments or additions to the rules; and

(d) The committee on absence of members from the sittings of the House of the Lok Sabha considers all applications from members for leave of absence from the sittings of the House. There is no such committee in the Rajya Sabha. Applications from members for leave of absence are considered by the House itself.

(iv) The Committee on the welfare of scheduled castes and scheduled tribes, on which members from both Houses serve, considers all matters relating to the welfare of the Scheduled Castes and Scheduled Tribes which come within the purview of the Union Government and keeps a watch whether the constitutional safeguards in respect of these classes are properly implemented.

(v) Committees concerned with the provision of facilities to members:

(a) The general purposes committee considers and advises the Speaker/Chairman on matters concerning the affairs of the House, which do not appropriately fall within the purview of any other parliamentary committee; and

(b) The house committee deals with the residential accommodation and other amenities for members.

(vi) The joint committee on salaries and allowances of members of Parliament, constituted under the Salary, Allowances and Pension of Members of Parliament Act, 1954, apart from framing rules for regulating payment of allowances and pension of members of Parliament, also frames rules in respect of amenities like medical, housing, telephone, postal, constituency and secretariat facilities.

(vii) The joint committee on offices of profit examines the composition and character of the committees and other bodies appointed by the Central and State governments and Union Territories administrations and recommends what offices ought to or ought not to disqualify a person from being a member of either House of Parliament; and

(viii) The library committee, consisting of members from both the Houses, considers matters concerning the library of Parliament.

***Ad hoc Committees*:** Such committees may be broadly classified under two heads : (a) Committees which are constituted from time to time, either by the two houses on a motion adopted in that behalf, or by the Speaker/Chairman to inquire into and report on specific subjects (for example, committee on the conduct of certain members during the president's address, committees on draft five year plans, etc.,) and (b) the select or joint committees on bills which are appointed to consider and report on particular bills. These committees are distinguishable from the other ad hoc committees inasmuch as they are concerned with bills and the procedure to be followed by them is laid down in the rules of procedure and the directions by the Speaker/Chairman.

Central Secretariat

Each House of Parliament has a secretariat of its own headed by a secretary-general who is a permanent official working under the over-all control of the presiding officer of the House.

The main function of the secretary-general is to advise the presiding officer, in the exercise by him of all the powers and functions that belong to his office. He also acts as the administrative head of the secretariat of the House.

Proceedings of both Houses begin at 11 a. m. When a correspondent enters the press gallery he can get a list of business for the day. This is the order in which the House will take up its business for the day. Two other lists are also available, one listing the oral or starred questions and the other of unstirred questions answers to which are laid on the table of the House.

If the member or members who have asked an oral question is/are not present in the House, the question becomes unstarred automatically and no other member is allowed to ask any supplementary question. A copy of the written answer which was to be read by the minister in the House is available to correspondents along with the answers to other unstarred questions.

The following example illustrates the form in which correspondents get the answers to questions. There are hundreds of such questions from which the correspondent has to select useful ones:

Rajya Sabha

Government of India

Ministry of

Information and Broadcasting (Unstarred Question No : 1147)

(To be answered on 02-08-85)

Appointments Sub-Committee for Unified Language News Agency

1147

Shri Amarprosad Chakraborty

Shri S.W. Dhabe

Will the Minister of Information and Broadcasting be pleased to state:

(a) Whether any meeting was called by his Ministry and a sub-committee appointed for making a proposal for unified language news agency;

(b) If so, what are the names of the members of the sub-committee and whether they have submitted any report; and

(c) What are the recommendations made by the Committee and Government's action thereon?

Answer

Minister of State for Information and Broadcasting (Shri V.N. Gadgil)

(a) (b) & (c):—Minister of State for Information and Broadcasting convened a meeting of the leading editors and proprietors of language newspapers for the purpose of obtaining consensus for formation of an Indian Language News Agency for dissemination of news in Indian Languages on June 25 and 26, 1985. At the outset the Minister of State for Information and Broadcasting made it clear that the Government do not propose to start any agency nor do the Government want to get involved in the management or functioning of any agency.

The consensus at the meeting was that there is need for an Indian language news agency to meet the requirements of newspapers in Hindi and other Indian languages. The participants also recognised that there is no possibility of reviving Hindustan Samachar and Samachar Bharati.

The meeting was of the unanimous view that it is for the proprietors and editors of newspapers themselves to operate such a news agency service. The proprietors and editors agreed to examine the possibility of raising resources for setting up a viable news agency service in Indian languages. It was also agreed at the meeting that if it was not considered possible to raise adequate resources to set up a separate Indian language news agency, an alternative could be for the existing English language news agencies to start services in Indian languages also.

Consequent thereto, a committee of eminent newspapermen under the chairmanship of Shri Ramnath Goenka was constituted to examine the various aspects of the matter. The following were the members of the Committee

1. Shri Ramnath Goenka (Convenor)
2. Shri K. Narendra
3. Shri Ramesh Chandra
4. Shri Narendra Mohan
5. Shri P. Mahapatra
6. Shri Somasundaram
7. Shri S.K. Aggarwal

The committee has submitted its report. The following are its specific recommendations:

(i) The creation of a full-fledged news agency with adequate technological back up will require at least Rs. 3 crores for capital expenditure and, in addition, recurring expenditure of Rs. 1 crore per year. The Indian language newspapers are not at all in a position to raise even 50 per cent of this capital. Further the running cost of Rs. 1 crore per year cannot be recovered from Hindi/Indian language subscribers.

(ii) On the other hand, if Indian languages service is added to the infrastructure of an existing news agency, the additional annual cost will be only Rs. 50 lakhs per year. There will be practically no capital cost. This level of annual expenditure can be managed both by newspapers and other subscribers like AIR and Doordarshan. If, however, there is still any deficit, the news agency concerned can bear it. The Government has not yet taken a final view on these recommendations.

Many a time several questions related to a subject form part of the same story. Sometimes all the important questions selected are put in a single story with the most important one coming first and making headline and others get two or three sentences with a subhead.

But these are occasions when a single question can make a good story with proper use of background and interpretation. Here is an example:

Hermes Sailed in—Uunstarred

Express News Service

New Delhi, April 24. The government confirmed today that it had signed an agreement with Britain for the purchase of the aircraft carrier *Hermes* at a cost of 63 million pounds.

The announcement was sneaked into unstarred questions in the Rajya Sabha in a style characteristic of the defence ministry.

On Wednesday, the defence ministry would not confirm or deny news reports from London that such a deal had been signed on April 19. The Indian people learnt of a major agreement to acquire a second aircraft carrier from British government officials.

The minister of state for defence, Mr. Arun Singh told Mr. Kalpnath Rai, Mr. L.K. Advani, Mr. K.K. Birla, Mr. Suresh Kalmadi and Mr. D.G. Prashant in written replies on Thursday that a memorandum of understanding was concluded on March 12 this year for the purchase of *Hermes.* The cost of the package was likely to be about 63 million pounds inclusive of docking and refit, spares, stores and services.

Mr. Singh said a second aircraft carrier was considered desirable in the light of the threat perceived. *Hermes* has the facilities for operating Sea Harrier aircraft and Sea King helicopter which are already part of the Navy's air arm. *Hermes will* be fully operational when it joins the Indian Navy and is expected to serve till the end of the century.

This is not the first time that the defence ministry has sneaked a major announcement through the unstarred question in

Parliament. It did this in the case of purchase of eleven Sea Harriers last year at a cost of 150 million pounds.

Several weeks ago news reports appeared that the government had signed an agreement to buy Swedish 155 mm guns for the army. In this case also, news of the agreement was provided by the Swedish company concerned to a news agency. Asked about it, the defence ministry spokesman would only say: 'I have not been asked to deny it. ' No official announcement has been made on this so far.

The way the *Hermes* announcement was made—five days after agreement was actually signed—goes against the assurance the Prime Minister gave during his reply to the defence debate in the Lok Sabha.

Mr. Gandhi said much had been made about the secrecy of defence contracts dealings and assessments. He said he had a feeling that documents were being over classified. "There is no intention at any time to keep Parliament or the country in the dark about any details," he said but added that performance limitations and evaluation reports of equipment could not be revealed.

Members of Parliament have expressed concern about the secrecy surrounding such deals because they involve hundreds of crores of the taxpayer's money and there have been a number of instances in the past of the defence ministry bungling these deals.

Earlier this month the public accounts committee of Parliament in its 29th report flayed the defence ministry for its lapses for import of defective communication equipment and insisted on fixing responsibility. This particular piece of communication equipment imported in 1976 from a US company for the army did not work for a single day. Ten years later, several engineers in Bharat Electronics Limited (BEL) are wasting time trying to make the equipment work, oblivious of the fact that the technology in the equipment may now be obsolete. The PAC noted that between June 1976 and June 1981, there were nine other cases of import of defective equipment.

Questions cover all the ministries and give authentic information. They should be kept by correspondents for future use as they may provide leads to other stories. The questions provide basic data on almost all subjects that deal with a nation or state's economy and development and various other projects. This information can be analysed to yield many good stories.

Zero Hour : Just after the declaration by the presiding officer at 12 noon that the question hour is over a large number of members get up from their seats and want to be heard. This is the beginning of zero hour, the most tricky period from the point of view of the coverage of Parliament.

Members raise most crucial issues during this period and if they want to make an issue of something they utilise it for such a purpose. Zero hour is the period most prone to walk-outs and sit ins in the well of the House. Several members speak simultaneously on different subjects. Many of them speak without the permission of the Chair and the Chair rules that whatever is being said without permission should not be recorded. Certain remarks made with the permission of the chair are later expunged by the Chair.

A correspondent has to listen with utmost care and take notes. Simultaneously he should have his ear on the presiding officer's ruling. Normally all unparliamentary remarks against members are not permitted to go on record. If something is not on record, it cannot be reported. For that a correspondent can be punished for the breach of privilege.

A reporter can describe the scene in the House without any contemptuous remark against any member or minister. He cannot say that someone behaved foolishly though one can describe what happened from which the readers may conclude that the behaviour was foolish. However, a statement cannot be written to later say that the Chair ruled that the statement may not be recorded. What has been expunged cannot be reported in any form. But it is permitted to write that certain remarks made by Mr. X against Mr. Y were expunged by the Chair.

Experienced correspondents know the names of most of the members who take active part in zero hour. It is always good to check the names of the members, if in doubt, while describing what he said or did.

Home-work is also necessary for coverage of zero hour. Though the subjects raised in the zero hour look like coming out of the blue but most of the issues raised normally come from the morning newspapers. The home-work for zero hour involves careful screening of newspapers. In about ninety per cent cases this will be of great help.

Breach of Privilege **:** In India each house of legislature, whether the Lok Sabha, the Rajya Sabha or a house of State legislature is custodian of its own privilege and is empowered to take action for its breach by any one including a newspaper or a news agency. However, the scope of parliamentary privilege has not been defined and therefore one should err on the safer side.

Legislatures are generally indulgent towards the press. They normally overlook minor lapses but are bound to take note of serious transgressions. Deliberate suppression or distortion of members' speech or other contribution to the proceedings, aspersions cast on a member's behaviour in the House, imputation of motives to him for his speech or behaviour in the House, seeking to bring pressure on him to speak or vote in a particular manner, or in any other way seeking to influence his functioning as a legislator are serious transgressions.

However, comment on the behaviour or speeches of a legislator unconnected with his functioning as a legislator does not attract privilege.

Papers laid on the table of the House **:** During the zero hour the Chair calls the ministers and they lay on the table of the House the papers mentioned against their names. This does not mean that the minister leaves his seat and goes to the central table of the House and lays papers there. He just gets up and says so.

The list of these papers is given in the order paper (list of business). A correspondent should find out which paper or report laid on the table of the House is important from the point of view of the news. Many annual reports, reports of various parliamentary committees, economic surveys, and plan documents fall in this category along with reports of enquiry commissions, etc. A correspondent should get hold of these reports and papers and do a story if the information is newsworthy. Such reports should be preserved for future reference.

Suo Moto Statement : Occasionally ministers make suo moto statements on an important issue in both the Houses. In the Lok Sabha members cannot ask any clarification while in the Rajya Sabha members ask clarifications on such statements. Almost always a minister says something more than what is there in the statement and therefore normally the story of such statements is made by the person covering the Rajya Sabha. The correspondent covering the Lok Sabha can add to it if there was something noteworthy before, during or after the statement—like clapping, walk-out, etc.

In news agencies the Lok Sabha reporter makes his story while the Rajya Sabha reporter prepares the lead story incorporating what happened in the Lok Sabha also.

Here is an example of such a statement:

Statement by the Prime Minister, Shrimati Indira Gandhi in the Lok Sabha/Rajya Sabha on October 5, 1982, regarding the Israeli invasion of Lebanon

No event in recent years has pained and shocked humankind as the Israeli invasion of Lebanon, atrocities committed by them, and the brutal, heartless and merciless massacre of the civilian population.

What is a matter of even greater shame is the state of helplessness of the international community in dealing with a member of the United Nations who has unabashedly invaded another member State. The Security Council has passed unanimous resolution calling for a ceasefire and withdrawal. These have been arrogantly ignored. World leaders have condemned these actions. This has had no impact on Israel. While withdrawing its military presence from West Beirut, the PLO was guaranteed that the Palestinian civilian population would be protected. Nevertheless over 1000 defenceless men, women and children were massacred in a manner reminiscent of atrocities committed during World War II. We have news of PLO prisoners being tortured in Israel.

As Hon'ble Members are well aware there has been massive public sympathy in India for the unimaginable sufferings of the Palestinian People. Our hearts and sympathies go out to them. Their lands were forcibly occupied. They are homeless, having been driven out of their hearths and homes. For over three decades theirs has been a life of humiliation, misery and sufferings.

We view this Israeli aggression and their acts of genocide with abhorrence. We have made our views known in public, at the United Nations, and in many chancelleries of the world. I have written to several world leaders. I have personally spoken to others whom I have met since the Israeli aggression. If universally accepted norms of international law and behaviour are to be observed and respected as they must be then due value must be placed on human life and property whether in Europe, America, Africa or Asia, and global peace, stability and security must not be further jeopardised. We have to work collectively for a just, equitable and durable solution.

A sense of urgency is also involved. A very heavy price has been paid in the form of military destruction, loss of human lives, and sufferings of hundreds of thousands of helpless human beings. Even today the atmosphere in West Asia is increasingly surcharged with emotions of anger and hatred, of revenge and reprisals. All this must be ended. The use of force never brought any lasting solution. Destruction and killing is self-defeating. The interest of all peoples is to live in an atmosphere of cooperation and friendship. We cannot cover or retain what does not belong to us. We must not deny to others their rights and what is theirs. Lands forcibly occupied must, therefore, be vacated. Peoples who have been uprooted and rendered homeless must be rehabilitated and provided a state of their own. Countries in the region must be assured of their security within internationally recognised frontiers.

Therefore we appeal to all, particularly those in a position to influence Israel, to spare no effort in prevailing upon Israel to withdraw from Lebanon without delay. This must be the first step in a long process of finding a solution to the larger problem. Our foremost priority must be to work collectively in initiating a new peace process towards a comprehensive and final settlement.

The tragedy of Lebanon has been grafted on the tragedy of Palestine. The UN peace keeping forces and others are there. There exist several resolutions of the United Nations Security Council and General Assembly and lately we have also had some noteworthy plans and proposals. We welcome any effort towards a peaceful settlement. We have to initiate and encourage trends of conciliation and negotiations. The parties directly involved which must include the PLO, need to play a major role. These efforts should also have the full involvement and support of the super powers. I should like to assure Hon'ble members that India will not be found wanting in this regard.

Debates and Discussions : General principle of speech reporting should be applied to the debates and discussions in the legislature. The story should be written depending on the importance of content and person.

Side lights can be described as separate stories. The correspondent should also be alive to the sense of humour of the members.

Central Hall : A few senior correspondents and editors are allowed in the Central Hall of Parliament where members and ministers can be found sitting in a relaxed mood. Many a time meeting these people in the Central Hall may give clues to major political developments. For political correspondents this opportunity is very useful.

On the first day of the budget session of Parliament the President addresses members from both the Houses in the Central Hall. Correspondents with the Rajya Sabha and the Lok Sabha.

Press gallery cards are allowed to sit in the galleries above the Central Hall. When some foreign dignitary addresses Parliament then also the Central Hall is used in a similar way. Occasionally, political parties also hold their parliamentary party meetings in the Central Hall.

8

News from Press Conference

Almost every day newspapermen get invitations for press conferences. Some press conferences are over crowded while some people keep on waiting for newsmen and sometimes they begin only when the newsmen who have arrived on time threaten them with a walkout. The variety of subjects is also unlimited. Anybody who thinks he has something to say can invite newsmen for a press conference.

The invitation for press conference is marked to the reporter or correspondent who deals with the subject. If the press conference is important and the reporter thinks that he would need help, then somebody else is also asked to accompany him. Sometimes even editors attend press conferences. The tradition has been that editors are just present and they do not ask any questions. But now this tradition is fading out.

Before going to the press conference a reporter should do his 'home work'. He should prepare himself for the event and read as much as possible on the subject. He should look for the questions which can yield news from the person who is to address the press conference.

Many reporters prepare a list of possible questions and actually write out the language in which to ask. The more confident ones normally have the subjects in mind and phrase their questions when the opportunity comes. But if a reporter does his homework properly there is no harm if he writes possible questions in advance. It is better that these questions be written in order of importance. All questions cannot be asked by a reporter. In fact many reporters who do very good copy do not sometimes ask any question.

Since other reporters present also think along the same lines on the subject some questions may be asked by them. Then if the reporter gets an opportunity he should ask a related question to get more information before the subject is changed. He should open a new subject if he thinks that enough has been asked on the subject on which the previous reporters had been asking questions.

A reporter should not hesitate to ask relevant questions even if they are uncomfortable for the person addressing the press conference. However, care should be taken to be polite. Even if the person gets rude the reporter should keep his cool. He must remember that he has come to get news and not to quarrel with the person on a point.

If the behaviour of the person addressing the press conference is unbecoming then the reporters can mention that in the story or make a small separate item. But this behaviour should be reported only when it has news value.

After the fall of the Janata government the leader of the Janata party Jagjivan Ram used to get angry if somebody referred to Mrs Indira Gandhi. Later when H.N. Bahuguna joined Mrs Gandhi even the name of the former irritated Jagjivan Ram. Many reporters described this behaviour of Jagjivan Ram in their stories.

The reporter should also try to use his sense of humour while asking questions if a suitable opportunity arises. But he should not overdo it as it becomes funny and irritating if overdone.

A reporter should not ask long questions. He should be brief even while giving the background. He should remember that he is attending the press conference and not addressing it. A long question confuses the person who is addressing the press conference and also indicates that the reporter has not done his home work. Sometimes the person addressing the press conference uses his sense of humour and asks the questioner to repeat his question, which he was unable to understand. He invariably generates laughter which is humiliating for the reporter who asked such a question.

For important press conferences it is good to have a taperecorder. But the reporter should also take notes to ensure that if some mechanical failure spoils the quality of recording he should be able to do the story without it. Further, these notes will be time savers when the story has to be filed. Entire replay will not be required and the reporter will play only that portion which he wants to check to make sure he is accurate. A similar problem arises with reporters who depend on shorthand. They concentrate on noting down each word and end up as confused persons. They read again and again what they have noted down in short hand and thus waste precious time and sometimes their copy is not in order because of the confusion in the mind.

One must remember that a tape recorder and shorthand are devices and skill which should be used to help the mind in retaining and analysing. They are not to be substitutes for an alert and lively mind. Care should be taken that shorthand and taperecorder do not become a burden on the mind of the reporter. It is better not to use them if they burden the mind. The decision should be made by the reporter himself and he should make his own assessment about the use of these devices and skills. A reporter should not become dependent on these devices also because there would be occasions when, despite his best efforts, he will not be able to get a tape recorder or his device may fail at the last moment.

During the press conference while taking notes and asking questions the reporter should also keep an eye on news value of what is being said. This simultaneous analysis is easy if it is done at the end of the conference. However, looking at the notes the reporter is free to revise his judgment.

Depending on the news value and the subject touched upon at the press conference the reporter may file just one report or he may file several separate reports.

If a team of reporters from a newspaper covers a press conference they should ensure they sit together so that they can communicate among themselves and decide which subject should be covered by whom. Normally, the possible subjects should be divided by reporters among themselves before the beginning of the press conference, but if a new subject comes up which they could not think of earlier it should be allotted on the spot to someone.

In important press conferences, like the one addressed by the prime minister, all available hands who get invitations (all accredited correspondents) are used. Better planning yields better results on such occasions.

Sometimes in important press conferences reporters from news agencies divide the work in a way that one of them conveys a major announcement on the phone to the desk and it is creeded immediately to the subscribers: Other reporters take notes and do the final copy.

Sometimes press conferences start with questions and answers but sometimes the person addressing the press conference makes preliminary remarks and then question and answers follow. Some people also supply a press note or a handout, say something to introduce the subject and then they take the question from newsmen.

As an example of what happens at press conferences, the transcript of Prime Minister Rajiv Gandhi's press conference (July 7, 1985) follows:

PM's Press Conference

Transcript of the Press Conference of Prime Minister Rajiv Gandhi

New Delhi, Asadha, 16, 1907

July 7, 1985

Friends,

I had wanted to meet you much earlier. But the last six months were so packed that it was difficult to find time. In between we had the budget session and the two foreign tours, there was the Air India tragedy. This has caused us all great agony and I want to express our sympathies to the bereaved families. We have done a good many things in the last six months. I had outlined our programmes and priorities in my first broadcast and in Parliament. We have placed before the country what we want to do. The most urgent task of all is to lift the people out of poverty, we have to remove poverty and move forward. We have to see how to ensure fuller social justice, how to strengthen our society.

There are many other problems. Punjab is a major problem. It loomed large at the time of the elections. As a result of the path we have adopted in the last six months to the measures we have taken, the tension has considerably reduced. You find that the Akali dal is coming forward again in Punjab. They are talking in terms of functioning within the framework of the Constitution. They are speaking out against extremists and against violence. Because of some of the recent incidents, the whole country stands against terrorists. It has been my effort all along to take the Opposition Parties with me in the work before the nation. Whichever major problem has been there, I have invited them and talked it over with them. We have met five or six times in these months and had serious, discussions on all the major problems.

We are looking ahead now to the Seventh Plan. Our priorities are before you. The biggest task is in agriculture and we shall address ourselves to it. We shall place even greater emphasis on poverty alleviation programme and on strengthening the infrastructure. In the last few months we have given a new thrust in several areas in licensing policy, in capacity utilisation in our industries, in electronics, in textiles, and in many other fields, in order to speed up our work. We are looking into the 20-Point Programme with a view to speeding up its implementation. We must give more attention to the public sector and we are doing so. We wanted the restructuring of the public sector to be done faster but some matters have arisen which require a little more time.

Our economic situation today is on the whole good. There is naturally, discussion about prices. On this matter I should only like to say that in the last three months the inflation rate has been only of the order of 3.·1 per cent which is lower than in many years. Prices are a matter in which we cannot afford to relax our vigilance. We are looking seriously into the matter, so that whenever there is any rise we at once contain it and bring the situation under control.

We have promised to clean up our public life and take steps to remove corruption. We have made a beginning, but it is not enough. We are planning some more steps. We have brought in the anti-Defection Bill and legalised donations to political parties and launched a two-pronged attack on black money-by simplifying licensing and taxation on the one hand and by tightening administration on the other.

We have set up the Wasteland Development Board. It is our hope that there will be vigorous plantation activity, as a result of which there will be more fuel for our people and fodder for our animals. We have also established the Ganga Authority to implement our programme of cleaning the Ganga. We shall make a beginning with Varanasi.

I undertook two foreign tours. Both have yielded considerable results and it is my earnest hope that as a result of these visits our bilateral relations with the countries I visited will be greatly strengthened, that there will be more friendship and more cooperation. In between the two tours I also went to Bangladesh for a day, as a result of which our friendship with this neighbour has improved.

I think I have spoken enough and now to your questions.

Q : It seems that the terrorist problem is being utilised by several countries to pressurise the Government. I refer in particular to the reports that the FBI arrested some terrorists, and some other terrorists were arrested who had received training, as it was said, in Eastern Europe. What comments do you have on this international pressure being applied on you through the terrorist menace?

PM : There is no way that the Indian Government is going to succumb to any pressure, whether terrorist or otherwise.

Q : Mr Prime Minister, this is about the reservation policy of the Government of India. You have just removed one Chief Minister in Gujarat yesterday. But the leaders of the agitation have said that they are not going to withdraw the agitation. Since the country has become independent, because of the reservation system, we have created, it seems, a new caste system and many people seem to have developed a vested interest in staying backward and we have different kinds of reservation systems in different States. In the South, you have reservations from 65 per cent to 75 per cent whereas in the North, you have several States where it is only 20 or 25 per cent. The Chief Minister of Gujarat was trying to increase it upto 50 per cent and he lost his job. All this is because of this peculiar reservation system which goes by the caste a person belongs to and not genuine economic backwardness. Now, what are you plans? Are you planning to call a Chief Ministers' Conference to discuss this and arrive at a national policy where you have a ceiling upto a maximum number of XY or whatever? What are your plans? This is what I would like to know.

PM : First, one point should be absolutely clear and that is that the reservations for the Scheduled Castes and the Scheduled Tribes are in no way under question and there is no question of changing or altering those at all. You have asked two questions, I think, One : What is going to happen in Gujarat? The new Chief Minister will tackle the problem. The agitation that has been going on in Gujarat, we have maintained, is a political agitation in which many Opposition parties are involved, and we would like that they do not exploit parochial feelings among the people for their political ends. They must rise above this and work for the political betterment of the country, not for their personal gains.

Regarding calling a Chief Ministers's Conference, we have no such plan at the moment. I have discussed this problem with the leaders of the Opposition. I will talk to them again about it and we will try and work out how we can start finding a solution to this.

Q : I would like to know, Mr Prime Minister, whether you have got any economic philosophy. If so, what is it? Is it Left or Right or is it Centre or Left or Right of Centre? If you have got any ideological background, would you kindly take us into confidence?

PM : Well, the question you have asked will take most of our time allotted to this Press Conference to answer. But just to put it in a few sentences. There is no question of Left or Right or Left of Centre or Right of Centre. It is a question of what is good for India today. The basis of our policy has been laid down by Panditji, by Indiraji, and we are not shifting from that. But we have to modify their ideology and their thinking with today's conditions on the ground which means the economic conditions in India, the improvements that we have made the progress that we have made, the financial constraints as we see them and the situation in the world monetary and financial systems. Today we have, to balance all that and produce a package which does not deviate from the basic Congress ideology and is dynamic and will take India ahead.

Q : Your Excellency, please evaluate the agreements signed recently between India and Pakistan. To what degree will they influence bringing of normalisation to India's north-western borders?

PM : We have always been in favour of normalising relations with all the countries, especially the countries in our neighbourhood. The progress that has been made in these talks has been good. We would of course have liked that we would have made some major advance in trade. Unfortunately, there were some differences. But we hope, in future meetings, that they will also be clarified. We have made progress in cultural exchange, in interchange of our peoples going to each other's country, simplification of various travel arrangements. In our talks, I think there has been a general understanding of each other's perspectives for the region.

Q : In your opening remarks you referred to your desire to clean up our public life. The Opposition parties, or a few Opposition leaders, presented to you a memorandum of charges against the Haryana Chief Minister, Mr Bhajan Lal. Do you propose to hold an enquiry into these charges and, if so, what is the nature of the enquiry you are going to order?

PM : The procedure that has been followed on all such complaints, and which we also propose to follow for this complaint, is that we will first ask the Chief Minister for his comments. Then we will evaluate his comments with the charges that have been made. On the basis of that evaluation we will decide whether to have an inquiry and what sort of inquiry to have. I have talked to the Opposition leaders who came, and I have promised them that if anything is substantiated in what they say, we will take action.

Q : If we can go back to Indo-Pakistan relations and the talks with Sahebzada Yaqub Ali Khan, for a minute, Prime Minister. During your visit to the United States, the question of Pakistan's pursuit of nuclear capability figured very prominently, and at the end of it, what we got were two contradictory statements. One that the United States has assured us that they will do all they can to dissuade Pakistan from going nuclear. Two, that the United States told us that they did not think that Pakistan was making or could make a bomb.

PM : I don't think they are contradictory at all.

Q : What is our own estimation of the state of Pakistan's nuclear pursuit and secondly if this matter was discussed with Yaqub Sahebzada Khan and, if so, with what result?

PM : While our assessment is that they are fairly close to manufacture of the weapon and that they do have a programme for manufacturing the weapon, their position is that they are not manufacturing the weapon. This has been brought to the notice of Sahebzada Yakub Khan and he has taken the stand that they are not making the weapon. We pointed out that if they have the weapon it will change the situation in this region and we would have to react in some manner.

Q : (Hindi) I have a short question. From coins to sugar, we are importing so many things. Is this a proof of our economic self-reliance?

PM : (Hindi) The meaning of self-reliance is not that we don't import anything from abroad. Japan is also a self-reliant nation but it imports a good number of things. This is not the only criterion. What matters is that we utilise our resources in order best to achieve India's progress and development. If imports help us to conserve our resources we should not hesitate to import. If we have to enlarge our domestic industrial capacity, we must do so. Sometimes, you will require something at once and importing it is the only way. But if you look at our economy and at our progress, you will then find that we have now achieved what we have not achieved earlier.

Q : It ?? months since you have assumed charge as the Prime Minister. You have not been able to organise your Cabinet fully. What is holding it up? There is a supplementary also which I would like to ask.

PM : What makes you think my cabinet is not organised? I think it is perfectly well organised.

Q : You have given additional charges to several of your senior Ministers.

PM : I see no fault in the functioning of the Ministers.

Q : You had talks with the Congress (S) President, Mr Sharad Pawar. Is there any likelihood of the Congress (S) joining your Party?

PM : Not at the moment.

Q : (In Urdu) Sir, let me first congratulate you on your having used Urdu, which is a forgotten language. We have been free for 38 years but the dependence on English continues. All your governmental media give preference to English papers over language papers, whether Hindi or Urdu. May I appeal to you to give encouragement to Hindi and Urdu papers instead of English papers.

PM : (In Urdu) Certainly. In whichever language the question is asked I try to reply in the language.

Q : (In Urdu) That is why I congratulated you. For the first time the Prime Minister has spoken in Urdu.

PM : (In Urdu) Thanks.

Q : It has been seen that many non-Congress (1) States, particularly in the South, take to what is called populist programmes. In one State, they spend about Rs 200 crores towards what is called a mid-day meal scheme. In another State, they spend about Rs. 180 crores towards what is called cheap rice scheme. A third State is also in the same way to supply rice and also cloth. Now my point is, all these constitute some kind of a non-developmental expenditure although they could be justified in terms of promoting human welfare? The real point to consider is that it causes erosion of funds for meaningful economic development. Now, this is putting pressure on the Congress (1). Parties in those States which are in opposition, and are likely to generate similar pressures for Congress Governments which are in power. Now, I want to ask you whether you have any intention to take up this matter either at the NDC or at any other appropriate forum so that there could be some kind of uniform norms and guidelines so that the poorer people in the Congress (1) States do not suffer also in the process.

PM : You missed one out. One State is also distributing power free. I know this is a very serious problem and it has to be looked at by all the States and the Central Government together. The fact is that such programmes are necessary and are required. But, as you said, they are not productive in the sense that they do not generate any returns which can be redeployed for development: So, they must be balanced with programmes which do generate such returns. And it is this balance which we must establish because if you spend everything on such programmes, our development process will come to a grinding halt. These States must realise that there is no goose that lays golden eggs. They have to generate the wealth that they have to distribute for development amongst the poor.

Q : I have two questions Mr. Prime Minister. You were very prompt in passing the Anti-Defection Bill, but the first defection has taken place in your own party in Bihar. The second question is Mrs Gandhi used to describe her Government as 'the Government that works. How would you like to describe your Government?

PM : One that works faster.

Coming to your first question, we passed the Anti-Defection Bill and if there is anything which contravenes that, there are provisions in the Bill which will come into action. The matter that your are talking about has been taken up in the court. There it will be sorted out. It is a legal matter. We have categorically given instructions that no people are to be inducted into our party. We are having some things like this in the North-East also. There too we have told them that nobody is to be taken in.

Q : Mr. Prime Minister, you said that' you are going to do something for the upliftment of the poor people of this country. What exactly are the specific steps that you are going to take to help them ?

PM : We have got our anti-poverty programmes. Our main thrust in development is agriculture, which is targeted to help the poorest in the country. We have to develop our infrastructure. These are the three basic thrusts that we are giving.

Q : Coming back to Punjab, you referred to some hopeful signs with regard to the attitude of the Akali Dal. What do you think, how do you rate the chances of complete return to normalcy and the chances of having elections before the deadline expires on the 6th of October?

PM : For normalcy, I give very high chances. As regards elections before October 6, it is very difficult to say at the moment because the situation is fluid and sensitive and we will have to watch it as we go along. We would, of course, like to have elections before October 6, so that we do not have to extend President's rule. But if it is necessary to extend President's rule, we will extend President's rule.

Q : In your talk with the leadership of USSR, France and USA; during your recent visit to those countries, did you find any accord in their approach towards the nuclear disarmament question and also what were the areas of discord?

The second part of my question is : are there any fresh initiatives in the offing from India to solve the Gulf crisis and'the Palestinian question?

PM : No, we are not taking any fresh initiatives at the moment. We are watching the situation. We are in touch with the various people.

The attitude of the countries on the nuclear question has been made very clear on a number of occasions. The non-aligned countries are for disarmament. The nuclear weapon States are rather more cautious when they talk about disarmament. The US has said that they are for complete disarmament. But they feel that the road to complete disarmament is via star wars. We feel that this is wrong and any escalation cannot lead to disarmament and we feel that this would be an escalation. France says that it has a very small deterrent which is only relevant to France and the Soviet Union and does not affect the total nuclear picture. This deterrent is also totally on submarines-the weapons are totally on submarines and thus are not covered under the purview of the present disarmament, talks. And their position is that if there is a substantial reduction in armaments by the major powers, they will start disarming themselves.

Q : I am Suman from Samachar Bharati. Mr. Prime Minister; the Kanishka tragedy has been a big disaster.

PM : (In Hindi) At least Samachar Bharati should ask questions in Hindi.

Q : (In Hindi) You are right, I shall ask questions in Hindi. Prime Minister, I want to say that the recent Kanishka mishap has been a big setback to the confidence in Air India. I want to draw your attention to the fact that all over the world hijacking and terrorism are on the increase. What guarantee is there that such incidents won't recur? I want to ask whether Government is considering any steps by itself and in consultation with the

Government of the United States and Canada to ensure that lives and journeys of passengers will be safe.

PM : (In Hindi) We have taken up these matters with both the governments. When I was in America, I had some talks with them. I am confident that the American Government will take suitable action. I think that the Canadian Government will also deal firmly with the extremists. Earlier they were not as firm with them as they should have been.

As regards the larger question of international terrorism, as long as there is no worldwide agreement and everyone does not exert himself to put an end to it, until then it will not end. We find that there are many who condemn terrorists but the same people are also encouraging them. If this ends then terrorism will also end. Meanwhile, we are taking all possible steps to ensure fullest safety on Air India, Indian Airlines and Vayudoot and also to have thorough search of luggage, goods and passengers.

Q : (In Hindi) Sir, a question arises out of your opening statement. When you took over the prime ministership you emphasised two or three matters. Among them the top priority was given to educational reforms. But you did not mention it at all in your opening statement: Would you please take the trouble of telling us what is your comprehensive vision of education in relation to the nation's progress and taking the nation to the 21st century?

If you will permit me, I will also add one other question connected with this. In one of your speeches during your recent visit to America you said that as regards scientists and technicians now working in America it was your attempt to create conditions which would make them come back and work within the country and that a time would come when they should be ready to come to India. What opportunities are you creating to enable them to come back and serve the country?

PM : (In Hindi) You will remember I had said that within five or six months we would come out with our educational policy, so that there could be discussion and debate on it as a result of which we could get a picture which could then be put into a final shape and implement it from next year. There is no change in this. The policy will be ready in the coming month or two. A draft was indeed prepared two months ago on which there have been discussions and there will be more discussions and there are also some other reports. These will be before you in the next two months. There could then be a full-fledged debate. We have to see that this policy will prepare workers for new industries in the next fifteen years and also our students for the technological innovations. We have to instil a work ethic in our countrymen, a sense of unity and a feeling that we belong not to a developing nation but to a developed country. This will be our objective in formulating a new educational policy. At the same time, we have to see that we do not forget our history, out traditions, our ancient values.

Regarding your third question, we shall try to bring back all our technologists and scientists. We are providing opportunities to them and are assisting them. We have formulated policies to enable them to come back to this country and work here. Many of them have now thought of coming back to India and I hope that they will return. But it is not our intention that none of them goes abroad. We would like them to go there for education, experience, so that they could use these on their return to India.

Q : Mr. Prime Minister, it is exactly ten years after the Emergency. Do you think at this stage that the declaration of the Emergency was the right step to have been taken and if similar conditions of unrest, as it was called, prevail, will you resort to the same measures?

PM : I think at that time it was the right step and there were various forces working. If these conditions are repeated, it might be necessary to have an Emergency. But that will have to be seen with the conditions that prevail. There can be no absolutely equivalent set of situations, there cannot be an equivalent situation. Things will be different. I, personally, am not in favour of using such harsh measures if they can be avoided. But, if it is necessary, they must be used.

Q : In reply to an earlier question, you said that an inquiry will be conducted into the charges against Mr. Bhajan Lal on receiving his comments. But, two days ago, we were told that the Government had decided to stop any further action on the Vaidialingam Committee report on the two former Prime Ministers. Now, if follow-up action is not taken and inquiry reports are not taken to their logical end, what will be the sanctity attached to such inquiries? That is No. 1. No. 2 : Do you have any alternative mechanism to ensure that people in high positions—the Prime Minister and the Chief Ministers—are not allowed to get away with whatever wrongs they may commit during their tenures.

PM : One : We will take action if any of the points raised is substantiated. Second : On the Vaidialingam report, although Justice Vaidialingam has said that a prima facie case has been made out on three issues, on three points and they should be followed up, we thought that since in 1980 elections, the people had given their decision on those very issues, it is not necessary to follow that up further. We are trying to see how to set up foolproof systems. We have seen the Lokayukta and Lokpal system working in various places. They are more successful in some places, less successful in some places and totally redundant in others. We would like to come out with a system which is effective and which works. And we are trying to see how this can come about.

Q : In the light of the forthcoming visit of the German Foreign Minister—after Mr. Gromyko's elevation to the Presidency now the most senior one in the Western world—how do you rate the state of relations between India and Germany?

PM : I think our relations are good. We have a good trade relationship. We have fairly good understanding of our political positions. And I see relations between our countries improving with more technological and trade exchange.

Q : (In Hindi) After the brutal assassination of Indiraji who was the beloved leader of not only this country but of the whole world, on what grounds is the government continuing to adopt a lenient attitude towards the Akali leaders and leaders of SSF who were responsible for converting the Golden Temple into a military base and headquarters of terrorists?

PM : (In Hindi) Partly on the grounds of their statements. We shall not allow them to repeat the same thing and if they try to do so we shall deal with them firmly right from the beginning. We will not let it happen again.

Q : Mr. Prime Minister, under your chairmanship, the Planning Commission has just sort of had a dream that overnight the resources gap has disappeared. I would like to know how, without any specific steps being suggested, such a scheme has been visualised.

PM : No, I don't think the gap has just disappeared and I don't think the Planning Commission has had a dream of their resources. They do have a dream of what they want to make India, yes. The resources gap has been closed after discussing with the States and evaluating the additional resource mobilisation that the States are willing to do and have accepted to do. On that basis, we have evaluated that we not only can but we will have a Plan of Rs 1,80,000 crores, and we are optimistic that we might even be able to do better.

Q : Mr. Prime, Minister, how do you react towards the efforts of Sant Harchand Singh Longowal towards Hindu-Sikh unity and amity in Punjab? Further, have you any plan to release all the Sikh detenus and for reinstatement of Army deserters?

PM : Well, the Army has its own rules. They have their own laws and they will deal with the deserters as per their rules. We are not going to interfere in that in any way. I think Sant Longowal has taken many steps, positive, to bring about normalcy in the situation and I congratulate him on that. And we look forward to, his moving even further ahead and bringing about complete normalcy in Punjab.

Q : At your press conference in Washington the, other day, you were asked whether you had any plans for removing

Government controls on radio and television and you replied "None at the moment" and went on to explain that, as you put it, India is not yet ready for the change. Sir, except for a mercifully brief period, we have been a functioning democracy for almost forty years. We' have a vigorous Parliament, we have an independent judiciary and we have an articulate press. All these have only enriched our democratic system. It is, therefore, rather too late in the day to try to convince the world that giving freedom to radio and television will be a risky venture. Mr. Prime Minister, my respectful submission in this: Will it not be more correct, credible and convincing to say that in this particular matter at least, it is the Congress Party which is not, and obviously will never be, ready?

PM : Well, that may be your submission. I don't think the Janata Party gave any autonomy to radio and television: neither did the BJP, neither did anybody else. . . .,

Q : That is not a precedent?

PM : I am not talking of precedents. I am talking of what is right for the country at the time. It is when you are in Government that your realise the responsibilities that you have to bear. It was very easy for the BJP to talk about autonomy for the radio and television but when they had the responsibility and they had to bear and shoulder that responsibility, they realised that the time was not ready for it and they did not do it. . ..

Q : Sir. .

PM : Do you want my answer or do you want. . . .

Q : I am sorry, I just want to ask supplementary if you permit me?

PM : You permit me and then after that I will permit you: . . . . As you say, India has been a vibrant democracy for 38 years now and if this was really an issue with the people, they would have raised it. They have not raised it. We feel and I reiterate that we are not ready for total autonomy for these two institutions and we are not going to give it at the moment.

Q : I know when the Janata Party was in power, they were busy quarelling among themselves and they had no time for these basic reforms. But my point is the Indian people were never consulted in this matter and how do you say we are not ready for this particular democratic reform? In what respect are we not ready? Is it a risk?

PM : By seeing the way that you people print and publish; I don't think you behave responsibly at all.

Q : But that has nothing to do with radio.

PM : Of course; but if it spreads to radio, there will be a tremendous danger to country. . .

Q : But is radio a counterblast to the Press or creative?

PM : Do you want a debate or should we carry on with the press conference?

Q : I have two questions : Is the Congress-I planning to withdraw its support to the G.M. Shah Government in Jammu and Kashmir since the Congress-I has been openly criticising that Ministry?

Second: Has the post of Principal Secretary to the Prime Minister been abolished? .

PM : 'No' to both. We are not withdrawing the support, and the post has not been abolished.

Q : There is the recent case of a Muslim religious court sentencing a woman to 101 lashes. There is also a demand for deletion of Article 44 from the Constitution. This brings out the danger of religious laws and civil laws diverging from each other. Will the Government move in the direction of a uniform civil code and, if so, how soon?

PM : No, we have no plan at the moment to move away from the systems that we have at the moment and where discrepancies come up such as you have pointed out, we have High Courts and the Supreme Court which will handle that.

Q : (In Hindi) Hon'ble Prime Minister, the Information and Broadcasting Minister had said recently at a conference of information ministers that there should be a code of conduct for the national press. This has been a moot point for a long time and the Press Council Act enjoins upon the Press Council to gradually formulate a code of conduct. This has been said at the instance of a Chief Minister who has now become former Chief Minister. His own record has not been good, because it is alleged that his police in Gujarat burnt a newspaper office and the Press Council was asked to look into it. For the last four months there are no members of the Press Council, their selection was done six months back, but the Government notification has not been issued as yet. I would, therefore, like to know as to what is the policy of the Government towards the Press?

PM : (In Hindi) I have already expressed my views regarding the code of conduct for the Press. This subject was raised when a delegation from the press had come to meet me and they had suggested this. I had told them that we could consider this suggestion, but we would like that it should be implemented by the press without the Government's interference.

Q : (In Hindi) Why has the notification not been issued?

PM : (In Hindi) I 'shall' find out the reason. I do not :know about it.

Q : Mr. Prime Minister, your recent mass exposure in five nations was on a cultural plank and according to reports, Indian culture through the Festival of India has been enhancing the Indian image. However, at home, eyebrows are being raised on the justification for this kind of expenditure. My question is: What steps are you proposing to take towards promotion of culture at home? In these troubled times, where culture in the past has been the only bond for many ethnic groups of vastly different backgrounds in this poor land, one finds that the budget for Culture is an abysmal 0. 3 per cent of the 3 per cent which is the allocation for the sister department of Education. Secondly, whatever funds there are, are spent on white elephants which do not reach out to the common people. I will give you an instance. You recently sanctioned the Patiala Cultural Centre rupees five crores. Now, one regrets to, say that it will probably end up as a big set of buildings and a couple of chairs for non-descript and obscure disciplines. Can you propose some steps whereby culture could come down to the common people through interaction?

PM : What makes you assume that it will end up like that when the foundation-stone has been laid only a few days ago?

Q : I am afraid previous experience says because of bureaucratisation of culture in the past.

PM : I am very sorry that you have such notions and I will guarantee you that it will not end up with a building and a few chairs, but it will end up as a vibrant cultural institution which will bring together the cultures of the whole region and not just one State. We have put aside in the Seventh Plan over two thousand crores of rupees for basic culture-related activities and this is fairly large. We have increased it to over two thousand crores in finalising the Plan. We are going to set up cultural centres all over the country to look into this. My personal feeling is that cultural and human resource development have been much neglected and we are going to pay much more attention to it.

Q : But if I may just point out, this regionalism and this regional clubbing together of cultures in these centres is not going to work as well as letting a hundred flowers bloom as in the past.

PM : This is not going to stop a hundred flowers blooming. In the past, we have seen that a hundred flowers have bloomed, but they have not grown. They remained what they were. There has been very little development.

Q : Mr. Prime Minister, you had indicated that there should be a new media policy in the country. The process of a national debate on the new media and communication policy has been started. I understand that this policy would help the Press grow and be ready for the 21st century with technology. However, in this case, recently in the new Budget, even the computerised photo composing machines which are to modernise the Press have been deleted from the OGL. I would like to know whether you have given this matter a thought and whether you envisage the kind of steps that will prepare the Press and support the Press for the 21st century.

PM : Deletion from the OGL does not mean prevention from your acquiring the machine. It only says that you have to acquire it through a different method, a different route and I do not think there is any extra restriction on your getting the machines. Increase and speeding up the functioning of the media is not limited to printing machines, but there is much more involved in that. As you will be well aware, one of the major thrusts of the Communications Ministry is to improve the functioning of data links between major stations and help the Press and other industries to communicate with each other much more efficiently and easily.

Q : How will you evaluate the election of Mr. Gromyko as the President of the Soviet Union for the development of relations between India and the Soviet Union?

PM : We think it is a very positive development. We have had very long contact and relationship with President Gromyko, and we see it as a positive development. We congratulate him on his new position.

Q : You have stated that the population problem is the No. 1 problem for the country. It is also fairly obvious that the programmes in place are not yielding good results at the moment. What new initiatives does your Government have, and when will we see them?

PM : This is one of our most serious problems. We too feel that the returns on investments are, not commensurate with what we are spending. This does not mean that what we have done so far is wrong. I just think that we are coming to a stage where a particular type of thrust is not giving us dividends that it should and we must look further to see where the problem is and how to overcome that. We have already done one exercise and we are doing a few more. But I am not in a position to tell you today, but may be in two or three weeks we will be in a position to tell you what we are doing in this. But one of the major factors which has come out is the social and cultural block and we are seeing how we can tackle that.

Q : (In Hindi) I am asking three questions. My first question is that you have just returned from two foreign tours-Russia and America. You discussed many things there. I would like to know as to how did you guess which country could be a better friend to us and to what an extent?

PM : (In Hindi) We have friendship with all. With Russia, our friendship has been long. They have stood by us in times of difficulties. We have faith in them and we have strong friendship. We have non-aligned friendship with non-aligned nations. We have old relations with Algeria. We both want to take the non-aligned movement and the world in a particular direction through a particular path and there is very little difference in our approach. We have an old friendship with France. They have also stood by us in our time of need and it is our endeavour to strengthen this friendship further. Because of America's policy in our region, we have some difference of opinion with them. We have discussed it in detail and we feel that we can develop this friendship further. Many problems between us can be sorted out mutually and we are both keen to do it. We hope that with America also, friendship and cooperation will grow and we will be able to work together.

Q : How do you take Amitabh Bachchan's criticism by your own Partymen?

PM : This is hardly a thing for me to answer. We are open to criticism from all quarters. We do not put a lid on criticism everywhere. And it is for Amit to answer that criticism and to face it.

Q : Will you define Rajiv Gandhi as Prime Minister?

PM : (In Hindi), It looks as though I made a mistake in allowing you three questions.

Q : My question is on the proposal for declaring the Indian

Ocean as a zone of peace. What are the obstacles to convening an International Conference on the Indian Ocean?

PM : We are very much for Indian Ocean as a zone of peace. And we are getting support from some of the major powers. But there are too many vested interests in the area, and we have to take a consolidated stand to face these, and to bring about a zone of peace in the Indian Ocean. We will be working towards this.

Q : My question is split into four parts. Mr. Prime Minister, yesterday. . . .

PM : I don't think we will make that mistake again.

Q : It is only split into four parts—(A), (B), (C) and (D). Yesterday, the AICC (1) headquarters had issued a press release which amounts to a written assurance to the former Chief Minister of Gujarat, Mr. Madhavsingh Solanki, that his services will be utilised at the national level. Does this mean that a reshuffle in the Cabinet is in the offing and he will be inducted at the Centre? (B) What steps do you propose to restore normalcy in Gujarat? (C) Do you propose to convene a meeting of all the Opposition parties to see that normalcy is restored soon? I will leave the D part of it.

PM : I think on A, I can very categorically give you a 'maybe'. On B, it is for the Chief Minister to decide how he will tackle the Gujarat problem. It is his problem, it is not our problem at the Centre. As regards C, I have already had a couple of meetings with the Opposition on the basic issues that have been raised there, not restricted to Gujarat, but on a national perspective and I intend to carry on with that.

Q : Picking up the question on Gujarat, spreading of communalism in India and doing anything that leads to communal rioting, is an offence. A serious charge has been made against Mr. Solanki that he fomented communal trouble in Gujarat to divert attention from his other troubles. Are you going to take any action against Mr. Solanki for spreading communalism in Gujarat?

PM : There are many charges which the press raises.

Q : Your own party has raised charges against Mr. Solanki.

PM : Charges are raised on all sorts of issues. Nothing has been substantiated. If anything is substantiated, we will take action. It is too easy to just level charges and to accuse people of doing things. We have to have a system where these must be substantiated in some manner and the persons who raise these charges should be willing to face some sort of action if the charges are proved untrue.

Shri H.Y. Sharada Prasad: There are still 45 to 50 flags waving there. Anyway, we will have two more questions. (Interruption).

PM : You must learn to ask questions quicker and sharper.

Q : The questions are lengthy.

PM : That is not my fault.

Q : Sir, time and again you have said that the unity of the country must be strengthened and in one of your earliest broadcasts to the nation, you referred to communalism as perhaps being the most and the biggest stumbling block in the way of the country's unity and progress and you have also said and I think I am using your words, that an ideological struggle would be waged at factory-gates, and at the doors of schools, and colleges, farms, everywhere in the country. But till now we have not come across any such measures but we have only found that the traditional law and order machinery of the police, which has been found wanting very often, has been used. Not even in the slightest a beginning has been made by way of ideological fight against the communal forces. Would you like to comment on it?

PM : This is a subject which we have taken up very seriously in all the branches of administration. We are seeing how we can improve the training and the ideological inputs into the training. The police, unfortunately, have had very inadequate input, not only ideologically, but also financially and in every possible way. We have not faced the problems of terrorism and extremism that other countries have faced. So we have managed to spend less on the police but I think now is the time when very much more attention has to be paid to the police. The quality of the police, the quantity, the number and their methods and equipment their training and many more things are to be improved and we are doing that now.

Q : In the field of telecommunication, Mr. Prime Minister, you would perhaps remember that you had called Mr. Thomas Kora to your residence and asked him to dial 100 and he could not get it. Now you promised in those days—and of course your mummy also promised in those days—that the telephone system would be improved in the country and perhaps an agreement was signed with a French Company and factory in Gonda has been installed to manufacture electronic exchanges. My first question would be: What are you doing for the second factory and whether the country is going in for another technology in the field of telecommunication which has the worst infrastructure in the country?

PM : One, we are looking very seriously at communications. But as you are aware, we are under tremendous resource constraints during this period. The specific question of what has been happening about the second telephone factory, you better talk to the Communications Minister. He will be able to answer that better. But as a matter of policy, what we are developing is our own technology. We are hopeful that it will be ready in a couple of years and we are hopeful that it will be as good as or better than what is available anywhere in the world. We have got the best brains working on it and we are optimistic.

Q : Mr. Prime Minister, you have been generous enough to allow more than one question to your own journalists. May I be allowed to ask three questions, Sir, I am from Pakistan. My first question is: What are the real difficulties in signing a No War Pact with Pakistan?

PM : There are many problems with this. We are in favour of a much more comprehensive treaty and we have put forward various proposals. We feel that a simple, pointed thing would not give the necessary results. .

Q : My second question is, Mr. Prime Minister, Pakistan has proposed joint inspection of nuclear installations. What is India's attitude towards it?

PM : We feel it would not be adequate to give us the guarantee that we need and it would give an excuse for clandestine development.

Q : My last question, Sir, there has been a general feeling among masses, both in India and Pakistan, that despite extensive clamouring and loud claims, nothing much could be achieved during the Indo-Pak Joint Commission's deliberations, particularly in the field of travel and trade.

PM : Well, we have been very positive in our attitude and we are willing to do much more. It is for the Pakistan Government to come forward and help us to do that.

Q : Mr. Prime Minister, there is a new disarmament proposal initiated by two political German parties-one is the Socialist Unity Party of GDR and the other one is the Socialist Democratic Party of FRG. Both have elaborated a common framework for governmental agreement on a zone free of chemical weapons. How do you consider this proposal in the context of worldwide endeavours of peace loving forces for disarmament?

PM : We are very much for a ban on chemical and biological weapons, and we would like to see some agreement between all the nations to bring this about. It is something which must be seen on its own and we are disheartened that certain countries are now starting development' of just such weapons.

Q : This is about cleanliness in politics. You did a very right thing at the time of the last Assembly elections by denying tickets to various partymen who were under some doubts and you had very good criteria and everybody appreciated that Indian people liked it and they gave you the verdict. But the point is the same persons who had been denied tickets are becoming Chief Ministers or they are inducted into State ministries. Is it consistent with your policy or do you feel that you have entered a chakravyooh and you cannot come out of it now? No. 2: There was a talk that you are sharing dual responsibility—one as the Prime Minister and one as President of the Congress Party—and there are a lot of things you have to do with many questions before the country as well as organisational problems. So, would you like to share your responsibility as President of the Party with somebody else?

PM : To the first question first there were many reasons why we denied tickets to people. Corruption or bad image was not the only reason. One of the reason was that if in their Assembly constituencies they had lost votes during the Parliamentary election, and some people, because we stuck rather rigidly to that, some people who were only down by a few hundred votes were denied tickets. And these are the sort of people that we have used after that. Where there have been serious charges of corruption, we have not rehabilitated those people.

About Party presidentship, this is for the party to decide. We are having party elections next year. We are building membership now. It is for them to decide.

Q : You are holding both the positions. So, you must be having your personal thinking about it. Are you feeling comfortable in both the positions?

PM : Yes, I am very comfortable. They put me here and they must decide.

Thank you very much.

From Different Stories

The Times of India, New Delhi published four different stories from this press conference.

Talks with Opposition Promised PM hopes Punjab situation will ease

New Delhi, July 7. The Prime Minister, Mr. Rajiv Gandhi, today sounded a hopeful note on Punjab, pledged a continuing dialogue with Opposition parties and noted that Pakistan was fairly close to manufacturing nuclear weapons.

Addressing a nationally televised news conference, his first in the Capital since assuming office, the Prime Minister indicated that "India will have to react in some way" if Pakistan develops nuclear weapons. He did not elaborate.

He explained the rejection of the proposal for joint inspection of nuclear installations in India and Pakistan, saying that it would provide no foolproof guarantee against clandestine operations.

It was the first time the news conference was held in the main hall of Vigyan Bhavan. Journalists were asked to pass through tight security checks. The atmosphere inside was one of ease.

Barring a question or two, there was full rapport. There was little attempt to parry any question.

In fact, Mr. Gandhi enlivened the session with pithy answers. As for instance when a Hindi news agency correspondent put his question in English, he remarked that at least the particular questioner should have raised the query in Hindi. He gave an enigmatic reply: "Categorical may be" when asked if' Mr. Madhavsingh Solanki would be inducted into the cabinet.

In reply to a subsequent question, however, he said if there were definite proven charges against the former Chief Minister, there would be an inquiry.

Answering a number of questions on Punjab, he said he was optimistic that the situation there would ease. While the government was keen on conducting the elections before October 6 when President's rule" expires, it might be continued if the situation warranted. He congratulated Sant Harchand Singh Longowal on several "positive steps" the Akali leader had initiated to promote Hindu–Sikh unity.

A correspondent reminded the Prime Minister of the emergency ten years ago and enquired if he envisioned a repetition of the situation.

Mr. Gandhi maintained that the then prevalent conditions justified the emergency. If these were to be repeated, it might be necessary to declare emergency again. He qualified his observation, saying he was not in favour of such harsh steps and "there could be no equivalent situation now."

On the issue of reservation, he made it clear that as far as Scheduled Castes and' Tribes were concerned the position could not be changed.

He had no plans to convene a conference of chief ministers to discuss the reservation issue. He referred to the talks he had four or five times with the Opposition in Punjab.

Asked why he had not yet organised his cabinet, he snapped back, "What makes you think so. We are perfectly organised." When the correspondent pointed out that the ministers were holding additional charges, he said "I see no fault in the functioning of the ministers."

To a question whether the Congress (S) was joining his party, he replied, "not at the moment."

Asked about his continuing in dual position as party President and Prime Minister, he thought it was a matter for the Party to decide the issue. Party elections would be held next year. "Yes, I am quite comfortable," he quipped raising laughter when asked whether he felt comfortable occupying the two posts. "It is they (the Party) who have put me in this position and they must decide," he said.

About his statement while in the U.S.A. that India was not ready for autonomous radio and television, he maintained the position, saying that electronic media could not function the way the press behaved.

He recalled the decision not to give such autonomy to radio and the Doordarshan when the Janata was in power. The other main points contained in the Prime Minister's replies were:

Punjab: In his opening remarks, Mr. Gandhi said Punjab was one of the major problems. As a result of the steps that had been taken, there was lessening of tension. The Akalis were also coming forward and now talking about finding a solution within the constitutional framework. They were also completely against terrorism and violence.

Replying to a question, he said holding election before October 6 was very difficult to say at the moment because of the fluid situation in the state. "We are watching it as we go along".

Replying to a question on the misuse of religious places, including the Golden Temple, Mr. Gandhi said: "We will not allow such activities to find a foothold in religious places. If these activities start again, we will take firm action." The terrorists within the country were getting isolated with the "positive actions" of Sant Longowal and others.

Army Deserters : The government would not interfere in the army rules and procedures in dealing with the Sikh deserters.

Gujarat : So far as handling the current law and order situation in Gujarat was concerned, it was for the new Chief Minister to decide how to tackle it. Asked if charges levelled against Mr. Solanki would be probed, Mr. Gandhi said it was easy to level charges. However, action would be taken if the charges were substantiated. Mr. Gandhi felt there should be some system under which charges were substantiated before they were hurled.

He felt that the current anti-reservation agitation was given a political turn in which many political parties were involved. He asked political parties not to exploit the agitation for whipping up parochial feelings and also not to use it for political gains.

So far as the question involving the political parties in finding a solution to the anti-reservation agitation was concerned, the Prime Minister said, "We will again hold talks with the Opposition leaders and try to find a solution."

In reply to a question on the crash of the Air-India jumbo jet, Mr. Gandhi said the U.S. Government had taken positive steps against terrorists. He was hopeful that the Canadian government would look more seriously into the activities of the terrorists and take firm action against them.

As the phenomenon of terrorism was new to India, the police force and other security agencies were not geared or trained to combat this threat to national security. "We are now planning to equip the police force with new equipment, training programmes and inputs to make it fully alert to the new danger."

India for Better Trade Ties with Pak

New Delhi, July 7. The Prime Minister, Mr. Rajiv Gandhi said here today that the recent Indo-Pakistani talks had further strengthened the general understanding between the two countries.

Addressing newsmen, Mr. Gandhi said, India would have, however, liked major advances in trade, but unfortunately some differences cropped up. India hoped that these differences would be clarified.

On signing of a no-war pact with Pakistan as suggested by that country, the Prime Minister said: "There are many problems with this. We are in favour of a much more comprehensive treaty."

The Prime Minister said that during his recent foreign tour, the issue of disarmament had figured in talks with the leaders of the USSR, the USA and France. Mr. Gandhi denied a suggestion of contradiction in the US approach as reflected in the statements that Pakistan was not making a nuclear weapon and that Washington was persuading Islamabad to abandon its nuclear weapon pursuits.

India's relations with the Soviet Union, which had, "stood by us in our times of travails", had further strengthened as a result of his recent visit to Moscow. "We trust the Soviet Union as a friend and depend on them." He said France had also helped India in the past and "Our friendly relations and cooperation with them would expand in future."

India was keen that there should be a global ban on the production and use of chemical and biological weapons. "We would like to see some governmental action" against such weapons, he said.

Mr. Gandhi said the election of Mr. Andrel Gromyko as Soviet President was "a positive development" in Indo-Soviet relations.

Gulf War : Mr. Gandhi said, India, as Chairman of the non-aligned movement, was not contemplating any fresh initiative at the moment to bring about an end to the Iran-Iraq war. India was maintaining close contact with the two warring countries which were members of the non-aligned movement. On the problem of terrorism, the Prime Minister said it could not be tackled effectively unless there'was worldwide agreement.

New Plan to Control Population Soon

New Delhi, July 7, A new programme for population control would be announced in the next three weeks, the Prime Minister, Mr. Rajiv Gandhi, said here today.

A new education policy would also be ready for public discussion in two months, the Prime Minister told a press conference during which he was also asked to explain his economic philosophy.

The Prime Minister said, the government's economic policies were governed by what was good for the country and rejected the suggestion that he should label his philosophy in the ideological terms of the right or the left.

He said, the basic economic policies were laid down by Pandit Nehru and Indira Gandhi and the government was not deviating from these. "But we have to modify our thinking to today's economic conditions in the country, the progress we have made, the financial constraints and the international monetary and financial systems."

He said, "the government has to balance these considerations to produce a package which did not deviate from the basic Congress ideology and yet is dynamic and will take India ahead."

Describing the population programme as a serious one the Prime Minister said the methods employed so far to deal with this had not proved very effective. The returns were not commensurate with the investment, he said.

The particular kind of thrust being given to it was not yielding the desired results because of certain social and cultural blocks, the Prime Minister said.

The Prime Minister set at rest doubts about the seventh plan outlay of Rs 1,80,000 crores which would be protected. He said he was optimistic that it might even be enhanced.

Resource Gap : When a correspondent commented that the planning commission just had a dream that there was no resource gap, the Prime Minister said, "I do not think the gap had disappeared. But the gap has been closed after talks with the states and evaluating additional resources that they are willing to raise and are expected to do. On that basis, we have concluded that we cannot only have a plan of Rs 1,80,000 crores but are optimistic that we may even be able to do better."

In his opening remarks, the Prime Minister described the economic situation as "good" and while taking note of the pricerise maintained that the rate of inflation at 3. 1 per cent had been the lowest in the last three months in relation to the past several years.

But prices of certain items were such that the government had to be vigilant to control the situation.

Mr. Gandhi said his government was considering how the 20 Point programme could be implemented more effectively. He said streamlining the functioning of the public sector was taking time.

In reply to a question, he said there should be a balance between the productive and non-productive expenditure by the states. The "populist schemes" evolved by some non-Congress states in the South should not hamper economic development.

When the correspondent referred to the midday meal scheme of Tamil Naduu, the Prime Minister reminded him that a state was even giving power free.

The Prime Minister said, some of the welfare programmes were necessary but a balance had to be maintained, otherwise the development would come to a grinding halt. Expenditure on populist programmes by some states was a serious problem which had to be looked into by the States and the Centre.

In reply to a question on the plan to buy technology from abroad for manufacturing telephone exchanges, Mr. Gandhi said our best brains are working to produce an indigenous technology which could be better than any available in the world. This would be ready in a couple of years, he said.

The Prime Minister said the government proposed to set up cultural centres all over the country. He pointed out that the seventh plan allocation on culture was Rs 2,000 crores.

Bhajan's Reaction to Charges will be Sought: PM

New Delhi, July 7: The Prime Minister, Mr. Rajiv Gandhi, said at his news conference here today that the government would decide on an inquiry if the Opposition charges against Bhajan Lal were substantiated.

In this regard the past practice of asking the Chief Minister first for his reaction to the charges would be adopted.

On dropping of charges against the two former Prime Ministers, Mr. Gandhi said it was done because the government thought the people had given their verdict on the issues in the 1980 elections.

Press Code : Mr. Gandhi said the government will not want to impose any code of conduct on the press and it was for the press itself to have self-imposed controls.

Regarding the civil code, the Prime Minister said, "We have no plans at the moment to move away from the system that we have at the moment. If there are complaints of discrimination, it is open for anyone to approach the high courts or the Supreme Court."

He said the post of Principal Secretary to the Prime Minister had not been abolished.

The Tribune, Chandigarh, carried three different stories:

P.M. for Punjab Poll by Oct 6

No Succumbing to Terrorism

New Delhi, July 7 (P.T.I)—Mr. Rajiv Gandhi told a press conference here today that he would like the Punjab Assembly election to be held before October 6 so that President's Rule in the state did not have to be extended.

However, President's rule would be extended if it was necessary to do so. Replying to a question he said it was difficult to say at the moment whether the elections could be held before October 6 because of the fluid situation in the State. "We are watching the situation."

The Prime Minister said he thought that Sant Harchand Singh Longowal had taken many positive steps to bring about normalcy in Punjab and "I congratulate him."

He said the Government would not interfere with the Army rules and regulations with regard to the trial or release of deserters.

He told another questioner that the Government would not allow terrorists to operate from places of worship, including the Golden Temple. "If they do we will take very strong steps in the initial stages."

In his opening remarks, Mr. Gandhi said Punjab was one of the major problems. As a result of the steps taken by the Government there was a lessening of tension. The Akalis were now talking of finding a solution to the problem within the Constitutional framework. They were also totally against terrorism and violence.

The country had stood up against terrorism recently, he said apparently referring to the bomb blasts and the Air-India plane crash.

He categorically declared that India would not succumb to any pressure from terrorists or others within or outside the country. In reply to a question, he said so long as terrorists received support from one Government or the other it would be difficult to curb the menace.

There must be an international agreement on the subject so that terrorist activities which had spread to almost all parts of the world, were checked.

Regarding the crash of Air India's jumbo jet, Mr. Gandhi said the U.S. Government had taken some positive steps against the terrorists. He was hopeful that the Canadian Government would look more seriously into the activities of the terrorists and take firm action against them.

As the phenomenon of terrorism was new to India, the police force and other security agencies were not adequately trained to combat this threat to national security.

"We are now planning to equip the police force with new equipment and train it to meet the danger." The force would be substantially increased.

Mr. Gandhi said Air-India, Indian Airlines and Vayudoot had taken fresh security measures in the wake of the Kanishka tragedy. The steps would be reviewed from time to time keeping in view the developing situation in the context of terrorism.

The Prime Minister expressed serious concern over the progress Pakistan was making in acquiring nuclear capability. "We will have to react in some manner" if Pakistan produced a nuclear bomb.

The Pakistan Foreign Minister, Sahabzada Yakub Khan, was told of India's concern during his recent visit here.

Asked to comment on Pakistan's offer of a joint inspection of each other's nuclear installations, Mr. Gandhi said India could not accept it because Pakistan had failed to give adequate guarantees in this regard, leaving room for clandestine preparations.

Mr. Gandhi said the Pakistan Foreign Minister maintained that his country was not producing a bomb, but "our assessment is that they are very close to making a nuclear bomb."

India had drawn the attention of the U.S.A. to Pakistan's efforts to acquire nuclear weapons.

Asked by a Pakistan journalist why much headway could not be made at the recently concluded India-Pakistan joint Commission meeting, Mr. Gandhi said India had adopted a positive attitude and wanted to have cooperation in areas such as trade. It was for Pakistan to reciprocate the gesture.

India was keen on further strengthening bilateral relations with Pakistan. The two countries had reached an accord on cultural exchanges and simplified travel and tourism formalities.

Mr. Gandhi said there was an improvement in Indo-U.S. relations, despite differences on the situation in South Asia.

The two countries tried to remove impediments in their relations during his recent visit to Washington and were now willing to have increased cooperation in various fields.

Mr. Gandhi described India's friendship with the Soviet Union as old and time tested. "The Soviet Union has stood by us in the hour of crisis and we rely on its friendship," he added.

He criticised the USA's "starwars" Programme and said it would not help contain the nuclear arms race.

Replying to questions on disarmament, Mr. Gandhi said the nuclear powers had now started talking of the need to curb the arms race. But the USA thought that the route to disarmament was via the "star wars" programme. This view, India felt, was wrong. Referring to India's relations with France, Mr. Gandhi said the friendship between the two countries was also old. In a way France, too, stood by us when we were in need of its support.

Cong (I) Not to Withdraw Support to Shah

New Delhi, July 7 (P.T.I.). Prime Minister Rajiv Gandhi said today that his party was not withdrawing its support to the G.M. Shah Government in Jammu and Kashmir.

The Prime Minister was replying to questions at a Press Conference here.

Mr. Rajiv Gandhi said the Government had no plans to draw up a Uniform Civil Code.

He was replying to a question whether the Government was thinking of evolving a Uniform Civil Code in the context of a woman in Kerala being awarded 1,000 lashes by a religious body for alleged adultery.

Corruption : The Government would evolve a foolproof system of curbing corruption in high political offices. Mr. Gandhi, however, justified the dropping of charges against former Prime Ministers Morarji Desai and Charan Singh on the ground that the people had given their verdict against them in the 1980 Lok Sabha polls.

Code of Conduct : The Prime Minister made it clear that the Government would not interfere in the formulation of a code of conduct for journalists. The code, he said, should be evolved by members of the Press themselves.

On granting autonomy to All India Radio and Doordarshan, Mr. Gandhi said, "We are not yet ready for giving total autonomy to the two media." The BJP which was a constituent of the Janata Government had not granted autonomy to the two media. It was easy for the BJP now to talk about autonomy, he said.

Harsh Measures : Mr. Gandhi said he was against the use of harsh measures like emergency but if these were necessitated by circumstances these must be used. The emergency imposed ten years ago was a "right step" in the circumstances prevailing at that time. If these conditions are repeated, it might be necessary to have emergency. That will have to be seen in the light of conditions that prevail. There can be no two absolutely equivalent situations. Things will be different."

He said that Congress (I) organisational elections were going to be held soon.

The Prime Minister said his government was a government that worked faster. When a newsman said his mother used to describe her government as a government that worked. How would he define his government? "The government which works faster," remarked Mr. Gandhi smilingly.

Cleaning of Ganga : The cleaning of the Ganga would begin at Varanasi soon. The Prime Minister referred to the setting up of the Central Ganga Authority in this connection.

Defection : The Prime Minister said he had given instructions to his party that nobody is to be taken into the Congress (I) in view of the Anti Defection Act. Citing an instance in Bihar, a correspondent said the Congress (I) had violated the Act. Mr. Gandhi said the matter was already in the court. He added that several people, particularly in the north-east, were keen on joining the Congress (1).

Cabinet Expansion : The Union Cabinet was likely to be expanded before the coming monsoon session and former Gujarat Chief Minister Madhavsingh Solanki find a place in it, Mr. Gandhi said A.I.C.C.(I) General Secretary Rajendra Kumari Bajpai has already gone on record saying that Mr. Solanki's services will be utilised at the national level. Asked if charges levelled against Mr. Solanki would be probed, Mr. Gandhi said it was easy to make charges. Action would, however, be taken if these charges were substantiated.

Mr. Gandhi said that action against Haryana Chief Minister Bhajan Lal against whom Opposition members had submitted a memorandum of charges would depend on evaluation of the allegations. The Chief Minister's comments would also be sought in this connection.

Mr. Gandhi said that the best brains were working to develop indigenous communication technology. The technology would be equal to, if not better than, that available in advanced countries. It should be ready in a couple of years.

Indian Ocean : He reiterated the need for declaring the Indian Ocean a zone of peace and said that India would support any initiative taken in this regard.

India as Chairman of the Non-aligned Movement was not contemplating any fresh initiative to bring about an end to the Iran-Iraq war. India was, however, maintaining close contact with the two warring countries which were NAM members.

No Deviation in Economic Policy

New Delhi, July 7 (RTI). Mr. Rajiv Gandhi said today that the government's economic policies were governed by what was "good for the country" and not by ideological consideration of Right or Left.

Asked to define the "economic philosophy" of his government Mr. Rajiv said, "Our basic policy has been laid down by Nehru and Indira Gandhi and we are not shifting from that. But we have to modify our thinking in terms of today's approach, financial constraints and international monetary and financial systems." "We have to balance them and produce a package which does not deviate from the basic Congress ideology. It will take India ahead," Mr. Gandhi said.

Earlier in his opening remarks, the Prime Minister described the economic situation as good and noted the price rise. He said the rate of inflation at 3. 1 per cent had been the lowest in the last three months in relation to past several years. But he agreed that the prices of certain items were going up and that the government had to be vigilant to control the situation.

The Prime Minister set at rest doubts about the Seventh Plan outlay which he said would remain at Rs 180,000 crore as envisaged in the approach paper. He said he was optimistic that "we may be able to do even better."

Asked about the reported resource gap for the Seventh Plan, Mr. Rajiv Gandhi said, "I do not think the gap has disappeared. But the gap has been closed after talks with the States and evaluating additional resources that they are willing to raise. On that basis, we have concluded that we can have a Plan of Rs 180,000 crore."

Asked if the Centre did not consider "populist" certain schemes of the non-Congress (1) Governments such as mid-day meal and cheap rice involving hundreds of crores of rupees that cut into funds available for economic development, the Prime Minister said: "It is a very serious problem and has to be looked into by all the States and the Centre together."

Such programmes, he said, were necessary but they were not productive in the sense they did not generate returns which could be redeployed for development.

"They must be balanced with programmes which generate returns. If we spend everything on such-programmes our development programmes will grind to a halt. The States must realise that there is no goose that lays golden eggs," Mr. Gandhi remarked.

Self-reliance does not mean that you do not import anything, Mr. Gandhi told a questioner who said the government was talking of self-reliance and at the same time is importing such items as coins.

There were many items that needed to be imported to meet the immediate needs and some that would enable the country to produce more and better things, he said. He pointed out that even developed countries like Japan could not do without imports.

In his opening remarks the Prime Minister said the first priority of his government was to uplift the poor. It had chalked out many programmes. The anti-poverty programmes would be implemented vigorously, he added.

Referring to the Seventh Plan, he said priority would be given to agriculture where a lot of work needed to be done and would be done.

He said many steps had already been taken to give a new thrust to improving infrastructure facilities. Greater attention would also be given to the public sector, he added.

9

News from Speeches

Speeches are a major source of news and every day many news items that appear in the newspapers can be traced back to some speech or the other. Sometimes several speeches form part of one report. This happens in reports of seminars, symposia and legislatures. In such situations the most important speech, normally from the most important speaker, gets prominence.

While covering political party conferences and international conferences on various subjects, one has to deal with several speeches in a row. Depending on the content and the speaker, a reporter has to decide who should come first. Effort should also be made to generalise observations if possible and then mention who said what. In such cases the most important things said by different speakers should be mentioned and there should be no repetition of ideas. If there are contrary opinions expressed by different speakers they should be mentioned and then supporters of different schools of thought should be quoted. Here again repetition of ideas should be avoided.

The Importance

The importance of speeches and speakers varies from occasion to occasion and relative importance of other speakers. A reporter must evaluate various factors and use judgment while writing the story. For example, if many ministers speak in a party their speeches are important and what they say will be important according to the content of the speech. But if the prime minister speaks and he touches upon points which have been covered by other ministers already and adds something to it, he will get the maximum space and the rest of the ministers will be mentioned in the story with very little of what they said.

In a special debate in a house of parliament the speech of a minister of state gets prominence in case the cabinet minister of the same department does not speak. If the cabinet minister also speaks, then the state minister is normally pushed out of intro. If the prime minister intervenes during the debate and says something on the subject even the cabinet minister is pushed below in the body of the story. So, while reporting multiple speeches, the reporter must evaluate all these factors.

There are occasions when copies of a speech may be supplied in advance. Sometimes the story is prepared based on the advance copy and a reporter goes to the site when the speech is made—just to check whether the speech was made and if so whether it followed the advance copy. The advance story is subject to an embargo which is released automatically at the time up to which it is embargoed (should not be used before/should be used on or after. . .). A reporter or sub-editor who writes the story from such a speech has enough time at his disposal and should read the speech carefully and write the story on the top of which 'not to be used before . . . (time) on . . . (date)' as mentioned in the embargo should be typed. Normally, this embargo time is the time of the event where the speech is to be made. News agencies sometimes creed the embargoed story in advance. It should be used only after the embargo is lifted.

Where advance copy is not made available, the reporter must reach the place where the speech is to be delivered and check from the organisers if they are supplying a copy of the speech. If the copy is supplied before the speech then the reporter should start working on it immediately. He should go through it carefully and mark what he considers as important points.

He should also mark the order of their importance so that he losses no time when he has to type or dictate his story. He should carefully check the copy when the speech is made and see if there are any major deviations from the text supplied. Sometimes what is said by the speaker outside the supplied text is more newsworthy than all what is given in the text. Such departures from the prepared text should find place in the intro or body depending on their news value.

Many a time a speaker does not read the prepared speech and says that the speech be taken as read while what he says is in addition to that. In that case the reporter is supposed to listen to the speaker carefully and read the text also before writing the story.

If the organisers promise that the copy of the speech will be supplied but it is not distributed when the speech begins, the reporter should start taking notes from the beginning of the speech imagining that the copy is not available. Many such promises of the organisers prove false and if the reporter does not take notes or record the speech when it is delivered, he will be in difficulty. Moreover, he will miss any departures from the text.

A reporter should make use of the copy if he gets it within a few minutes after the event, otherwise he should rely on his notes and do the story. The copy can be used for quotations from the speech.

But there are occasions when the copy of the speech is not supplied. This happens in seminars and almost all the public meetings of political parties. A reporter can record them on a tape recorder. He must take care to take down important points in his notebook. In this way he can do the story quickly, for he will not have enough time to replay the full speech and then write. A tape recorder is useful for it helps the reporter in reproducing exactly what the speaker might have said on a controversial or important issue.

A speech can sometimes yield more than one story. In certain circumstances a reporter can add colour to the story by describing the atmosphere or some sidelights. Such opportunities should not be missed.

It is interesting to see how the same speech is covered by different newspapers. Following is the address by the President of India to Parliament (February 20, 1986).

Presidents' Speech

Honourable Members,

1. It gives me great pleasure to welcome you to this first session of Parliament in 1986. I felicitate the new members.
2. The year has seen Parliament transact its business in a purposeful manner and in an atmosphere of cooperation. I extend to you all my best wishes for the successful completion of the budgetary and legislative business that lies ahead.
3. In July, 1985, the Government took a major initiative to resolve the complex and difficult problems in Punjab. Our prime concern was to strengthen the forces of unity and integrity. Policy was governed by the perspective of serving the highest national interest. The democratic process triumphed over terrorism. The peaceful elections in Punjab testified to the desire of the overwhelming majority of the people for peace and normalcy in the State.
4. A great responsibility rests on those who have secured the mandate of the people. Their supreme task is to isolate those who are resorting to violence to disturb communal harmony and peace. In this task they will have the support of all political forces committed to the unity and integrity of India. There cannot be and must not be, any compromise with the forces of disintegration. It is imperative that all secular and democratic forces join hands in a mass campaign to safeguard the values enshrined in our

Constitution—nationalism, secularism, democracy and socialism—the bedrock of India's unity.

5. The Assam settlement was followed by elections to the Legislative Assembly and the Lok Sabha. A new Government has taken office.
6. Government are committed to the fullest implementation of the Punjab and Assam Accords.
7. Government express their deepest sympathy with the families of all those who lost their lives, or were injured, or suffered loss of property in violent incidents in different parts of the country. Violence in public life is the very antithesis of the ethos of our civilisation. The frequent resort to violence to settle what are perceived as grievances of one group or another should deeply disturb those who uphold democratic values. While governments must firmly put down violence wherever it may occur, it is essential that political parties committed to democratic values should deal with the root causes of violence through purposive and sustained work among the people. The temptation to seek short-term advantages from communal and other types of violence must be eschewed.
8. Communalism continues to pose a serious threat to national unity. It is being reinforced by religious fundamentalism and fanaticism. These trends represent a reactionary social outlook, directed against the struggle of the poor and the under-privileged against the vested interest. The reconstituted National Integration Council will have to act decisively and systematically to strengthen secularism.
9. In my Address on January 17, 1985, I had outlined the major policies and programmes of the Government. I recapitulate the main points:

   (i) Commitment of a clean public life

   (ii) Administrative reforms

(iii) Judicial reforms

(iv) A new national education policy

(v) A new national programme for women

(vi) Participation of youth in programmes for promoting national integration and achieving excellence

(vii) Establishment of a Wasteland Development Board

(viii) Formation of a Central Ganga Authority

(ix) A new textile policy and

(x) Thorough examination of safety measures for industrial establishments.

10. My Government have fulfilled in substantial measure the tasks they had set for themselves for the past year.

11. The anti-defection Act is now on the statute book. Contributions to political parties by the companies have been permitted by law. Government has endeavoured to set a new tone in public life. This has strengthened national confidence. A strong sense of involvement in public affairs among all sections of the people and a buoyant spirit have characterised the year that has gone by. We have to build on these assets to raise the standards of public life.

12. Vigorous steps have been taken to combat corruption and to improve the performance of the public services. Strong emphasis has been laid on sound personnel management and training of personnel at all levels. Machinery for redressal of public grievances is in place. Its results are being continuously evaluated. A new Ministry has been set up to monitor the implementation of various programmes. All Departments of Government have been directed to formulate detailed action plans for the coming financial year, against which their progress will be judged. Administrative reform is a continuous process. Detailed exercises are under way to reorient the system to speedier decision making and better implementation.

13. Government is determined to eliminate delays in dispensation of justice. The experiment of Lok Adalats has proved that an innovative approach is required to cure this malady. The establishment of Administrative Tribunals will also lighten the burden of the courts, enabling them to devote more time to the liquidation of arrears. However, these are just the first steps in tackling the basic problem of making justice inexpensive and easily accessible to the poor. Drastic changes are needed. Government have entrusted to the Law Commission the task of recommending such changes.
14. Government published in August 1985, a status paper entitled "The Challenge of Education". This was intended to stimulate wide and intensive national debate on issues and alternatives. Government note with satisfaction that the debate has involved all sections of the people and many useful ideas and approaches have emerged. A draft of the new Education Policy will be presented shortly to Parliament.
15. Government have set up a new department to look after the development of women. A comprehensive national programme for women is being worked out. It will aim at enabling women to play their full part in developing a strong and modern nation.
16. Programmes for youth development have made considerable headway but much more has to be done in this area.
17. The Wasteland Development Board has been set up and has started work on an ambitious programme of afforestation. In a recent meeting, all the State Governments endorsed an integrated approach to a National Land Use Policy as well as the strategies and policies for wasteland development.
18. The Central Ganga Authority has come into existence. With the cooperation of the concerned State Government,

work has started in full swing on stopping the pollution of the Ganga.

19. A new textile policy was announced in June 1985. It aims at production of cheaper cloth for the people. An equally important objective of the policy is to protect the interests of handloom weavers. It is envisaged that in the Seventh Plan the entire production of 700 million sq. metres of controlled and janata cloth will be transferred to the handloom sector. The Handlooms (Reservation of Articles for Production) Act, 1985 has been passed to strengthen this vital sector which provides livelihood to millions. Steps are being taken to ensure full and efficient implementation of the policy.

20. Government have completed examination of issues relating to industrial safety and management of hazardous substances and legislation will be introduced in this session of Parliament.

21. Government will establish seven zonal cultural centres—three have already been set up—to promote a sense of cultural cohesion. These centres, cutting across territorial and linguistic boundaries, would project the rich diversity of regional cultural traditions and their underlying unity. They would take the best of our culture to the masses, harmonising it with their lives and struggles. Their essential thrust would be to break the artificial barriers created during the colonial era between the masses and the living tradition of India's age-old culture in all its forms. The centres will also aim at revitalising folk art which has enriched the country's cultural life.

22. I would now refer to the major trends in our economy.

23. The seventh Five Year Plan was approved by the National Development Council. The basic strategy of the Plan is cast in a longer term perspective of eradication of poverty and building a strong, self-reliant and modern economy. The plan sharpens the focus on the anti-poverty

programmes which will have an expanded coverage. It also envisages adequate investments in the core sectors to strengthen the growth potential of the national economy.

24. The fulfilment of the Plan required total commitment and determination to mobilise adequate resources for investment. To translate the vision of a strong, prosperous, self-reliant India into reality requires unremitting toil and capacity to sacrifice and to bear hardship. Adequate savings have to be mobilised to pursue a non-inflationary path of development. More importantly, these savings have to be used effectively. The challenge has to be met. There are no shortcuts to development, no alternatives to hard work.

25. Vigorous implementations of anti-poverty programmes yielded significant results. The Sixth Five Year Plan aimed at assisting 15 million families under the Integrated Rural Development Programme; 16. 6 million families were actually covered, of which 6. 4 million belonged to the Scheduled Castes and Scheduled Tribes. These programmes are being strengthened and surplus foodgrains stocks will be used in 1986–87 to expand the national Rural Employment Programme and the Rural Landless Employment Guarantee Programme to cover one million additional families. An amount of Rs. 100 crores has been provided annually during the Seventh Five Year Plan for the construction of housing for the Scheduled Castes/ Scheduled Tribes and freed bonded labour.

26. By the end of March, 1985, of a total of 2. 31 lakh problem villages lacking safe drinking water supply, 1. 92 lakh villages had been provided with at least one source of water supply. During 1985–86 the programme was further accelerated.

27. In 1985–86 agriculture continued to make steady progress. In November 1985, foodgrains stocks with Government were higher by nearly 15% over 1984. This has enabled Government to offer subsidised rates in tribal areas and

to other vulnerable sections, especially the Scheduled Castes, expectant mothers, children, etc. A comprehensive crop insurance scheme has been introduced in specified areas for the kharif crop. Government are considering further expansion of such schemes.

28. During the first seven months of 1985-86, industrial production grew at the rate of 6. 3%. The policy initiatives of Government have created a buoyant investment climate. The infrastructural industries have performed well. Compared with the first nine months of the last year, power generation was up by 8. 2%; saleable steel production by 12. 9%; fertiliser production by more than 10%. Our ports handled 13. 2% more cargo and the railways created an all time record in freight traffic movement.

29. In 1985–86 the Central Plan outlays were stepped up by 15% over 1984–85, especially on anti-poverty programmes human resource development and infrastructure. There was considerable increase in the outlays of State Plans. Government will have spent in 1985–86 Rs. 1,650 crores on food subsidy and Rs. 2,050 crores on fertiliser subsidy. Public distribution system was strengthened and prudent management of supplies prevented shortages. It is gratifying that a significant increase in public investment was achieved.

30. Tax collections have been buoyant belying gloomy forebodings. The collection of direct taxes is up by about 23% compared to the corresponding period last year, Indirect tax collection has increased by 22%. Total tax collections have increased by 22% which is the highest in the last decade. An effective drive was launched against tax evaders, smugglers and blackmarketeers. Action has also been taken against personnel found guilty of colluding with economic offenders. Government is determined to cleanse the economic life and to fight the evil of black money.

31. For the first time, a long-term fiscal policy co-terminous with the Five Year Plan has been announced. A long-term direction to economic policy has been provided. Government is confident that the policy will ensure economic growth and speedier expansion of productive investment and employment opportunities.

32. It is necessary to focus attention on the structural problems of the economy to further our basic objective of growth with social justice. India's development depends upon steadily rising levels of public investment. How are these investments to be financed? Massive investments made in the previous plans must yield adequate returns. Costs of production have to be reduced. Every paisa of national savings has to be put to the most productive use. Otherwise it will be difficult to find real resources for the larger and larger investments required for maintaining the tempo of self-reliant growth, for enlarging our anti-poverty programmes and for preserving our economic independence. Sooner or later, sooner rather than later, we have to face the realities of the situation. No one should be under the delusion that growth, social justice, price stability and self-reliance are achievable without efficiency, discipline and sharing of burdens. Contemporary history warns us of such pitfalls.

33. We must reduce the costs of our inputs and prices of final products and services. We cannot afford the luxury of pricing ourselves out of both the domestic and the export markets. A modern industrial society cannot rise on the basis of continuing low levels of productivity and high costs of production. New jobs cannot be created if existing enterprises incur losses year after year. Operational inefficiency increases the cost of production and is inevitably reflected in increased prices which are a burden on the people. It raises costs all round, reducing real investment.

34. The future of the planning process depends on our capacity

to face up to difficult questions and to take hard decisions, that may involve sacrifices but without which forward movement will not be possible. Growth is absolutely vital to raise the standards of living of the poor. Can we evade decisions that protect and strengthen this development process? Nations are built by generations that sacrifice for a better tomorrow.

35. The balance of payments position poses a similar challenge. Our exports have remained sluggish in 1985-86 but our imports have increased. The imports of petroleum products and edible oils are well above the limits the country can afford. The question basically is whether we want to stand on our own feet or not. If we do, there is no question that we have to curb the growth of consumption of petroleum products and we have to be self-sufficient in oilseeds. We also have to have a fresh look at our imports of capital goods. We do not want to shut out new technology because that will harm us, but we have to make sure that such technology meets the rigorous criteria of essentiality. External financial flows are needed but Government are determined that India must never be at the mercy of foreign banks and institutions. Economic independence and self-reliance are central to our philosophy of development. We shall pay whatever price is required to maintain our economic independence.

36. The primary objectives of our foreign policy continue to be the promotion of non-alignment, advocacy of peace and nuclear disarmament, enlarging the area of friendship and cooperation and building of a just world order.

37. We welcome the resumption of high level dialogue between the USSR and USA. It is imperative to take urgent steps to bring about a freeze in the nuclear arms race and a comprehensive nuclear weapon test ban treaty. The six nation initiative has called for these measures. The Delhi Declaration of January, 1985 had a good impact on public

opinion throughout the world. The leaders of the six countries are in touch with one another about further steps.

38. During the last one year the atmosphere in the subcontinent has distinctly improved. We have succeeded in making progress with our neighbours in many fields. But we remain concerned about the ethnic situation in Sri Lanka and Pakistan's continued pursuit of a nuclear weapon capability. We remain convinced that the situation in Sri Lanka can be settled only through political means; attempts to seek a military solution will fail and will only result in the loss of a large number of innocent lives.

39. The Government welcomes the establishment of South Asian Association for Regional Cooperation (SAARC) launched in Dhaka in December, 1985. We expect that it will help strengthen forces of friendship and cooperation in our region.

40. The Government have made untiring efforts towards the resolution of the major areas of tension. At the Commonwealth meeting in the Bahamas in October, in which the Prime Minister participated, our delegation played a leading role in the adoption of the Commonwealth Accord on South Africa. We continue to demand comprehensive mandatory sanctions against the racist regime in South Africa. If the authorities there, and other Governments in a position to influence South Africa, do not act in time, violence on a large scale will become unavoidable.

41. The Prime Minister also attended the 40th anniversary of the United Nations. The Nassau Declaration on World Order adopted by Commonwealth leaders, contained a strong plea for adherence to international norms and principles and the strengthening of the United Nations. Support for the United Nations system is one of the cornerstones of our foreign policy. We are concerned at the growing threat to the multilateral institutions and the

increasing tendency to resort to unilateral action. Government supports international efforts to combat international terrorism, while recognising the rights of people under colonial occupation to use all means to attain their just objectives.

42. The Government deplore the fact that the Palestinian people continue to be denied their inalienable rights, including the right to an independent homeland of their own. Until this problem is tackled, West Asia will not see a basic lasting peace.

43. The Prime Minister paid official visits to the USSR, Egypt, France, Algeria, the USA, Bhutan, the UK, Cuba, the Netherlands, Vietnam, Japan, Oman and Maldives. Our traditionally close and friendly relations with the USSR have been further strengthened following the Prime Minister's discussions with Soviet leaders in Moscow. The visit to USA has significantly enlarged the content of our bilateral relations with the USA. The Prime Minister visited Dhaka to express our solidarity with the people of Bangladesh during the cyclone disaster and participated in the meeting of Heads of State and Government for launching the South Asian Association for Regional Co-operation. The Prime Minister addressed the UNESCO during his visit to France. He addressed the annual conference of the I.L.O. in Geneva. We had the privilege to host visits by the Kings of Nepal and Bhutan, the Queen of the Netherlands, the Presidents of Mexico, Maldives, SWAPO, Sri Lanka, Tanzania, Indonesia and Pakistan, the Chairman of PLO, the Head of State of Ethiopia, and the Prime Ministers of Poland, Yugoslavia, Mauritius, Britain, New Zealand, People's Democratic Republic of Yemen and Trinidad and Tobago. The Crown Prince and Princess of Norway and the Pope also visited India.

44. Let me now outline some priority areas for 1986–87 and beyond.

45. The need of the hour is to enable the poor to better their lives. Science and technology have to support this fundamental objective. To this end, Government are mounting technology missions in the following areas:
    (i) Drinking water for all villages
    (ii) Eradication of illiteracy
    (iii) Vaccination and immunisation of children
    (iv) Production of oilseeds and manufacture of edible oils
    (v) Improved communications.
46. In the course of the year more thrust areas will be identified with the object of using technology for improving productivity in industry and agriculture. In selected areas science and technology missions will endeavour to place India in the front rank of scientific activity.
47. A comprehensive agriculture policy will be formulated to promote an optimal cropping pattern, to improve water and soil management, to increase productivity of all crops to enhance the incomes of small and marginal farmers and to enlarge our hard-won self-sufficiency in foodgrains through production of oilseeds and pulses. A time-bound action plan will be drawn up to take the green revolution to the eastern region.
48. It is gratifying that a national consensus has emerged on treating water as a national resource. Government attach high priority to the evolution of a national water policy which would optimise the use of water for agricultural, industrial and other social needs.
49. Government have carried out an indepth analysis of our family planning programmes. Profitting from the experience of the past, an effective strategy for family planning is being worked out and will be announced shortly.
50. The focus on anti-poverty programmes will be sharpened. A new programme, which builds on the success achieved

by the revised 20-Point Programme, is being formulated and will be announced soon. It will bring together all the elements, policies and programmes for a major national effort to tackle the problem of mass poverty in all its manifestations, specifically the problems of Scheduled Castes and Scheduled Tribes. Programme for the social, economic, educational and cultural development for the Scheduled Castes, Scheduled Tribes and other weaker sections will be vigorously implemented. The implementation of the 15-Point Programme for the development of minorities, with special emphasis on increasing economic opportunities will be closely monitored.

51. To rapidly increase employment to stimulate development in backward areas and to enhance the efficiency by Indian industry to serve the masses better, a more comprehensive framework of industrial policy is required. Many changes have already been made in our industrial policy which now reflects the new thrust for modernisation, absorption of new technologies and promotion of indigenous technologies. High cost and inefficient industry hurts the poor, because it absorbs resources that are needed to create new jobs for them. A vast increase in the production of goods and services for the masses in-rural and urban areas is central to our strategy for the removal of poverty. This necessitates a fresh look at policies governing the scale of production, capacity utilisation, the role of indigenous technology, labour productivity, the detailed regulatory mechanism, the future perspectives for small and medium industry and the existing administrative and management apparatus. Industry must serve the large masses.

52. To meet the challenge of maintaining a viable balance of payments position, a major thrust for promotion of exports and tourism is called for. Any slackening of progress on this front will jeopardise our overall development strategy. Government will take new initiatives in this critical area.

53. It is imperative to effect changes in our administrative system to bring it in tune with the objective of growth with social justice. Management in Government has to be imbued with a new social outlook. It is not a question of imposing something from above. The impetus to reform must come from within. The national community as a whole must debate issues affecting the working of the administrative system. A concrete agenda of action will thus emerge for implementation. Our watchwords must be improvement of efficiency and enforcement of accountability.

54. To safeguard the health and vitality of our basic political institutions, changes will be needed in our electoral and other laws. Government will hold wide-ranging consultations with the leaders of political parties with a view to formulating concrete proposals to ensure cleaner public life.

55. The vision of a mighty India will be realised only in the actual lives of men and women who have strength of character, tenacity of purpose and commitment to excellence. Government's strategy for human resource development aims at developing these qualities in our national life. The new education policy will be an integral part of this strategy. It will aim at the physical, intellectual, cultural and moral development of society in a harmonious fashion.

56. It is not enough to state objectives. A national mobilisation is essential to ensure that the resources required to implement the education policy are forthcoming. Even more important is the involvement of the youth, students, teachers, the intelligentsia, workers and farmers in giving a new direction to the national effort in this area. Education has to be transformed from an activity in the classroom to a social process for building the India of our dreams. It has to be integrated more closely both with production

and our commitment to conserve and enhance our cultural heritage to make us proud to be Indian.

57. The years ahead are years of challenge. Government have taken a number of measures to accelerate growth, to modernise the economy and to give new content to our programmes for achieving social justice. It is imperative to impart a sense of urgency to the task of implementation.

58. Much has been achieved this past year, and the hopes and expectations of our people are high. As their representatives, you have the onerous duty to fulfil their aspirations. Above all, people's representatives and organisations of all political persuasions should work together to strengthen the secular and democratic foundations of our society. The forces of violence and fanaticism have to be fought. The economic capabilities we have built up since independence have brought us to a point where determined and concerted efforts to take us forward and to remove poverty are feasible. Now is the time to ensure greater political cohesion so that the battle against poverty and backwardness can be won. I wish you all success in the tasks ahead. Jai Hind.

Model Report

Now let us examine how this address is covered by newsmen. The copy of this speech was made available to all correspondents when the President began to read it. Given is the report of the speech published in the *Times of India,* New Delhi:

Opposition Boycotts Address

Isolate terrorists, says President

New Delhi, February 20. The President in his traditional address to the joint session of Parliament outlining the agenda of the government today pointed to the "inevitability of hard decisions without which forward movement will not be possible."

The address promised a comprehensive agriculture plan to promote an optimal cropping pattern, a more effective strategy for family planning and sharpening of the anti-poverty programme.

Technology missions will be mounted to ensure drinking water for all villages, eradication of illiteracy, immunisation, oilseeds production and improved communications.

New initiatives will be made for promotion of exports and tourism with a view to maintaining a viable balance of payments position.

There will be wide ranging discussions to formulate concrete proposals for changing electoral and other laws. Administrative reforms calculated to improve efficiency and enforce accountability will be introduced.

The joint session, with its usual ceremonies, was still shorn of the excitement and rapture which featured in the function only a year ago. Most non-Congress groups stayed away as announced leaving gaps in rows.

Not since 1973 have so many groups joined in such a boycott. Even Congress members did not find any cause to cheer during the entire reading of the address. They thumped the desks only at the end, as the President resumed his seat.

There was a moment of suspense when the President paused at the beginning. It was then noticed he was looking for his reading glasses.

At the same time, the President's address made it plain that "hard decisions" were inevitable in the pursuit of self-reliance, economic independence and eradication of poverty.

"Sooner or later we have to face the realities of the situation. No one should be under the delusion that growth, social justice, price stability and self-reliance, are achievable without efficiency, discipline and sharing of burdens," Mr. Zail Singh said.

The President began his speech with a reference to the "triumph of democratic process over terrorism in Punjab" and held that the supreme task now was to isolate those resorting to violence.

He reiterated the government commitment to the fullest implementation of the Punjab and Assam accord.

Communalism: He acknowledged that communalism continued to pose a serious threat to national unity. "It is being reinforced by religious fundamentalism and fanaticism." The reconstituted National Integration Council will have to act decisively and systematically to strengthen secularism," he said.

He recalled the policies and programmes of the government outlined in his address last year and claimed "these have been fulfilled in a substantial measure". He cited the anti-defection law, enunciation of a new national education policy, establishment of a central Ganga authority, creation of a wasteland development board as cases in point.

As for trends in economy, agriculture made steady' progress with grain stocks going up nearly 15 per cent. He described the investment climate as buoyant. Power generation, fertiliser production, steel output have all gone up.

Tax Collection: He said tax collections have been buoyant, belying gloomy forebodings. The collection of direct taxes is up by about 23 per cent compared to the corresponding period last year. Indirect tax collection has increased by 22 per cent which is the highest in the last decade.

The Tribune, Chandigarh, used agencies and published the following story:

President Assures Akalis of Support

New Delhi, February 20 (PTI, UNI)—The President Giani Zail Singh, today asked the Punjab Government to isolate "those who are resorting to violence to disturb communal harmony and peace" and assured the ruling Akali Dal that in its "supreme task" it would have the support of all political forces committed to the unity and integrity of the country.

There cannot be, and must not be, any compromise with the forces of disintegration, Giani Zail Singh said in his address to a joint session of Parliament which all national and regional. Opposition parties, barring the AIADMK, the Muslim League, the Kerala Congress and the Assam Gana Parishad boycotted in protest against the recent hike in the prices of petroleum products and other commodities.

Some of the front seats earmarked for leaders of Opposition groups in the high domed Central Hall of Parliament House were empty when Giani Zail Singh began his address in Hindi.

The President said a great responsibility rested on those who secured the mandate of the people in the Punjab elections and recalled that in July 1985 the Central Government had taken a major initiative to resolve the complex and difficult problems in Punjab.

"Our prime concern was to strengthen the forces of unity and integrity and our policy was governed by the perspective of serving the highest national interest."

The democratic process triumphed over terrorism and the peaceful elections in Punjab had demonstrated the desire of the overwhelming majority of the people for peace and normalcy in the State.

Giani Zail Singh also recalled the Assam settlement followed by elections to the State Assembly and the Lok Sabha.

He reiterated the Government's commitment to the total implementation of the Punjab and Assam accords.

Referring to incidents of violence in different parts of the country, Giani Zail Singh said the temptation to seek short-term advantages from communal and other types of violence must be eschewed.

He said communalism continued to pose a serious threat to national unity and it was being reinforced by religious fundamentalism and fanaticism.

These trends represented a reactionary social outlook. The reconstituted National Integration Council would have to act decisively and systematically to strengthen secularism.

The implementation of the 15-point programme for the development of minorities with special emphasis on increasing economic opportunities would be closely monitored.

Expressing the Government's deepest sympathy with the families of all those who lost their lives, or were injured, or lost property in violent incidents in different parts of the country, Giani Zail Singh said violence in public life was the very antithesis of the ethos of civilisation.

The fact that violence was frequently used to settle what were perceived as grievances of one group or another should deeply disturb those who upheld democratic values.

While governments must firmly put down violence wherever it might occur, it was essential that the political parties committed to democratic values dealt with the root causes of violence through purposive and sustained work among the people.

Referring to the vigorous steps taken by the Government to combat corruption and to improve the performance of the public services, Giani Zail Singh said strong emphasis had been laid on sound personnel management at all levels.

A system for the redressal of public grievances had been put to work and the results were being continuously evaluated. Listing the achievements of the Government on the economic front, the President said the Government had taken a number of measures to accelerate growth, modernise the economy and give a new content to its programmes for achieving social justice. It was imperative to impart a sense of urgency to the task of implementation he said. The President underscored the Government's determination to achieve economic self-reliance without placing the country at the mercy of foreign banks and institutions.

Although the Opposition boycott was to protest against the recent price increases, the President's address made no direct reference to these even in the course of outlining the major trends in the national economy.

However, the President sought to justify the increases when he emphasised the point that larger investments were required for maintaining the "tempo" of self-reliant growth.

The President said the focus on anti-poverty programmes would be sharpened.

"A new programme which builds on the success achieved by the revised 20-Point Programme, is being formulated and will be announced soon," he said.

The need of the hour is to enable the poor to better their lives, he said adding, "Science and technology have to support this fundamental objective."

He said the Government would mount "technology missions" in five areas in 1986-87. These were drinking water for all villages, eradication of illiteracy, vaccination and immunisation of children, production of oilseeds and manufacture of edible oils and improved communications.

The President said a comprehensive agriculture policy would be formulated to promote an optimal cropping pattern, to improve water and soil management, to increase the productivity of all crops, to enhance the incomes of small and marginal farmers and to enlarge the self-sufficiency in foodgrains through higher production of oil-seeds and pulses.

A time-bound action plan would be drawn up to take the Green Revolution to the eastern region.

Giani Zail Singh spoke of a "more comprehensive framework" within the industrial policy to rapidly increase employment opportunities and stimulate development in the backward areas.

He called for a major thrust for the promotion of exports and tourism to maintain a viable position of balance of payments. Any slackening on this front would jeopardise the overall development strategy.

"The Government will take new initiatives in this critical area," he promised.

The President said the Government would hold wide-ranging consultations with leaders of political parties to formulate concrete proposals to ensure a cleaner public life.

Changes would be needed in our electoral and other laws to safeguard the country's basic political institutions.

He also said that new water policy and an effective family planning strategy were on the anvil.

Surveying the foreign scene, the President noted that the atmosphere in the subcontinent had distinctly improved. We have succeeded in making progress with our neighbours in several fields, but we remain concerned about the ethnic situation in Sri Lanka and Pakistan's continued pursuit of a nuclear weapons capability.

The primary objective of the Government's foreign policy continued to be centred around non-alignment, peace and nuclear disarmament, enlarging the area of friendship and cooperation and building a just world order.

It took Giani Zail Singh 52 minutes to read his address.

The Vice President and Rajya Sabha Chairman, Mr. R. Venkataraman, who read the English version of the Address took 34 minutes.

The President's Address was marked by the absence of any applause except the customary one at the end.

The Presidential entourage entered the Central Hall at exactly 11 a. m. It was led by the Presiding Officers of both Houses—Mr. Venkataraman and the Lok Sabha Speaker, Mr. Bal Ram Jakhar. Mr. Rajiv Gandhi walked behind the President.

10

News from Elections

If all editors have not hailed the development with hosannahs, and if all journalists have not hurled themselves headlong into the breaking statistical waves, that is only characteristic of the innate skepticism of the profession. However, progress is being made.

Qualified Reporters

There are, throughout the land, a modest number of reporters who have the qualifications to conduct a reliable scientific study of public opinion, who are adept at analyzing masses of statistical data and who are not afraid to work with computers and learn computer language. There are, as well, an increasing number of editors who are willing to employ them, news organizations that use their work regularly and sophisticated public officials and business and industrial leaders who know how to evaluate polling results.

Whom Do Polls Influence? : ocial science has shown us that, except in cases where public opinion is almost evenly divided, polls in and of themselves seldom can make perceptible changes in the mass mind. This is, of course, also true of much editorial opinion published in newspapers and newsmagazines and broadcast locally or by the networks. What polls can do in the vast majority of cases, is to reinforce opinions that are strongly held.

Whom, then, do polls influence mainly? As nearly all responsible social scientists agree, the people who commission polling research are the ones who are most likely to change their opinions and their public positions to conform to the public opinion findings. This is more true, naturally, of the vendors of commercial products than of others. And yet many a political leader and nearly all recent American presidents have been powerfully influenced by the findings of their private poll-takers.

While the "bandwagon vote" conjured up by James A. Farley has little substance-even though the old master of the first two Franklin Roosevelt presidential campaigns fervently believed in it-many a politician still clings to the notion that last-minute voters will flock to his or her standard just to "ride with a winner." And they try by every conceivable device to create the impression that they are certain winners.

The main reason for this exercise in atmospherics is to keep wealthy corporations, individuals and labour unions in a mood to continue to make large financial contributions to particular campaigns. Senator Hubert Horatio Humphrey was convinced to the end of his days that a California Field Poll, which showed Jimmy Carter ahead by 25 percent before the California Democratic primary of 1976, prematurely dried up contributions and crippled a last minute TV effort in the state by the Humphrey forces. Humphrey lost the primary by less than 5 percent.

Enormous Influence

Where the polls do have an enormous influence on voters is in the network projections of winners, based in poll on the random sampling of voters' choices gathered immediately after they cast their ballots. In the 1980 presidential Carter conceded defeat while the polls on the Pacific Coast were still open. The result, according to most reliable political estimates, was that a certain number of voters didn't even go to the polls in that area. Although this could not have changed the outcome of the presidential election, it could have had an effect on other close races in states in the Pacific time zone.

Polls: Their Nature : It is not in politics alone that poll-taking is of importance. The Nielsen ratings, to a very large extent, determine what we see on television. Nielsen and other commercial poll-takers are well into the critical surveys of whether old products should be changed or withdrawn and whether new products can be sold.

Polls also are taken on every conceivable subject. Within a few days in a recent year, poll-takers covered these issues.

- An Opinion Research Corporation Poll showed 75 percent of respondents mistrust big business.
- A Harris survey showed 62 percent of respondents mistrust big government.
- A United States Census Bureau study indicated that American women will continue to outnumber men for the rest of this century.
- A *New York Daily News Poll* determined 77 percent of respondents had lost trust in public officials.
- And a *Los Angeles* Time survey disclosed that most jurors in a poll were against judicial press gags.

That was, by the way, only a small sampling of the American news media.

The Researchers : It merely proves, if proof were needed, that the public opinion survey and social statistical analyses have become the basis for a major industry.

Within a little more than a generation, the news media, the universities and the commercial polling organizations have established a formidable network for measuring the frequent and sometimes dizzying shifts in public sentiment. However, it is still true as it was a century ago when Lord Bryce wrote that "the obvious weakness of government by public opinion is the difficulty of ascertaining it." Wide differences of opinion may be caught very quickly, it is true, nut when the margin of error approaches 3 percent on either side, most poll-takers agree, however reluctantly, that the acceptable margin of confidence usually has been reached.

No one, therefore, can quarrel with Winston Churchill's celebrated dictum "Nothing is more dangerous than to live in the temperamental atmosphere of a Gallup Poll, always taking one's temperature. There is only one duty, only one safe course, and that is to try to be right and not fear to do or say what you believe to be right."

Two of the pioneering polling organizations still remain in the forefront of public opinion research—George Gallup and his American Institute of Public Opinion and Elmo Roper's organization. Among the other, Louis Harris and Daniel Yankelovich are both prominent and widely used.

Of equal importance are the university research centres and the numerous social science researchers in academe, who are so often sought out to help with the various types of polls and other statistical studies. Among the oldest are the Michigan Survey Research Center and the National Opinion Research Center.

Finally, some of the stronger and wealthier news organizations are doing much of their own work, as witness the rapid adaptation of social science methods by the Knight Ridder Newspapers. Others have joined forces and thereby shared costs as well as services, the CBS News-New York Times polls being one example. Then there are the statewide polls, some going back for many years including the DesMoines Register's Iowa Poll, the *Minneapolis Tribute's* Minnesota Poll, the *New York Daily New's* New York State Poll and the MIRVing Field organization's California Poll.

The Significance

Everybody recognizes the importance of public opinion in an open society but few agree on what it i s or how it operates. Nor is it easy to define, even by social scientists.

Public Opinion : In a far smaller and less complicated United States nearly a century and a half ago, Alexis de Tocqueville called ii the "predominant authority" that acted by "elections and decrees". In a moment of disillusion with the vagaries of the British Public, Sir Robert Feel was less admiring to him, it was "that great compound of folly, weakness, prejudice, wrong feeling, right feeling, obstinacy and newspaper paragraphs which is called public opinion." In the early 1920s. Water Lippmann argued that it was "primarily a moralized and codified version of the facts," and that" the pattern of stereotypes at the center of our codes largely determines what group of facts we shall see and in what high we shall see them." In our own time, a social scientist, W. Phillips Davison, has concluded that public opinion should be treated as a "consensus that influences the behaviour of individuals who contribute to the consensus... a form of organization [that] is able to coordinate the thought and action of a large number of people."

Of one thing there is no doubt. Whether it is the "predominant authority" a "great compound of folly," a "pattern of stereotypes," of a "consensus," the measurement of what is called public opinion has become of transcendent importance in modern mass communications. It forms the basis of much advertising and merchandising practice, determines what shall and shall not be seen on television, locates new enterprises as varied in character as food markets and newspapers, provides trends for the illusion of trends in political campaigns at all levels of government and dominates the coverage of national elections. Journalists have not been able to escape the implications of this expanding activity. It has placed them squarely in the middle of the computer age.

Since newspapers have taken up "precision journalism," polling assignments have become a part of the regular routine. The Chicago Tribune, for example, has found that nine of 10 persons surveyed in Chicago favoured mandatory hand-gun registration. The Dayton (Ohio) *Journal Herald* forecast the outcome of a city tax referendum with less than 2 percent error. In a survey of "white flight" to the suburbs as a result of school integration, the *Milwaukee journal* found that the trend was exaggerated. And the Associated Press, in one of a number of surveys, looked for a relationship between death rates and the rate of spending for research.

Rise of the Pollsters : The practice of poll-taking goes back to 1824 when a Harrisburg *Pennsylvania* straw poll indicated Andrew Jackson was ahead in the presidential campaign. Over the course of the next century, such newspapers as the *Boston Globe and New York Herald* conducted street corner polls. And at the beginning of the 20th century, advertisers began experimenting with market surveys, the true forerunner of the modern public opinion poll. The first "social scientific" poll of public opinion was conducted in 1907-1908 by the Pittsburgh Survey, with the support of the Russell Sage Foundation. Another first was the *Kansas City Star's* quadrennial selection of "sample precincts," from which it would calculate the winner of the presidential election and banner the result soon after the closing of the election booths in the land.

But none of these was as spectacular a success — and failure — as the *Literary Digest Poll* which began in 1916. For most of the presidential elections through 1932, the *Digest* sent out postcards to millions of persons and predicted the outcome with reasonable success. By 1935, there was so much concern over polling that a bill was introduced in Congress to prohibit the use of the mails for polls and stop this "vicious practice." The bill failed. But in the same year, Elmo Roper began his poll in *Fortune* magazine and the first Gallup's Poll was issued by George Gallup's newly founded American Institute of Public Opinion.

In the 1936 presidential campaign, the *Literary Digest* calculated on the basis of more than 2 million postcards received mainly from telephone users and automobile owners, that President Roosevelt would lose to Alfred M. Landon, his Republican challenger, by 42.9 percent of the vote to 57.1 percent. The outcome gave Roosevelt 62.5 percent of the vote, which enabled him to carry 46 of the 48 states. The *Digest* Poll thereby racked up a polling error of 19.6 percent, the largest ever known for a presidential election, and the magazine went out of business.

The Gallup Poll based on a scientific sampling of a few thousand respondents, called the election correctly but itself registered an error of 6.8 percent, larger than any it has since made. Of course the difference between the two was that the Digest sampled only prosperous people in a time of depression, those who had phones and cars, while Gallup reached a better cross-section.

Despite a relatively good record set by Gallup. Roper and other pollsters, the polling industry had to struggle for years to overcome the Digest debacle. Just as it was regaining public confidence, however, it came a cropper in the 1948 presidential election, when President Truman upset the favoured Thomas E. Dewey. The picture of a grinning Truman holding up the Chicago Tribune, with a banner headline proclaiming a Dewey victory, is a favourite in every journalistic album of the era and one the pollsters will never forget.

In 1948, Gallup was in error by 5.3 percent, Crossley by 4.7 percent and Roper by 8.4 percent and all understated the Democratic vote by these respective amounts. The Social Science Research Council blamed errors of sampling, interviewing and forecasting. Gallup himself argued that he failed because he stopped polling "about 10 to 14 days" before Election Day and thereafter Democrats who had been "leaning" toward Dewey changed their minds. He changed his sampling methods and began polling up to two days before Election Day.

The pollsters had some rough times after the Truman disaster, and some bright moments as well. In the close presidential race between Senator John F. Kennedy and Richard M. Nixon in 1960, both relied heavily on private polling advice, Kennedy on Louis Harris and Nixon on Claude Robinson of the Opinion Research Corp. Kennedy always gave credit to Harris for the findings on which his successful campaign was based. In the 1968 election, last minute Gallup and Harris surveys indicated that there was a trend toward Senator Hubert H. Humphrey, the Democratic candidate, that was reflected in Nixon's narrow victory.

Luck as a Factor : All poll takers are well aware that they ignore the usual 2.5 to 3 percent margin of error in any national survey at their own peril. And this was particularly apparent in the exceedingly close 1976 presidential election, when most major polling organizations came up with predictions of 1 percent or less in favour of jimmy Carter, George Gallup, the dean of pollsters, picked Ford by the same figure. However, Gallup and others covered themselves—pointing to the margin of error— and said the election was "too close to call."

The only one daring enough to make an unqualified forecast was Burns Roper, for the Public Broadcasting System, whose final survey Carter 51 percent, Ford 47 percent and the minor candidates 2 percent. He came within 1 percent of complete accuracy, the final vote giving Carter 51 percent, Ford 48 percent and minor candidates 1 percent. Said Reporter "Polling is part science and a helluva lot of human judgements. Fortunately, we made the right ones. "And Gallup commented drily.' "The plain fact of the matter is that you have to be lucky. You have to repeal the laws of probability."

Yet, poll-taking and election forecasting have become so deeply imbedded in the American political system—and in American journalism as well — that they have continued to develop despite all setbacks. Their credibility has suffered from time to time, particularly when hired pollsters of some repute issued findings that tended to support the positions of those who paid them. Yet on the whole, this has not seemed to affect their public acceptance.

As a result of their 1976 experience, most poll takers were overly cautions in the 1980 election and called it a toss up, a close election and some even refused to predict a winner because their samplings showed such an even division. The only major poll-taker to break out of this bind was Louis Harris, who went on national TV in the closing hours of the campaign and forecast a large Reagan victory. A few hours after the polls opened, the news leaked out of Washington that Patrick Caddell, President Carter's private poll-taker, had told him that he could not win.

The Reagan landslide was thus a surprise to almost everybody in the polling business except for Ronald Reagan himself and his closest advisers. They had assurance from their private polls that the victory would be theirs and that it would be very large, indeed.

Reasons for Forecasts : It may well be asked why the news media go in so heavily for surveys of public opinion with the reporting of politics and government, and elections in particular. One very good reason is that such forecasts, and the basis for them, are a part of the legitimate business of political reporters and their news organizations. An even more compelling reason is that no news organization worthy of the name can act as a mere recording device that plays back speeches and rival claims but does not undertake to evaluate them. When the public asks, "Who's ahead?" the question is worthy of a serious reply by trained reporters commentators.

Applied Techniques

The oldest, least sophisticated and least dependable type of public opinion poll is the reportorial survey in which an editor sends several staff members out to talk to almost anybody they think will give them a good quote. Before the rise of the feminist movement, it used to be called the "man-in-the-street poll, and it is still used by editors here and there."

The notion is that any reporter, unschooled in the simplest statistical procedures, can talk to 20 or 30 persons and come up with a valid reflection of the view of the community. Such exercises, no matter how carefully reporters go about their work, come near the truth only by the sheerest accident. The sample has not been picked at random according to the rules of probability and therefore can't be truly representative of the views of all persons in the region under consideration, known in statistical terms as the "universe."

Random Sample : Many journalists still believe that a random sample consists of picking anybody you want to talk to on the street. The folly of that approach is readily apparent in a place like New York city, for example, where people picked at random at the fashionable corner of 50th Street and Park Avenue, in front of the Waldorf Astoria Hotel, will be no more typical of New Yorkers as a whole than those selected at the corner of 125th Street and Lenox Avenue, the cross roads in Harlem.

The definition of a true random sample specifies that everybody living within a given "universe" that is to be surveyed must have an equal chance of being selected for interviewing. If the selection is properly done, the sample need not be large. As statisticians are fond of pointing out, if an experimenter draws 100 balls from two casks of black and white balls, one with 100,000 and the other with 1,000 and each divided into a ratio of three black balls to seven white balls, the likelihood is virtually the same that the drawing will yield 70 white and 30 black balls from each cask. Thus, Gallup's usual random sample is about 1,500 and his and other national polling samples during a political campaign run to no more than 3,000 persons.

In any event, reliable research and news organizations always go to considerable trouble and expense to develop; a random sample that will represent the "universe" whether it is a village, a country, a state or the nation as a whole. In some instances, a "universe" may consist of groups of people taken by irregular areas depending on the type of survey and the desires of the person in charge.

Probability Method : The most difficult, time-consuming and costly technique is the probability method. It is also the most widely accepted.

In this process, nothing is left to chance that the sample will be truly selected at random. Trained interviewers are given a list of carefully prepared and pretested questions, certain addresses in specified areas, a list of selected apartments in such buildings and a group of persons to be interviewed in order (the oldest male, the oldest woman and so on) at certain times of the day or evening.

They are given a choice if the address turns out to be an empty lot, or an apartment is vacant, or the type of person to be interviewed isn't available after repeated calls. Then the interviewers are given a list of alternatives, the whole following a statistical pattern developed will in advance.

Various refinements are applied to increase the representative nature of the sample, including stratification. This means simply that where the "universe" includes several identifiable groups of persons, samples will be drawn separately from each group to make certain they are properly represented. This helps maintain the accuracy of the sampling process, whereas clustering — interviewing several designated types of persons in one house or apartment — tends to reduce it.

Question of Confidence **:** Using statistical tables of probability, polling organizations invariably determine the size of their samples on the basis of what is called a "confidence level" — in other words, a test of accuracy. If Gallup sample totals 600 persons, for example, he calculates that the chances are 95 in 100 that a poll which divides 60 percent in favour, 40 percent opposed (or the reverse) will be within four percentage points of the true figure. This means that the number in favour will be somewhere between 56 percent and 64 percent. By doubling the sample to 1,200, Gallup holds that the error factor (using the same 95 in 100 criterion) is reduced to 2.8 percent. Doubled again, there is a further decrease to 2 percent.

It isn't any great mathematical feat, using statistical tables and relatively basic mathematical procedures, to work out the confidence level for any sample size and confidence level. Most surveys make it their goal to operate within 4 percent error at the 95 in 100 confidence level, which means a sample of 600 persons is adequate. At 3 percent, a sample of 1,067 is needed, 2 percent, 2,401, 1 percent, 9,605. These figures assume, of course, that there is an absolutely true sample based on probability. As for the size of the "universe" involved, those figures don't make much difference until they get below the 10,000 level.

For many years, it seemed to many that it was sheer madness to try determine national trends by polling a handful of citizens in a town, a few score in a state, and between 1,200 and 3,000 nationally. And yet, barring technical and human failures that now are usually kept to a minimum, the system works. The Bureau of the Census has been using the probability method of random sampling for years to determine population growth (the house to house enumeration process occurs only once a decade).

Sampling Techniques : The basis of most sampling techniques consists of maps and other data from the Bureau of the Census. If these are reinforced with city directories or comparable tabulations, the raw material for establishing a sample is in hand.

In the probability method, the primary sampling units may be drawn at random (using a table of random numbers) from a list of all the countries and metropolitan areas in the United States. These are then further reduced to urban blocks and rural segments, also selected by the random process as it is known in statistics. Next, within each selected block or segment, every dwelling unit is listed and a fixed number is selected at random. Finally, in the selected dwelling unit, all adults are enumerated, from each, one person is chosen, again at random.

The sample thus selected has a high probability of reflecting all the characteristics of the "universe" from which it is drawn. Factors of age, sex, economic status, ethnic and religious group and other relevant items are all represented in the sample. It is in this manner that interviewers are provided with their list of persons to be located and asked the precise list of questions drafted by the polling organization.

In telephone polls, which are faster and cheaper, the number of names in a telephone directory in a particular city is divided by the size of the sample (600, 1,067, 2,401 or whatever). The quotient shows the number of names to be skipped, from the beginning to the end of the directory, to produce a true random sample. Then, the designated telephone numbers are called by researchers. To cover unlisted numbers, some social scientists advocate adding one digit at the end of each telephone number on the list.

Uses of Polling : It is a familiar argument among pollsters, particularly those with an academic background, that the poll is more sinned against than sinning and that news organizations misuse polls by attempting to extract more information from them than they are able to give. To a certain extent this may be true. However, as long as polling organizations offer their wares for sale and as long as they announce certain results within a given range of probabilities, it is only logical to hold them responsible for their output.

No one can claim absolute accuracy for any public opinion study, whether it is done person-to-person, by telephone or questionnaire. The allowance of 3 percent error on either side is fairly standard in political poll-taking, but the public tends to overlook it in a close political fight when there is perhaps only a 1 percent difference between the chief rival candidates. Moreover, some polls are put to grotesque uses toward Election Day when one side or the other will claim victory on the basis of a lead of as little as one half of 1 percent.

While political polling is a hurry-up-job with a considerable element of risk, and while TV ratings are also under constant criticism for the same reason, the social issues type of poll can be much more leisurely and of tenjust as useful. The *Detroit Free Press*, in a study of black attitudes after the Detroit riots, took three weeks. A University of California study of the Watts riots took two years to produce. The *Miami Herald took* a considerable period for its inquiry into the militancy of blacks in the Miami area. And academic studies always take a great deal longer.

Depth Interviews : There are some practical minded social scientists and political experts who have faith in a few depth interviews — solicited from various types of persons at specific locations—as a means of judging the mood of a particular "universe," which may be a small voting unit or even the entire nation. Such depth interviews may be conducted for two or three hours and encompass a variety of subjects. It is hardly fair to say that this kind of work is a protection of the "man in the street interview, done at a highly sophisticated level. These depth interviews require a rare combination of journalistic skills and social science background, plus shrewd political judgements.

One of the most successful practitioners of the art was the political analyst Samuel Lubell, who did most of his own interviewing and calculated his own results. Lubell might select for a depth interview a man who resides in a low costing housing development and works in a factory, a housewife who lives in the center of an area torn by controversy over school busing or another emotional issue, a farmer in the center of the Midwestern grain belt, a small home owner and other such typical American citizens. Out of the mix of their opinions and his own judgement, he shaped his conclusions.

United States Overpolled? : Although a Gallup survey has indicated that six out of seven Americans over 18 have never been interviewed in a poll, polling organizations agree that there is rising public resistance to their surveys. The work not takes much more time, it is more costly and more people simply don't want to be bothered. The reason is evident. In addition to polls by the government, universities and the news media, more than 1,000 commercial organizations are now in the business — which means the public is being asked to do a lot of the pollsters' work for free. "Perhaps, " one pollster suggested, "we are not treating the respondent with respect as a human being".

Checking Trends : The use of selected national or state voting units is a favourite indicator of political trends. Every major polling organization has a well guarded list of such precincts, picked because they have accurately reflected the outcome of elections over a period of years. Of course, in landslides such as 1964 and 1972, it is easy to pick a winner by using the results in the model precincts and projecting them. Sometimes it can even be done before the polls close by taking a random sample among voters as they emerge from casting their ballot. But in a close election, model precincts are a risky guide.

Among newspapers, it is a time honored custom for political writers to publish their forecasts on the Sunday or Monday before election. Necessarily, this is nowhere near as informative as it used to be because the publication of weekly surveys before Election Day has taken the edge off what used to be "the last word." Once again, it is no big deal to pall a one sided election as for the close ones, predictions continue to be a gamble regardless of when they are made.

Polling Standards : Here is a checklist of the information that should accompany any poll.

1. The sponsor of the poll.
2. Exact wording of all questions.
3. Definition of the population sample.
4. Sample size and, where needed the response rate;
5. Allowance for sampling error;
6. Proportion of "don't knows" and others in sample who may not vote;
7. Method of interviewing and, where done;
8. Time period for interviewing.

Predictions : Any election forecast should have suitable qualifications throughout, even though the result may seem to duplicate many years of similar preelection accounts. This is a sample of the usual type of forecast lead.

Mayor Hammond Garvell appears likely to win re-election on Tuesday if the vote is as large as expected.

A sampling of typical voter opinion, plus talks with professionals in both parties and the findings of private polls, indicated today that the mayor was expected to defeat his opponent, Hereford Cates.

But even Mayor Garvell's closet aides empliasized that as an independent running for re-election, he must count on a heavy turnout at the polls-always a sign in this city that the independent voter is making his influence felt....

"Foregrounding" Politics : A considerable segment of political writing in newspapers and news-magazines and analytical comment on television is based on the summation and interpretation of coming events. The holding of conventions, listing of known candidates and issues and analysis of rival claims are subject for reports of this type. Another is the planning for a campaign during a given period and the conclusions that may be drawn from it in terms of objectives.

Best known of all is the pre-Election Day summation giving the time, places and candidates involved in the voting the registration figures, probable vote totals, analysis of issues, weather and whatever conclusions the writer or analyst wishes to make. On television, this type of information can only be give the voter all the material he needs to make a decision on numerous candidates, propositions and referenda. This, certainly is the place where a good newspaper is priceless and the electronic media are at a complete disadvantage.

Poll Coverage

The early part of the 20th century was the golden age for political reporters. They were regarded as seers in their own right the travelling companions of the great and near-great, the oracles who—in their own time at their own pleasure—gave the people the Word Arthur Krock of the New York Times, Charles Michelson of the New York World, Edward Folliard of the Washington Post and their associates were national figures. However the coming of television changed all that.

Reporters' Job : Today, the exposure of TV and its astronomical costs limit political campaigning in all except the marathon races of presidential years. The wise candidates try to save their principal pronouncements for TV and get by the rest of the time with a stock speech. But they are constantly on the move.

Consequently, political reporters for major news organizations outside TV are up against an almost impossible job. Their work is so concentrated that they have little time to talk to the candidates or their managers, let alone the voters. In a national campaign, if they try to see anybody at an airport or train or motorcade whistlestop, they risk being left behind. Now a days candidates will cover several states at a time in a single day. And because most candidates rely on the basic speech that isn't news after the first few times it is used. Except in the hands of experienced reporters who know how to dig for the unusual in a political campaign coverage tends to become a humdrum affair. More and more, it is the analysis that counts with many a newspaper.

Team reporting based on surveys of public opinion is being used by news papers that can afford it. And where research is needed one or two reporters may be assigned to do a lengthy background report on a candidate or an issue. Much of the news, therefore becomes a matter of reportorial initiative rather than the rewriting of political handouts or the stale coverage of last night's TV appearance. For newspapers and wire services, it is more of a challenge and, on the whole, it leads to better reporting over a period of time.

Political Routine : The electronic revolution that is reshaping the news media has enabled political reporters and commentators to use new and far more effective instrument in their work. At the beginning of the century, the task of obtaining and analyzing registration figures for all but the smallest elections was so time consuming that only a few great newspapers and the top echelons of wire services made much of an attempt to do it. Now the computer has made statistical analysis of registration figures almost a routine matter. This, plus social science's new knowledge of the habits of the nation's voters, has given public officials, journalists and office-seekers alike new insights into the operation of the machinery of self-government.

There is no excuse today for any political reporter who does not know the geographical social and ethnic backgrounds of the various areas of the nation. Nor can the journalists who cover politics ignore the need for a broad academic preparation for their work. It all may seem very glamorous to the beginner, who sees television floor reporters running around national conventions and buttonholing the elect of the country for interviews in front of the ever-present minicams with their instant replay videotapes.

Actually, that is only a small part of the job. Regardless of electronic advances in journalism, a certain amount of routine remains for every political reporter, and it has to be done well. For coverage begins with registration and proceeds through the nominating process preconvention manoeuvers, the conventions themselves or the primary elections that have replaced them in many states and then the coverage of the campaigns for all major candidates. What is involved here is a lot of traveling, interviewing research and writing at all hours of the day and night, the reporter doesn't exist who can cover politics on a regular basis within the neat framework of a seven or eight hour day.

Political Conventions : The old tradition of the "Smoke filled room", from which candidates like Warren Gamaliel Harding emerged and were thrust upon an astonished electorate in presidential elections, has been shattered by the growth of television. While many a politician sighs and wishes for its return the "smoke filled room" is now a part of history. Undoubtedly there will be what are known as "brokered" conventions of the two major political parties in the future, as there have been in the past but it will be next to impossible to keep the wheeling and dealing secret.

This is the main reason for the dramatic changes in the national political conventions at which presidential candidates are nominated. At the 1960 and 1964 conventions of both major parties, the presence of television cameras and TV reporters and commentators led to continual disorder as publicity conscious candidates and delegates crowded each other for exposure.

That, however, was but a foretaste of what was to come at the disastrous 1968 Democratic National Convention in Chicago, when masses of antiwar activists, seeking to punish the Democratic leadership for the escalation of the Vietnam War disrupted the proceedings with riots and other demonstrations before the television cameras. The Chicago police, surging to attack the demonstrators helped produce what turned out to be a political disaster for the Democratic nominee, Senator Hubert H.Humphery. He was defeated by former vice-president Richard M.Nixon, the Republican candidate in the November election.

Both parties tried, without much success to reduce the confusion on the convention floor in 1972 by attempting at restrain

television coverage. In 1976, finally, despite the use of hand-held minicams and videotape TV people were ordered from the floor of the Democratic National Convention several times in order to disperse the crowds around the cameras.

Calm, order, and dullness were the rule of the day at the 1980 conventions. At the republican convention, Ronald Reagan, the frontrunner during the primaries, was nominated in what amounted to a coronation. At the Democratic convention, with the exception of a lst-gasp effort from Senator Edward M. Kennedy, who made a brilliant speech, President Carter wrung an easy renomination from the reluctant Democratic leadership and went down to overwhelming defeat in the November election.

Election Day : The proceedings on Election Day, once so boisterous in the average American city are reasonably quiet today. In big cities, with few exceptions, there is almost a holiday air with banks and bars closed and often schools as well. It is seldom that there is news of such chicanery as stolen ballot boxes, the multiple voting of floaters and other tricks of the bad old days. If an election is being stolen the few remaining political bosses try not to make a public announcement of it. Trickery at the polls, in consequence, is rather difficult to detect except in Illinois, as the 1982 gubernatorial election showed.

This does not mean that news staffs have an easy time of Election Day, however. On the contrary the arduous business of interviewing voters after they have cast their ballots now begins with the opening of the polls. And as the voting progresses, the news no longer is based on an hour-by-hour estimate of how many have voted but on projections at sample precincts of the standings of the various candidates. Of course not every news organization is equipped to do this, because it takes a major outlay of funds and commitments of staff and electronic gear. But those that do can make an Election Day story much more exciting than it has been in recent years.

Election Night : The important thing about Election Night work is the effort that goes into organizing it. In the press and in the electronic media the news staff that generally does the best job

is the one that prepares for it with the greatest care. Sometimes the preparations for an Election Night begin as much as six months in advance. During the final weeks, the compilation of background figures, campaign materials data covering everything from biographies to party platforms and the outlining of actual assignments are almost as important as the day-to-day cover age of the news. No good news organization goes into Election Night without complete, pretested planning and batteries of the best calculators and computers available with trained personnel to run them.

Election coverage is the kind of thing the American news media do best. Once the polls close and the first figures start flowing from the newsrooms, partisanship is nearly always forgotten by the working journalists and all effort is concentrated on reporting who won how victory was achieved and what it means. The union of wire services and the three major television networks for Election Night coverage has reduced the public's uncertainty over the outcome in all but the closet elections.

Tabulating the Vote : The public's attention is riveted on the television screens on Election Night and the announcements as soon as possible of the winning candidates. The electronic performance is risky, but it is in the journalistic tradition, Gradually, the major television news organizations have learned the bitter lesson that newspapers absorbed in the years before the electronic media took primacy in such spot-news reporting. They have become far more careful with the announcement of who won— and why—and have generally adopted a stance of responsibility that befits the journalist far better than a wild-eyed claim of exclusivity. Their cooperation on presidential elections is in the public interest.

Even though television is first with the results and often first with the announcement of the winners, it cannot — by its very nature — provide the detailed tabulations of the voting down to the smallest districts and the totals amassed by every candidate in the various races. That is something good newspapers have always done superbly and they still continue to do so. Without

this kind of service, it would be difficult for a democratic system to operate as well as it does.

Handling the Figures : The basis of any voting announcement, whether it is given by the wire services television or rival media, is the vote total itself, the number of districts it represents and the identities of these districts. No fragmentary vote is worth anything unless the source is identified, so that it can be compared at once with previous records. Thus, any voting result that is important enough to be made known should contain the number of voting districts, the area and — if possible — the time as follows.

442 out of 1,346 election districts in Great Bear Country, on the state's northern border, gave these totals at 10.32 p.m.

lones (D)	60,024
Smith (R)	50,555

26 election districts in the 64th Ward, in the heart of Central City's south side, gave these totals at 9.30 p.m.

Brown (D)	2,022
Green (R)	2,366

The names of election units change, of course, from one place to another, nut whether they are wards or districts the practice is the same. On the basis of a sufficient cross-section of the voting, and a knowledge of past performance in the same area, a projection of the figures can be computed and an indicated voting result can be given. Thus, on the basis of a 25-percent voting return, an experienced political analyst can calculate what will happen and make an announcement that reads something like this:

> On the basis of returns from one-quarter of the city's districts two hours after the polls closed, Smith led by 40,622 to 32,634 for Jones, his Democratic rival. This gave him an actual plurality of 8,028 over Jones and an indicated plurality of more than 30,000 if the same vote ratio continues.

Political analysts know if it is possible for the same ratio to continue. They have all the statistics of past performances and they have tabulating machines and computers, with operators, so that it takes little time to work out a proper projection in all but the closest contests.

Where cities are heavily Democratic and rural districts are overwhelmingly Republican, as is usually true in such states as Illinois, New Jersey and New York, the initial returns from cities, being tabulated faster, often show Democratic candidates far in the lead. But this is where the analysts take over. They point out that the early figures may be misleading. As the returns come in from rural areas, they make projections of the vote to see if the usual Republican majorities are being piled up; if they are, then it is a relatively simple matter to match this projection against those of the cities and arrive at a tentative winner if the swing between the candidates is wide enough. But where the difference between the candidates vote percentages comes to 3 percent on either side, the familiar danger point for most statistical compilations, the wise analyst concludes that it is best to await virtually complete results.

It has happened, although rarely, that candidates have conceded defeat on the basis of projected returns and gone to bed, only to find upon arising in the morning that they have won because of a surge of late returns in their favour. And sometimes, when only a handful of votes separates winner and loser, a recount may reverse the result. So caution in close elections is an article of faith in every newsroom on Election Night.

The stories of the election results-written and verbal—are based on the tabulated figures, and the majorities and pluralities are calculated accordingly. A majority is the difference between candidates where only two are running; a plurality between two candidates is the difference where more than two are in the race. A candidate may have aplurality over the second person in a three-way race and a majority over the combined total of the opposition.

Anchor persons on TV need judgement, stamina and verbal skills to a high degree, but they don't have to worry too much about organizing their remarks. Newspaper work is different.

The key to the successful newspaper story on Election Night is the organization of the piece. It should be assembled in such a way that it need not be completely rewritten every time a voting total changes. Often figures are left out of the lead for this reason. The lead is merely based on the fact that one candidate is leading, the actual returns being given immediately afterward in tabular style so that they can be changed quickly by substituting an insert.

Qualifying the Story : Until a vote is decisive, it is well in reporting on Election Night to use such qualifications as, "On the basis of scattered returns," or, "Partial and unofficial returns showed Smith had a narrow lead 30 minutes after the polls closed." Until the election has been decided, a careful writer qualifies the lead in this manner:

> Robert J. Epperson apparently was elected mayor last night by an indicated plurality of 40,000 votes.
>
> Although no concession of defeat came from his rival, Arthur Ahlgren, Epperson claimed victory on the basis of returns from half the city's districts which gave him a commanding lead....

Sometimes, in a close election, a candidate may be the victor on the basis of final and unofficial returns and the loser may charge fraud, demand a recount or both. Circumstances dictate how the story should be presented, but it is only logical to report that one candidate has scored a victory that is being contested. The charges of fraud should be used in a lead only when there appears to be some basis for them.

When elections are very close, news organizations sometimes have to wait until the entire vote is counted before declaring a winner. In rare cases, the decision has to await the filing of official returns a week to 10 days after the election. But generally, an election is considered final when the rival or rivals of the successful candidate concede defeat.

There have been instances in which a candidate conceded defeat only to learn, when complete returns were in, that he had won. But that doesn't happen often..

Styles vary in the reporting of election results in newspapers. Some carry the actual figures in a box preceding the story, where readers can see them before they look at anything else. Others like to use a lead saying who won, and then immediately summarize the salient figures, even though television has already done the job. Here is a general style in use on many newspapers and wire services, which is also familiar to television audiences who have heard it present-tensed and read by exhausted second-string announcers late at night after the first team has gone home.

Arthur J. Wintage scored victory last night over his Democratic opponent, George Berling, who was seeking a third term as governor.

The Republican triumph in the state, which ran counter to a nationwide Democratic trend, was the result primarily of deep inroads that Mr. Wintage made into normally Democratic pluralities in Central City, largest municipality in the state.

Governor Berling conceded defeat at 11:15 last night. The concession followed a conference with Gunnar Dahlquist chairman of the Democratic State Committee, and Mayor Franklin Quest of Central

At 12.32 a.m., with nearly complete statewide returns in, 10,132 out of 11,110 districts gave:

Wintage (R)	2,834,263
Berling (D)	2,378,767

Nearly complete returns from Central City at that hour indicated that Mr. Wintage, 54-year-old industrialist from Willow Grove, had cut the usual Democratic plurality there to less than 400,000 votes. Four years ago, Governor Berling was able to carry the city by almost 700,000 votes...

The unofficial results, reported on Election Night by the news media, are seldom upset by challenges, charges or recounts, but the final result must await the official canvass. When there is an election upset, it is major news.

Basics on Polls and Elections : Here are some of the main things to remember about reporting on public opinion, polls and elections:

- Polling is based on the scientific use of statistics and must always include an announced probability of error, based on the number of people involved in the sample and the method of interviewing. No poll is ever going to be perfect.
- The least effective, and least scientific, poll is the one in which a reporter asks any dozen or so people for an opinion. That kind of poll is useless scientifically.
- A proper poll is based on the selection of a true random sample, in which everybody in a given polling area or group has an equal chance of being interviewed. The usual national telephone sample is about 1,500 which has a 3 -percent margin of error on either side, in 95 out of 100 instances.
- The two main methods are (a) probability, in which the interviewer is given specific instructions on exactly where to go and whom to interview, and (b) the quota method, in which the interviewer is told the types of people to interview (young, old, men, women, etc.) and the number of each and left to his or her own devices. The probability method is generally used.
- Polling reports should include the population sample, the size and response rate, the wording of questions, the poll sponsor, allowance for error, the time period for interviewing and when the interviewing was done.
- Any poll that shows a narrower percentage of support between two candidates than the margin of error for the poll itself is not really worth much. It shows an election too close to call.

- In writing about elections, any partial vote total must include the number of voting districts reporting, the area, the time, the partial totals and the part of the vote that is still missing as to area and, if possible, past voting performance.
- Until an election has been decided by the concession of one or another candidate or the completion of the vote, all reporting of returns must be qualified. Vote projections, as used by the networks and major newspapers, should be announced with the margin of error involved.
- In very close races, the official returns—which may take a week to 19 days-are often the decisive count. It the case of recounts, court actions may be involved, and the final decision could take months to determine on Election Night on the basis of projections of partial returns and should be so labeled.

11

Academic News

Science News

Our near the San Andreas Fault in California, you don't wait for earthquakes to happen if you're in the news business. You prepare for them.

David Perlman, science editor of the *San Francisco Chronicle*, has covered earthquakes in California since 1952 and has a contingency plan for local emergencies. He knows how because he is a specialist and his paper and staff associates depend on him.

Useful as general assignment reporters usually are, they are the first to recognize when they are out of their depth. That is when the specialists are absolutely necessary in science, medicine, law and economics — to mention only four fields in which special knowledge is mandatory for practicing journalists.

In such newer fields as consumerism, the environment and atomic energy, a certain amount of special training, background knowledge and experience also are necessary particularly for investigative reporters.

Leaders among the news media are applying greater resources, both in human and financial terms, to satisfy the public's increasing demands for more competent coverage of these and other specialized areas. And more young journalists are persuaded that it is worth their while to develop an interest in a speciality.

There is nothing theoretical about David Perlman's interest in earthquakes in California. And people who read the *San Francisco Chronicle know* it. Forever since 1906, when a great quake razed a large part of the city and set the shaking ruins afire, people in the area have been well aware that their only real defense against a recurrence is advanced knowledge. And Perlman has it, to the extent that anybody can in so unpredictable an area. He writes.

I covered my first major earthquake at Tehachapi in California in 1952 - flying down in a Red Cross plane to the tiny town where 14 people were killed in a temblor registering 7.7 on the Richter scale. We slept in the open for several nights on army cots which shivered and shook with every aftershock, and we filed stories via the railroad telegraph.

Today our earthquake coverage involves continual contact with the seismologists at Caltech in Pasadena, at the University of California in Berkeley, and at the U.S. Geological Survey in Menlo Park usually write scientific "explainers" when a quake strikes, while we send as many reporters and photographers as needed to the sites of significant damage — be it San Fernando, the High Sierra, the imperial Valley, or wherever.

Contingency Planning : Like 120 million Japanese, who accept the reality of daily earth shocks as a part of their lives, people in towns and cities near the San Andreas Fault in California know that earthquake reporting is serious business. These are a part of the *San Francisco Chronicle's* plants for any serious contingency. Perlman writes.

We assume that phone lines and even power will be out, but that somehow cars will be able to roll. So we have preassigned photographers (whose cars are all equipped with radios) to drive as quickly as possible to the highest spots around San Francisco, where they would serve as local command posts and communications links to our central radio in the city room.

And if the city room is inoperative, our chief photographer's car would be parked in an open lot next to our building—there to serve as a focus for all city desk activities. (In 1906, the San Francisco papers all printed a joint edition in Oakland and we could probably find a newspaper plant somewhere in the Bay Area that would be similarly operable.)

It is noteworthy that the *Chronicle* apparently does not place major reliance on the Federal Emergency Management Administration, which didn't function as well as the news media in covering the Mount St. Helens eruption. But FEMA for as long as it is able to continue in existence in the face of continual budgetary cut-backs, is bound to be a source in any disaster operation.

Covering a Quake : The way a specialist covers an earthquake is some-what different from and a lot more detailed than the way a general assignment reporter would go about the same job. This was how the *San Francisco Chronicle* led off its coverage of a "moderate" quake that took no lives (issue of January 25, 1980).

By David Perlman

Quake results	Rumbling aftershocks shook the Bay Area last night as damage
	assessment and repairs continued in the wake of a rolling earthquake that swept through much of Northern California yesterday morning.
Timing and damage	The initial quake, lasting nearly a minute, caused minor injuries and damage near its epicenter and forced 7,100 workers to leave the huge Livermore nuclear weapons laboratory.
Danger discounted	Last night, laboratory officials said a 30,000 gallon container of "very, very

	low level" radioactive tritium was leaking at the rate of four gallons an hour. The material, used infusion research, was leaking into an asphalt container and was not considered by lab officials to be dangerous.
Magnitude of quake	The" moderate" quake struck in a remote section of south-eastern and aftershock Contra Costa County at ten seconds past 11 a.m., with a Richter magnitude of 5.5. It was followed within the next three minutes by two after shocks — one with a magnitude of 5.2 and the other measuring 4.8.
	Two more aftershocks occurred yesterday evening— one of 4.6 magnitude at 9:12 p.m. and the second of 4.4 at 9.24 p.m.
Extent of quake	During the bigmorning quake residents reported feeling the ground roll beneath them as far away as Reno, nearly 200 miles east of San Francisco; Monterey, 150 miles south, and Santa Rosa, 50 miles north.
Trains still run	The BART system halted all its trains for five minutes after the quake, but trains in the tunnel beneath San Francisco Baby were allowed to go to the nearest station before the shutdown. No damage was reported on the lines.
Road damage	Country roads and some larger highways near the epicenter buckled and repairs and cracked and an overpass along interstate 5880 at

Greenville Road became impassable when earth-works and paving on the east side of the structure slumped three to eight inches.

The structure did not break but traffic had to be diverted off 580 and cars soon backed up several miles. Highway crews began clearing away chunks of tar and concrete. Resurfacing was completed and the bridge was reopened by late afternoon.

General damage

Throughout the Bay Area, shattered windows, swaying high rises and groceries piled in the aisles of markets provided typical marks of the kind Northern California experiences ....

Most of the rest of the story was taken up with interviews with earth scientists in the area, both governmental and academic, to determine what caused the quake and whether a recurrence could be expected in the immediate future. This was, to the science writer, one of the most important aspects of the staffs coverage. He commented on his own experience.

It was easy enough writing the first-edition story because the aftershocks obligingly subsided in plenty of time. But when more of them hit during the night, I had to rush back to the office and patch up the new information in a hurry. But that's the fun of the newspaper business.

***Progress in Science Writing* :** Humankind's giant vault into space has done as much as anything to stimulate the trend toward specialization in journalism. When Neil Armstrong in 1969 stepped on the moon's surface and said, "This is one small step for a man, one giant leap for mankind," he also marked a major development in the reporting of science news.

Through all six moon journeys in which manned landings were made, and all the subsequent experiments that were climaxed by the trips of the space shuttle, the journalists told the story behind the marvelous TV pictures in terms that a mass public could understand. These, plus the space explorations of distant planets, have broadened the methods the news media use to communicate science news. Such experiences have given the trained newscasters and science reporters an advantage over their less skilled colleagues. As a young general assignment reporter observed ruefully, "You can't explain what you don't fully understand."

What is Covered : Out of the enormous amount of material that is published in scientific and scholarly journals, it is obvious that only a small part can be translated into popular terms and used widely by the news media commanding a mass audience. Consequently, a considerable volume of science news of a technical nature appears in specialized publications first. Scientific conventions account for almost as much news of science, being prime sources of new developments and new ideas. Entirely on their own, science writers study almost anything bearing on the development of atomic energy and space exploration for the germ of a significant news account. Sometimes they learn of such developments from their own sources in government and industry, on other occasions, they may be able to deduce clues to future developments from their own background and knowledge.

The increasing emphasis on studies of air and water pollution has deepened public interest in such matters and broadened the scope of the writer of popularized science. This is also true of the emphasis on medical reportage and progress in improving conditions in hospitals. But whole areas of mathematics, physics and chemistry and other natural sciences are still relatively uncovered in the daily and periodical press because the developments are so far above the level of public understanding.

Energy Crunch : Nowhere is there greater need for informed and dispassionate reporting than in the field of energy, on which the United States and other industrialized countries are so dependent. To put the case directly.

Today, electric power provides about 30 percent of the energy consumed in America. Of that total, a little less than half is generated by burning coal, 15 percent by burning gas, 13 percent by burning oil, 12 percent by hydroelectric power and only 11 percent from nuclear reactors. Thus, in the first half of the 1980s, only a small part of America's energy needs — if that much — comes from nuclear power, and there are no more than 72 operable nuclear power plants in the land.

Yet nuclear power has generated major demonstrations against the "nukes" from coast to coast and has resulted in wide public fear and misunderstanding. In consequence, no informed person believes we can now come anywhere near building and operating the 250 nuclear plants we were expected to have in the year 2000. Moreover, the cost of building such plants has virtually tripled.

The accident to the nuclear facility at Three Mile Island and its aftermath have done much to undermine public faith in nuclear power. But what happens now? This is the conclusion of a report by the National Academy of Sciences entitled "Energy in Transition, 1985-2010.

A balanced combination of coal and nuclear electricity is preferable on environmental and economic grounds to the predominance of either Coal and nuclear power are the only large scale alternatives to oil and gas in the near term, before about 2000, as the use of fluid fuels begins to wane.

It is going to take a lot of informed reporting, based on hard scientific evidence, to change the public's mood, however. And today there are few industrial giants who are willing to take the risk of undertaking to build more nuclear plants than are currently scheduled for construction.

The Consumerism : When Pete McKnight was editor of the *Charlotte* (North Carolina) Observer, he warned his colleagues in the American Society of Newspaper Editors, of which he was past president," Consumer reporting is one of the big new fields that change has forced upon us. Consumer protection is a fact of life. It is not going to go away, even if it does set your advertising manager to trembling."

The Challenge : To a profession whose support is so dependent on advertising, that indeed is the challenge. It can scarcely be met by a few general assignment reporters, sent out at random, as consumer stories emerge, to cover each one separately. The more responsible news organizations have found it necessary to maintain a group of knowledgeable consumer specialists, who are reinforced from time to time with staff people; even among smaller newspapers with an interest consumer news, there is usually at least one reporter whose regular assignments the consumer beat.

More than in any other subject area of journalism, consumer news required the strict separation of the editorial department from the advertising and business offices if the press is to maintain its credibility with the public. For consumer news cuts across all the traditional departmental lines, from life style pages to financial from real estate to sports, and more often than not it dominates Page .

Growth of Coverage : A few pioneering consumer organizations, with pitifully small resources and skimpy publications, struggled for years to awaken then interest of the public in a crusade against shoddy products, overpricing, misleading advertising and the other signs of an overly commercial age. But for much of this century, few consciences were stirred except among the more progressive editors and managers of the news media. Along Madison Avenue, it was even hinted darkly that people who suspected the good faith of big advertisers were dupes of Communism at best and plotters against the security of the republic at worst.

The first to break through the barrier of indifference and neglect was a public spirited lawyer. Ralph Nader, who managed to marshal the support of a group of a talented young adherents in a whole series of campaigns to protect the interests of the consumer. Then, in a period of soaring inflation that sent the cost of living rocketing, the public itself began to face up to a distressing situation. The nation's campuses, ever sensitive to such movements, became staging areas for consumer groups that sought new recruits. And consumerism, at last, became a fact of life for the American Press. Even the broadcast media had to take notice when the crusade against cigarettes reached such a pitch that cigarette commercials were eliminated from the air by law. Health news, on a day-to-day basis, became important to a large and demanding public.

Range and Methods : Editors approach consumer reporting in various ways. The larger news organizations use specialists who do nothing else. Those who want consumer news but can't afford specialists expect their regular reporters to contribute pieces of interest to consumers. Business writers, for example, can do specialized pieces on how consumers can get satisfaction for their complaints. Sports writers can give much more advice than they do on such consumer details as where to park cars outside stadiums, the best methods of travel to various contests, costs, availability of meals and other details. All receipts in the family pages should carry approximate costs. And in travel and entertainment stories, costs should be included as a matter of course.

As the case was put in a report by Jack Foster, editor of the *Palm Beach* (Florida) Times, "Consumer reporting is all around us. It is no loner something out of the ordinary, if indeed it ever was."

Consumer Campaigns : Consumerism has been effective in journalism in several different ways. Leading newspapers are originating their own inquiries in response to complaints, one of the by products of the various Action Line columns of recent years. And all newspapers, even the most sluggish, are being obliged to reexamine their policies on using material that formerly was considered a harmless bonus for an advertiser. In this respect, television, usually so timid wherever advertisers are concerned, lags behind the printed media.

Campaigns that once were considered taboo are now being undertaken with the helpful resources of a news organization. The *Des Moines Register*, for example, gave full support to Nick Kats' s examination of unsanitary practices in meat packing plants, the result being the passage of the Federal Wholesale Meat

Act and a Pulitzer Prize for the reporter. Campaigns against unsanitary restaurants now are considered almost routine in some cities of the nation. And major papers like the Wall Street Journal do not hesitate to expose unscrupulous business practices wherever they are found. The 1982 Tylenol scare was a national sensation.

The automobile industry, despite its heavy advertising budgets, has been forced on the defensive in numerous instances to justify its safety standards and merchandising practices. The food sections of family pages, so long immune from critical inspection, have undergone an even more searching examination. And phonyphigs to advertisers and the acceptance of favours that have been so disgraceful a part of some financial, real estate and sports sections have come under fire from both within and outside the ranks of professional journalism.

Just how far consumer reporting will develop depends entirely on the skill and devotion of the journalists who undertake this speciality and the amount of support they receive from their news organizations. Several hundred of them are on the job today. But certainly, now that so many barriers have fallen, there can be no return to the comfortable situation where major advertisers felt that the average newspaper would always try to make up in departmental news for whatever injuries they may have received in the headlines on Page. No less than consumerism, the relationship of people to their environment and the increasing public concern over pollution have generated broadening interest in the news. The great industries that recklessly contaminated the atmosphere, despoiled the earth of its beauty and polluted the water supply arc being called to account. Cities that casually dumped their sewage in rivers, lakes and inland seas are finding themselves threatened by their own filth. New York City, a special case, has learned to its cost that it must cease dumping sludge in the ocean because it contaminates beaches for miles around. And even well-meaning citizens have learned that, through their own foolish disposal measures, they are among the worst polluters of all.

A Measure of Progress : There has always been a certain amount of interest in the conservation of natural resources in the United States and the development of the resources of the earth for the benefit of all peoples. But for more than a century after the founding of the nation, the constructive measures undertaken by the press were limited to such innovations as those of the editor of the *Pennsylvania Gazette.* Benjamin Franklin, who introduced the yellow willow to America and devised a practical system of lightning rods.

The muckrakers of the early 20th century were the forerunners of the environmentalists of today. Butcher influence, in general, was limited to the period of. The odore Roosevelt's presidency, primarily because he had a deep interest in the protection of natural resources and was not afraid to attack "the malefactors of great wealth." However, it was no newspaper, but an indignant novelist, Upton Sinclair who attacked the meat industry' in *The Jungle.* And it was no national columnist but a little know chemistry professor and editor. Edwin Fremont Ladd of the *North Dakota Farmer and Sanitary Home magazine,* who was among the earliest agitators for pure food and drug legislation. The press, with few exceptions, was preoccupied with the political economic scandals of the day.

Environmental developments were covered of course but there appeared to be no special concern over the state of the earth and the atmosphere even after World War II. Once again, it was a book, *Silent Spring by* Rachel Carson, that called public attention to a development of consequence — the effect of the pesticide DDT on wildlife. Out of the national debate that ensued, a new consciousness was created of the precarious nature of humankind on earth. It was a time when the public also began paying attention to the historical warnings of overpopulation, diminishing resources for sustaining life and the rising threat of pollution on every side.

But when the Love Canal scandal broke in New York in the late 1970s and editors realized thousands of families were living over or near abandoned chemical dumps that threatened their health, local reporters did not have to do a great deal of investigating to find that similar situations exited in their own area. The upshot was the issuance of a national list of dangerous abandoned chemical sites that had to be cleaned up. It was a major step forward in the development of environmental reporting as a daily newspaper assignment in many parts of the country.

Environmental News

When Henry Ford succeeded in manufacturing his first automobile, it was a revolution in the means of transportation on the personal and commercial level — an achievement which changed the world. Decades later, scientists have begun to realize that cars also emit harmful gases through their exhaust systems which affect our health and environment.

The issue of protection of the environment becomes a matter of awareness. Most of the projects and problems in the developing countries have their basis in their relationship to the scientific and environmental facts. These facts should be recognized by decision-makers as well as by the public.

The environment reporter's role is to keep up a continuous effort to inform the public and to make a constant effort to increase this awareness about the environment. The environmental reporter should also have the ability to understand the technical and highly specialized scientific information and to rewrite, or reedit it in a simple style suitable for the public. This should be done without losing any of the scientific facts. It may be useful and helpful to the environmental reporter to have a scientific background. Photography is another desirable skill for the environmental reporter. Frequently the priority for the assistance of a photojournalist usually goes to covering politics, crime or sports events. Assistance for the environmental reporter comes last. Hence the need for that reporter to take his or her own pictures.

Among the environmental problems which need special attention in the Third World are the problems of air pollution, especially in the big cities; the manufacture and use of pesticides; and the misuse of agricultural land and forests.

For a long time, competition between economic development and preserving the environment has existed. Everyone seemed in favour of economic development all over the world. In the so-called "Silicon Valley" in California, U.S.A., the first-class, fertile, highly productive agricultural lands were sacrificed to developers to build a base for what was once thought of as the "safe-to-the-enrolment" electronics industry. But that same industry after a time was proven unsafe, too, and those involved in agricultural food production were forced to move far away to the Central Valley of California where transportation was more of a problem for fertilizers and for getting fresh fruits, vegetables and other products to market. Water was also more of a problem for those who were forced to move.

In India, the Bellhop disaster exposed the problem brought about by some big industrial multinational pesticide companies. They shipped the hazardous and banned pesticides as separate chemical compounds to a developing country, then reassembled them into a pesticide under another commercial name.

In most of the capitals and large cities of the Third World there is serious air pollution, and this does not get the proper attention or research in an effort to put it under control or at least to lower the level of pollution.

In Egypt, an ancient practice was using mud bricks for building since the time of the Pharaohs. The Nile River annual flood brought a fresh supply of millions of tons of mud and silt, but after the Aswan High Dam construction, mud sediments were deposited in front of the dam, not making their way down the river as previously. Then farmers began to sell layers of their topsoil to persons deprived of their usual supply of mud for bricks. This practice led to the loss of fertile top soil in large areas. Others, to solve their housing needs, began to build on agricultural land. But recent laws have banned both practices of building on farm land or excavating topsoil for production of mud bricks. Now there are severe penalties for doing this.

In Colombia, in the vast Amazon forest, illegal coca plantations have had a large-scale development with big profits for labourers and farm owners who produce cocaine in laboratories in the forests. The government has used airplanes and Army troops to fight this practice. But the problem has had a negative effect where there has been damage to the tropical forests, and of course in the exporting of the drug to other countries.

A Veteron Journalist Observes : Investigative reporting sometimes could be a suitable way to deal with environmental issues, as when in a report on air pollution in Coria I had to get the number of cars, trucks and buses running on the streets from the Traffic Department. One can depend on relatives or friends to get information which may not be available through official channels all the time. They I had to get the chemical analysis of the air quality from the air pollution laboratory at the National Research Center. I also obtained information about the amount of fuel burned in that year from the Department of Petroleum. Then I had to contact the Department of Public and Industrial Health at the School of Medicine of Coria University to get information about the effect of different components in the gases emitted in the exhaust. These particles included lead, hydrocarbons, etc.

Then I had to go the Meteorological Department to add to the report weather conditions and how they affect the amount of pollution in Coria. I also had to obtain photographs and to read abou air pollution in science magazines and in reports.

Finally, I had a good report available to me about air pollution problems in Coria. Other studies which are typical of what a reporter might use for background might include guides about the effect of lead particles on mental processes of workers in printshops using lead and studies about the effect of air pollution on traffic policemen exposed for eight hours daily to air pollution.

In basic environmental reporting the reporter can get ideas from his or her own interests or personal observations. In 1976, the noise level was very high in Coria because of traffic jams and the misuse of car horns. This observations which I made was followed by some regarding about noise. Also, there was a comparative study available concerning three cities and a remote village in the south of Sudan. In this study the medical team found that noise has had a bad effect on health causing loss of hearing, high blood pressure and tension which can lead to heart disease.

Another field of environmental reporting is that of wildlife protection. Third World countries are the home of many wildlife species which are becoming endangered because of development and expansion of agricultural land uses, taking away their natural habitat. Efforts should be made to preserve the wildlife species and native plants. Man kind should avoid the direct competition with these wildlife species. In addition to the pleasure we receive from watching wildlife creatures, these animals (and plants) are considered to be storehouses of natural genetic materials which could be very useful to the survival of mankind. In Egypt, I wrote several times about the importance of the As Mayhemed area, the southern triangle of the Sinai Peninsula surrounded by the Gulf of Suez and the Gulf of Aqaba, where the fantastic coralized formations attract drivers from all over the world. This area is also the home of the osprey, the fish-catching eagle; and the northern border where mangrove trees growing in the shallow water of the sea have the ability to extract fresh water from the sea water.

Now As Mahamed has been declared the first Natural Reserve and National Marine Park in Egypt.

For environmental reporters, scientific background is an advantage. But an interested reporter can obtain a good knowledge in the field by reading environmental materials published by international organizations, such as the United Nations Environmental Programme. Contact with the U.N. programme can put a reporter in touch with the organizations working in the field and with their publications. For example, the international journal for environment and development entitled Mazingira is available.

The environment is a multi-disciplinary subject, which includes science, medicine, public health, meteorology, engineering, city planning, economics, and many more facets of man's life. So a stream of continuous awareness is needed until we reach the point of the optimum development of our resources with a minimum disturbance to the environment. Having that awareness is the job of the environmental reporter.

Economic News

When rocketing interest rates threatened both the automobile and housing industries in the early 1980s and helped spin the nation into recession, many a news organization asked, "why'? The answers were not easy to come by because economic news, for the most part, had never been a staple of American journalism even in the Great Depression. More often that not, it was relegated to the business section of newspapers and given to reporters who couldn't or wouldn't get excited about covering fires and playing cops and robbers.

The seriousness of the American economic situation, however, prompted a turn about in general economic reporting. Efforts were made to find reporters who knew the difference between a bond and a stock, an expense budget and a capital budget.

When the Wall Street Journal became the largest newspaper in the land with more than two million daily circulation, and TV programmes like Loúis Rukeyser's Wall Street Week pulled in four or five million viewers weekly, a lot of newspapers got the message. While economic reporting wasn't in it at least became a necessary part of the daily coverage of events.

The long deferred recognition of economic news was accompanied by equally important changes in the way it was written and told. There is no longer an excuse for making economic dull. In professional hands, such a story can be told in informal, popular and often uninhibited style. Whether the subject is business or labour, the stock market or foreign trade or the innumerable off shoots thereof, the innovators on the Wall Street Journal are often the first to show their irreverence for stuffy old forms of writing. This, without doubt, is one of the reasons for the phenomenal growth of the journal into the largest daily newspaper in the land.

Nor is the journal alone in profiting from changes in the

presentation of economic news. All the leading business pages in rival newspapers have been affected by the movement toward improved content and livelier style. The McGraw-Hill magazines, headed by Business Week, and the Fairchild group, of which the daily Women's Wear is the most prominent, both have found prosperity in their sponsorship of the unorthodox.

Labour News

When the principal effort of the federal government was designated as an attack on inflation, the local headlines and local evening news programmes very soon reflected worsening unemployment. Many reporters throughout the land found themselves assigned to interview government officials, plant managers, university professors and union leaders. But relatively few have much knowledge of the labour movement in this country, let alone the complicated economic issues that have resulted in scary unemployment figures.

The problem is not new in American journalism. During every economic turndown since World War II, there has been agitation at professional conferences for the improvement of reportorial training in the coverage of problems affecting the labour force. But once recovery begins, the urgency for better labour reportage appears to wane.

It is perfectly true that the nation's leading newspapers and newsmagazines have had labour reporters for years and have, on the whole, told the labour story fairly and impartially. It would be unthinkable today for a newspaper of stature in New York, Chicago, Pittsburgh, Detroit or Los Angeles, for example, to fail to maintain regular and detailed coverage of labour affairs. But elsewhere in the country, until very recently, the labour story has usually been told as a series of disconnected episodes. While many smaller newspapers and even a few local stations have tried within their resources to keep a fair balance between labour and management in the news some have not.

In the columns of a good newspaper, news of labour affairs is by no means confined to unemployment, strikes and lockouts or violence on the picket lines. A more sophisticated approach to the reporting of conflicts between industry' and labour has developed, so that a good newspaper takes care not to label itself a proindustry partisan in every dispute but tries to give both sides of the story.

Educational News

With more than 60 million Americans going to school, the coverage of education today is a challenge to all the news media. There is a greater room for progress in the reporting of education news than in many another speciality. But it will take well-trained journalists to do the job-men and women who understand the problems of the schools and know how to write about them.

The old journalistic weakness for emphasizing trouble rather than achievement in only a part of the difficulty in achieving a balanced presentation of the news of education. In many cities, the extreme sensitivity of school administrations to criticism handicaps even their defenders when they embark on a purely fact-finding mission. Such sensitivity often is exceeded only by that of the press itself when it is under heavy community criticism. In such situations, there is little possibility for a constructive dialogue and school and pressdrift into postures of mutual hostility. This is particularly true in some of the struggles over school integration and busing in Northern cities.

When the schools are in the forefront of the news, however, cool, careful, impartial reporting must become the order of the day.

This was the pattern to which both the Boston Globe and the Louisville Courier-Journal and Times adhered when integration crises gripped the schools of their respective cities. What they did provide guidance for both hard-pressed parents and teachers as well as much-needed support for the children who went to class daily under difficulty.

It would be well if the noncrisis news of education were covered in the same spirit, but often it is given only minimal attention. Some universities in America are covered by student stringers for major papers and wire services, but not at all by the broadcast media, except when there is a riot or some other disorder. Many an education writer has tried to devise some better method for the daily coverage of higher education, but not many have succeeded.

Religious News

The news of religion for many years suffered an extremely low priority in the daily press except on weekends and religious holidays. The changed attitude that is so apparent today in a large section of the press, including television, scarcely means that the editors have suddenly "got" religion.

What has happened is that the extreme conservative wing of American religious leadership—the " Moral Majority"—has found a new outlet for its frustrations in political activity. It boasted that it helped elect Ronald Reagan as president and did much to defeat liberal Democratic senators. It also threatened to boycott television programmes of which it disapproved, and the threat was enough to get a small amount of reform in blatantly violent programming.

Thus, while news of religion in general still was given minimal coverage, the activists of religion repeatedly made Page I and the network evening news programmes. They were held up to critical examination on programmes like 60 Minutes, and created amingled atmosphere of controversy, criticism and fierce partisanship.

The conservative movement stirred up controversy in other areas as well. Its political supporters in Congress made renewed efforts to establish a prayer routine in the public schools despite constitutional bars against the mingling of religion and secular affairs. To get around that prohibition, President Reagan proposed a constitutional amendment. And book-banning in public libraries became news in some communities because conservative preachers made an issue of books they particularly disliked for various reasons.

Religious leaders became involved in political in other ways.

Editors specializing in news of religion for the wire services and the larger newspapers dealt with many issues beyond the regular religious observances. Nor was it unusual for reporters on all news organizations i n the land, large and small to find themselves engrossed in an assignment dealing with issues arising out of deeply held religious beliefs. The struggle waged by the forces for and against abortion, for example, was probably the single most emotional issue in American life during the 1980s and it deeply involved communities in every part of the land. It was a symbol of changing times.

Cultural News

The audience for cultural affairs in the United States now is larger than the sports audience in most major metropolitan centers, but the news media have been slow to take advantage of it. Most of the reviewing and critical writing about the lively arts appears in the larger newspapers, the weekly magazines and thewire services. Smaller newspapers use syndicated copy for the most part, but may run a few locally written reviews of books touring theater and musical attractions and occasional art exhibits. Films are more widely reported on and reviewed than anything else on the cultural scene. And only the smallest papers neglect to run the daily and weekly television listings.

While television itself does very little reviewing and criticism of a serious nature, it is the one universal medium with the capacity to bring great theatre and great music to nearly all American homes. That kind of TV programming doesn't occur very often. But when it does, it is nearly always a national event of importance.

Editorials : The editorial page is undergoing a much -needed revival in importance and editorial voice of radio and television is a little stronger. Even some news magazines are coming around to the need for a separate section for editorial comment. The new stress on editorial opinion is due in large part of the expansion of public-service journalism; for, without the strongest kind of editorial support and the total mobilization of the resources of the entire news organization, many a crusade would wither and die in a few days.

There are many definitions of what editorial opinion should be, and how a properly conducted editorial page or editorial programme should operate. Certainly, it must be something more than the voice of the proprietor, the vehicle for promoting his own interests and prejudices and those of his leading editors. Properly conducted, an editorial section should represent a community or region of the country; many, of course, contend that they speak for the nation but not very many could prove it if challenged. Moreover, such a section should be a marketplace of ideas, and not a grab-bag of columns and reprints intended to please all segments of the audience.

What Editors Believe : It is customary, in any discussion of the editorial function to note that editorial pages rank comparatively low in any survey of readership of newspapers, and programmes devoted to editorial opinion are close to the bottom in radio and television audience measurements. What these surveys do not show, however, is the quality of those who read the editorial page and listen to editorial programmes. In most communities and regions, it is primarily the leaders who pay the closet attention to editorial content and who are the most likely to be influenced by it. Thus, despite low total diffusion, the editorial section can have an impact on the decision making process and community leaders are well aware of it.

Tips for Specialist in Journalism

- Every young reporter should begin, as early as possible, to cultivate a speciality. In today's complicated world journalists with specialized knowledge are very much in demand.
- Science writing is of importance in everything from the coverage of earthquakes to claims

  about instant cures for the common cold. It is of special interest in anything having to do with atomic power and other aspects of the energy crunch.

- Consumer reporting cuts across all departmental lines in a news organization. A consumer reporter has to have specialized and dependable sources and the strength and courage to stand by the reporting of unpleasant and controversial facts.
- Environmental reporting was given a big boost through the discovery that hidden sites for the dumping of chemical waste, much of it toxic, existed in most parts of the United States. The reporting of water shortages, the opening of national lands for private exploitation and other aspects of environmental concern are regularly in the news.
- Any recession brings renewed interest in the reporting of economic news. It is no longer something that can be safely relegated to the financial page and it can't be done solely by the Wall Street Journal.
- Every news organization now is trying to find better ways to tell the economic story and it is going to take specialists to do it. The same is time of labour news, particularly in times of high unemployment.
- News stories about education, religion and cultural affairs all have their specialized aspects and are important on larger news organizations. In smaller organizations, the reporter with all interest in any one of these often does work on such stories without being specially assigned. Many give their own time to the job, even though it is not demanded of them.
- It is a rare beginner who makes the jump from school or a first job directly to the editorial page or a spot as a columnist. It has been done, but each case is extraordinary. It pays to how an editorial page operates and what makes columnist run, but the one thing young reporters cannot do is to let the paper's editorial policy guide their reporting. No reporter can go out on a story with a fixed idea of what he or she is looking for and expect to do a fair and honest job.

12

Investigative News

There is a school of journalistic thought that curls its lip and sneers at the very mention of the words 'investigative reporting'. It argues that, since all reporting is investigative, the phrase is meaningless. If only that were true. But some reporting is investigative only in the most basic sense. It is the journalistic equivalent of the single-cell creature and bears about as much resemblance to the subject of this chapter as amoebae do to humans.

Investigative Reporting

Investigative reporting is substantially different from other kinds and there are four features that distinguish it.

Original Research : Investigative reporting is not a summary or piecing together of others' findings and data, but original research carried out by journalists often using the rawest of material. It can be extensive interviewing, or matching and comparing facts and figures and discovering previously unknown patterns and connections.

The subject involves wrong doing or negligence for which there is no published evidence

Often you have suspicions of wrong doing or negligence but have no proof and neither does anyone else. You need to accumulate evidence and this requires far more time and prolonged effort than ordinary reporting. It may also involve more than one reporter.

Information Secret : This is true of a lot of reporting, but in day-to-day work, there is often a point at which you have to stop and report what you have found or not found. Investigative reporting starts at the point where the day-to-day work stops. It does not accept the secrecy and the refusal of officals to give the information. It finds out for itself.

The Stakes : The kudos and pride you get when the story works out can be considerable, but so can the amount of dirt hitting the fan when it all goes wrong. Consider the *Cincinnati Enquirer's* experiences in 1998. In May of that year they published a front page story and an 18-page section devoted to a year-long investigation into the international banana firm, Chiquita Brands. Headlined 'Chiquita Secrets Revealed', the paper alleged that Chiquita secretly controlled dozens of supposedly independent banana firms, that it and its subsidiaries used pesticides that threatened the health of workers and nearby residents, that employees engaged in bribery in Columbia and that its ships had smuggled cocaine into Europe.

All, however, was not quite as it seemed. In the issue of 28 June, the paper carried a six-column apology to the company across the top of the front page, totally repudiating the investigation. It fired its lead investigative reporter and it agreed to pay Chiquita no less than $10 million.

The problem was not the veracity (or otherwise) of the evidence, but the methods employed to obtain it. These involved access to internal voicemail messages of the company and the issue was how this access was obtained. The company alleged that the reporter posed questions and then tapped into their mailboxes to eavesdrop on their internal discussion on the issues the reporter had raised. The paper, in making the apology and settlement, appeared to accept the thrust of these allegations. In a published statement, the paper said that the reporter had misled them over the source of the voicemail messages. It was never clear, however, if there was any substance to the published stories.

The loss of credibility, plus the $10 million, made this a very costly investigation. Fortunately, for every episode like this, there are many more which were rewarding. They range from Nellie Bly's exposure of appalling conditions inside asylums for *New York World*, *W.T.* Stead's exposure of child prostitution in the *Pall Mall Gazette;* and the unmasking of the violently racist Ku Klux Klan by Roland Thomas in the *New York World;* to the uncovering by Seymour Hersch of the My Lai massacre in 1968; the *Sunday Times'* campaign for the limbless victims of the drug thalidomide; and Carl Bernstein and Bob Woodward's Watergate investigation in the *Washington Post.* They also include many more localised stories, which exposed neglect and so changed lives for the better. A classic case is the *Alabama journal's* investigation into the state's infant mortality record in 1987 - at 13 deaths per 1,000, it was the worst of any state in the union. The paper ran a 20-part series which led to the State Medicaid agency quadrupling funding for pre-natal programmes and a determined drive to bring better health care to poor mothers. By 1994 Alabama's infant mortality rate had shrunk by 20 per cent. By the end of the century, there were nearly 1,000 children who owed their very existence to this series. It's difficult to imagine more productive reporting than that.

Finally, what is at stake can even include your personal safety. In countries where organised crime is widespread, investigative reporting is a potentially lethal profession. In Russia, the *Moskovski Koinsolets* reporter, Dimitri Kholodov, was investigating army corruption. An anonymous source rang him one day in the autumn of 1994 and said that a bag of documents had been left for him at Kazan Station. Kholodov collected them and took the bag back to his office. When he opened it, the bag exploded, killing him. And in the summer of 1992, Peruvian reporter Adolfo Isuiza Urquia was investigating drug dealing for the daily *La Republica*. In August he named a major drug trafficker who was being protected by the armed forces. 'The army does not want to fight terrorism because it lives off drug trafficking', he wrote. A few days later, on 27 August, his body was found in the River Huallaga. He had been tortured and stabbed. Anyone considering digging around in these areas should carefully weigh any risk involved. Dead reporters can't report.

Sniff of a Story

Investigative reporting starts with a sniff of a story, or the hunch that in some subject lies the seeds of one. The main thing at this stage is to think carefully about the 'best case' outcome and consider whether the story will be worth the effort and time required. If it is not going to be page one, forget it. Specialised investigative units in particular can easily get obsessed with a story that is far too narrow to be of importance to general readers. Submit your planned inquiry to the headline test: if the anticipated outcome does not make a startling headline, then you are probably going to waste your time.

Potentially, good investigations can be found in almost any area of public life. Two broad categories, however, are particularly fruitful: activities and organisations that do their work in remote places or otherwise away from the public gaze; and people and institutions that suddenly get thrust into the spotlight, appear to have 'come from nowhere' and around which a mythology has speedily grown. They are people and institutions which seem to have no background. But they will, and in that background there is almost sure to be a good story.

Companies and financial institutions, especially of the 'get rich quick' variety, are a highly fertile ground for some journalistic digging. Sink your spade into a newfangled and highly publicised investment scheme and you can bet your salary that there will be dirt there. The Romanian pyramid funds of the early 1990s are a prime case of a missed opportunity. One that was not missed, and a classic example of this type of reporting, was the story of Charles Ponzi, or, as he liked to call himself, The Great Ponzi.

A lot of people believed him. More than 40,000 Americans plunged their savings into his scheme, lured in by his pledge to pay them, within 90 days, $2.50 for every $1 invested. Despite warnings from financial experts that his sums did not add up, Ponzi was, at one point in 1920, raking in $200,000 a day. In 18 months, he collected more than $15 million.

It was all based on currency exchange rates. His company would take your investment, and send it overseas, where his agents would buy International Postal Union reply coupons at depressed rates and then sell them in other foreign outposts at a higher rate. That was Ponzi's story and thousands joined the rush to have their investment earn money faster than they could. The reality, of course, was that he was paying new customers with the money from old ones. In the whole life of his company it traded in foreign currency with only $30 of the original $15 million.

But the flood of people who crowded the sidewalks outside his offices, queuing for the chance to invest everything they had, did not know that. It seemed, in the words of one of these hopefuls, that he 'had discovered money itself. He hadn't, of course. He had merely found that if you offer people a big enough return on their money, and wave a few libel writs around, you can postpone the day of reckoning for a long time.

But not indefinitely; for other things were being discovered. Reporters from the *Boston Post* newspaper were discovering his past. 'The Great Ponzi', it turned out, was better known to the authorities in Canada as prisoner no. 5247, the number he bore while jailed for forgery. He had also done time in Atlanta for smuggling aliens. The *Post* ran the story, Ponzi's company duly collapsed, and he went to jail for four years.

Reporting Skills

Investigative reporting can be undertaken by anyone with the determination both to see the job through and to handle all the inevitable frustrations. It requires no greater skills than those demanded by general reporting. But there are a few things that make the job easier and which will make you more efficient at it.

Public Access : What is the law on this in your country? Do you know what public records and documents you are entitled to see% This is vital. Some investigations have resulted from secret documents being passed to journalists, but many more have resulted from reporters discovering that certain records or registers are kept and that they have a right to consult them. Most bureaucracies do not exactly advertise the existence of such information and they erect all kinds of barriers to prevent people consulting them-by making them available only at certain times, or by storing them in out of the way places.

A reporter who once worked with me in London discovered in the small print of a government report the existence of a certain register. It listed all the rights of access to private estates that had been granted in return for the wealthy owners of the estates receiving tax concessions. Neither the officials (because they had given tax concessions) nor the owners (because they did not want members of the public tramping all over their estates) were keen to have this register publicised.

Once the reporter learnt of its existence and established that we had the right to examine it, she went through the lengthy process involved and consulted it. She was then able not only to report what access could be gained to these estates, but also to investigate the deals done between the owners and the government. None of this would have been possible were it not for her finding out about the register in the first place and insisting on seeing it.

This was in Britain, which has a tradition of secrecy about official documents. It is not exactly alone in this, but there are other countries that now have freedom of information laws which have opened up a vast amount of records to citizens. Very few ordinary people will know of these records and even fewer will consult them. All the more reason for journalists to make it their business to know what is kept and what can be seen.

In the United States, the 1966 Freedom of Information Act, strengthened in 1971, has opened up all kinds of documents to journalists. As a result of their use in investigations, all manner of scandals have been uncovered by the press:

- Unreported accidents at nuclear sites.
- X-ray machines at cancer-detection centres which were emitting 25-30 times the correct level of radiation (within months of disclosure, all such centres in the United States had reduced amounts of radiation).
- Anaesthetic drugs routinely given during child birth even though they could - and did - cause brain-damage to babies.

There was also the paper in Louisville, Kentucky which obtained federal inspection reports on nursing homes showing the abuse of residents. As a result, new state legislation was introduced, many homes were closed and the owners of several were charged with fraud.

There are many, other cases that could be cited. They all show the value of journalists discovering what records are kept, examining them and using them in their investigations.

Standard Reference Sources : In all but the most furtive of societies there is much more information available than the average journalist realises. A lot of this can be traced through standard, if not commonly available, reference sources: lists of official publications, reports from legislatures, lists of public bodies, company ownership reference books or registers of bodies receiving government funding. Any reporter intending to carry out investigative work should make it his or her business to know what information such reference sources hold.

The Contacts : All reporters obviously need contacts, but investigative reporters more so. And they need a particular type of contact - not just those who can give them information or point them in the right direction on a specific story, but those who can be useful on a range of stories. People like lawyers, officials in telephone services, car registration centres and those who can give advice on, and access to, official records.

Computer Literacy : This means not just the ability to search effectively online, but also the ability to use database software. Examples of the value of this in investigations now abound. One of the most instructive was that by the Atlanta Journal-Constitution in Georgia, which won a Pulitzer Prize in 1989 for a series analysing racial discrimination in bank lending.

This investigation, by Bill Dedman, repays study; not because its subject has any great global significance, but precisely because it hasn't. It is a piece of local city reporting, although a particularly fine example. It did not bring any governments down, reveal any criminal corruption or save any lives. To someone who is white and living a long way away from the United States, it might appear to be small beer compared to the problems that affect their country. But the Journal-Constitution series is worth looking at for its methods, organisation and attitudes. It is the story of a journalist determined to report a situation into print, rather than wish it there or just repeat the hearsay that was coming his way.

The investigation started with an off-hand remark by a white housing developer. He said he was having trouble building houses in the black areas of South Atlanta because banks would not lend money there (something that would be illegal, if done for discriminatory reasons). He added that he had been told that loans were hard to come by even in affluent black areas. It is the kind of remark that reporters hear every day - general, unsubstantiated and seemingly impossible to prove. But Dedman's curiosity had been aroused. He wanted to see if the charge could be substantiated.

First he talked to some academics who worked in this field, and they told him that banks and savings and loan companies must file to the government the location of every home loan, by amount and census tract. As Dedman later wrote: 'All we at the paper did, to put it simply, was to cross-index the federal computer tapes with a federal census tape, looking especially at comparable black and white neighborhoods.' This was easier said than done. The first three days were devoted entirely to putting spaces between the numbers on the computer so they could be read properly.

For the next five months, Dedman checked loans made by every bank and savings association in Atlanta over a five-year period - a total of 109,000 loans. There was also another study looking at real estate records. But the effort was worth it. Dedman discovered that banks and other institutions were making five times as many loans in white areas as in black areas. By examining bank policies and practices, he also found t hat they were not looking for business in black areas and were otherwise discouraging black borrowers. Blacks, in turn, could only resort to unregulated mortgage companies and loan sharks. As he says, 'Only then did I turn to anecdote.' He collected personal experiences, which gave his series real lives, and showed how the policies of banks affected people.

When he went to the banks, they were predictably reluctant to talk. One replied to Dedman's request for information thus: 'Some of the material you have asked for does not exist. Other parts of the material exist but are confidential. The rest of the material exists and is not confidential but is irrelevant to your subject matter.' It is the unmistakable voice of someone with something to hide. Another bank tried sneakily to combine an appeal to local patriotism with a thinly-disguised plea to the paper's publisher, Jay Smith, to kill the story. He wrote: `I'm sure that Jay Smith would recognize any article alleging racial discrimination by Atlanta financial institutions as another unmerited potshot at our great city...'. And he sent a copy of the letter to Smith.

Finally, when Dedman had enough material for a series (which he would call 'The Color of Money' after the Hollywood film), his editors came into the picture. As Dedman wrote later:

> I think I know the key to the effectiveness of 'The Color of Money'. The editors took out what I thought

> were the good parts. When I wrote that Atlanta's banks were red-lining [a pejorative word for marking off areas to be discriminated against], editor Bill Kovach marked through it. 'Just use the numbers,' he said, 'Let the facts speak for themselves.'

On Sunday 1 May, the series began with a story of several thousand words headlined 'Atlanta Blacks Losing In Home Loans Scramble'. It began:

> Whites receive five times as many home loans from Atlanta's banks and savings and loans as blacks of the same income - and that gap has been widening each year, an Atlanta journal-Constitution study of $6.2 billion in lending shows. Race - not home value or household income - consistently determines the lending patterns of metro Atlanta's largest financial institutions, according to the study, which examined six years of lender reports to the federal government.

The story went on to contain the following: explanation and denial from bankers, details of the survey with further news points (including the fact that the only bank which specialised in lending to blacks had the lowest default rate in the whole country), explanation of the law relating to bank loans, etc. Elsewhere in that day's paper was a story about individual blacks who were well-qualified for a loan but had trouble getting one. The rest of the series was as follows:

- Monday 2 May: Detailed story on bank policies, the history of discrimination by them, plus more case histories including the black Vietnam veteran who was refused a loan which would have cost him $100 a month less than his rent. The article also detailed the process of home purchase and how it related to blacks.
- Tuesday 3 May: Detailed explanation of the law on banking and its regulation and practice over the whole country, plus the history of efforts by black groups to change Atlanta's banks' policies. There were also follow-

up stories which established that discrimination was being practised nationally.

The results of Dedman's series were immediate. Nine days after it ended, Atlanta's nine largest banks began pouring $ 77 million into low interest loans into black areas. Some institutions also went positively into black areas looking for business, hiring black staff, advertising in black media and even taking their executives on a bus tour of the areas. Eleven months after the series was printed, the US Justice Department began investigating 64 Atlanta financial institutions for possible breaches of the discrimination laws.

Investigative Operations : The subjects for investigations come to papers in all kinds of ways: tips from contacts; by accident; a seemingly routine story that subsequent information indicates is far bigger; a reporter's own observations; a run of-the-mill story which escalates bit by bit, or one where every question you ask throws up other, increasingly important, questions.

This was the case with perhaps the most famous journalistic investigation of all - Watergate. It began in June 1972 with a break-in at the Democratic Party's headquarters in the Watergate Building in Washington. It ended just over two years later with the resignation of the most powerful man on earth, President Richard Nixon. The role of the President and his staff in the original burglary and much else besides (phone-taps, slush-funds and, most important of all, the cover-up of these illegal activities) would never been known had it not been for investigative reporters. The two main ones were Carl Bernstein and Bob Woodward of the Washington Post.

When they started working on the story, in a mood of mutual distrust, it was a routine crime story. Five men had been caught breaking into the Democrat's HO to plant a listening device. Woodward went to the courtroom the following day and noticed a prominent lawyer taking great interest in the case. What was he doing there? Woodward also learnt at the court that several of the men had worked for the Central Intelligence Agency. They were also carrying large amounts of cash on them when arrested and two of them had note books, inside one of which was a telephone number for a man who worked at the White House.

From these slender-but promising-beginnings was launched a series of stories that were finally to prove the Nixon administration's complicity in a whole raft of illegal activities. Bernstein and Woodward were feted, wrote a best-selling book and a Hollywood film was made of their investigation. But that was the final outcome. Before that were a thousand frustrations, abuse from Nixon supporters and officials who feared and suspected their reporting, wasted days, weeks and months pursuing false leads, mistakes (some of which got into print), countless hours searching records for that one vital piece of information, self-doubts, criticism and envy of colleagues, and late nights, all nights and weekends of their own time spent on the case.

There are valuable lessons to be learnt from their experiences. Their book, All *The President's Men, is* probably the best detailed description of reporting in the English language. It tells the story of two reporters edging slowly, and not always in a straight line, towards the truth by painstaking research and a healthy obsession with accuracy. The following guidelines on investigative reporting are based on their work, the study of other cases and my own limited experiences.

The moral of every investigation ever mounted is to lay your hands on every document that you can and throw nothing away. You never know when documents, notes, reports - indeed anything you accumulate - will be useful. Months after you acquire that apparently innocuous report, something might give it sudden significance. Bernstein and Woodward, the Watergate reporters, filled four filing cabinets after just a few months.

This is especially important if there is more than one of you working on an investigation or if it is a lengthy one. It pays to swap notes of interviews to see if you have missed something of significance. Typed (and filed) notes are also a lot easier and quicker to consult. This practice also allows executives to participate better in the discussions of the story.

Be Persistent : Read the story of any investigation and the persistence of the reporters is the thing that strikes you. During the Watergate investigation Woodward and Bernstein often spent days going through records, sat at their desks making phone calls all weekend, or waited outside lawyers' offices all day for the chance to see a perhaps vital source. On one occasion they obtained a list of the hundred-or-so people who worked at the Committee to Re-elect the President, the seat of much of the wrong doing. Since they obviously could not visit these people at their offices, they spent many weeks calling on them at their homes after their normal day's work at the paper.

Old Sources

As long as an investigation is in progress, there is no such thing as an 'old source'. People working in the area you are investigating will often remember things they should have told you, receive new information, or are able to make sense of new information you get. Each one of these is reason enough to call them regularly. Woodward and Bernstein each kept a separate master list of phone numbers of contacts. This eventually amounted to several hundred names. They were each called at least twice a week, every week, for well over a year. As they wrote in their subsequent book: 'Just the fact that a certain source would not come to the phone or return calls often signalled something significant.'

Cultivates Sources : During the Watergate investigation, Woodward contacted a man who worked at a senior level in the government to ask him if any word of the wrong-doing had reached him. It had. He knew an enormous amount and clearly regarded it as his duty to assist the exposure of the conspiracy. However, he had the bureaucrat's natural suspicion of the press and was also concerned lest stories based on knowledge only he and few others had was used without confirmation by other sources.

He therefore agreed to help Woodward, but only on certain conditions: he would only guide the reporter in the right direction, anything he told them would have to be corroborated by another source. Meetings between him and Woodward took place in underground car parks, late at night and were only arranged at his behest. Such was the quality of his assistance that Woodward agreed to these conditions.

The source revealed his identity to no one, and an executive at the *Washington Post* christened him 'Deep Throat' after the title of a fashionable pornographic movie which featured a woman whose speciality was oral sex. Deep Throat's identity still remains a mystery to all but Woodward.

It is an opportunity few reporters experience, to know and have the cooperation of such a well-placed source as Deep Throat. But the moral of Woodward's dealings with him is that if such a source sets certain rules, you should stick by them. That does not mean you should accept everything they say; Woodward argued with his contact frequently. But whatever is finally agreed should be adhered to.

Executive Support : The news editor/editor must commit staff and other resources to the project. The editor should be prepared for the project to take a long time and possibly result in no story. Publishing something just because a lot of time has been spent on it is a sure way to have a disaster on your hands. When it is finally printed, the story should be water tight.

The executives and reporters will also have to make a decision early on about whether the investigation will be a series of stories published as they are written, or a 'big hit' operation printed only when all the research is complete. If it is the latter, a deadline should be set. It is easy for investigations to drag on for months, with the reporters always claiming that they need 'just one more week' to finish their research. You should also remember that interim stories can sometimes encourage people to come forward with more, or even the vital piece of, information.

Yet whichever way it is being published, the investigative operation should be closely monitored by an executive. A key part of this role is to ask questions continuously of the reporters about the story. Such executives should act as devil's advocates and also keep going over evidence with reporters. They should be the fresh mind on the case.

Going Undercover : Most of the time there is a better way of collecting information than going undercover. But occasionally, very occasionally, it might be the only way to write the story. Investigating the situation inside some 'closed' world, like a secretive group, organisation or company is the most usual pretext, and there may be others. But the story had better be worth it, because it is very time-consuming and comes with a lot of risks, the least of which is the embarrassment if you are discovered.

The other hazards will take a lot more living down. First, undercover work always involves some deception, so the wrong-doing you are reporting needs to be serious enough to justify that dishonesty. Second, the physical dangers in such a situation can be immense and last long after you have surfaced to write your story. Third, if you are investigating criminal activities undercover you may well be drawn into participating, which makes your actions even harder, if not impossible, to defend.

There is an additional risk when you are investigating an illegal trade and posing as a buyer or seller, in other words as an agent provocateur. Apart from the dubious morality of that, you also become part of the story and so change it. This, to me, means that you have already passed beyond anything recognisable as journalism. The most flagrant case of this was in 1994 when stories began to emerge of weapons-grade plutonium being offered for sale on the German black market. A number of reporters thought they would make a name for themselves by probing this trade. Some posed as sellers, others as buyers with unlimited money. As if this was not bad enough, some journalists working undercover as 'buyers' then ran into others impersonating sellers. None discovered the true identity of the other and so their published stories were not of the 'trade in death' as they claimed, but of two over-enthusiastic journalists fooling each other and themselves.

Yet there are instances of undercover investigations producing memorably good stories. At the end of the nineteenth century, *New* York World reporter Nellie Bly (real name Elizabeth Cochran) feigned insanity to get inside the asylum at Blackwell's Island and wrote a shocking expose. Her findings were later published in her book Ten days in a *Madhouse.* The reward from her publisher, Joseph Pulitzer, was an assignment to beat the round-the-world journey time of 80 days set by the fictitious Phileas Fogg in Jules Verne's novel Around The World In Eighty *Days.* She did it in 72 days 6 hours 11 minutes and 14 seconds.

Less well-rewarded was the editor of the *Pall Mall* Gazette, W.T. Stead. He exposed child prostitution in Victorian London by 'buying' a 13-year old girl from her mother and, under the strictest of supervision, spent enough time alone with her to prove that she could have been put to almost any immoral purpose. His campaign to change the law on child prostitution had the support of many leading figures, including bishops. They, however, could not prevent Stead subsequently being prosecuted. The authorities jailed him for three months on a technicality for buying the girl at the centre of his story. This strange, red-bearded and eccentric man (he sometimes caught mice, fried them and ate them on toast) went down with the Titanic in 1912.

Since then, journalists have gone undercover mainly to expose the treatment - or maltreatment - of various 'victims' of society like the homeless, mentally ill or drug addicts. This involves a degree of acting and perhaps the adoption of disguise. The master of this genre is a German called Gunter Wallraff. His aim is to enter worlds forbidden to a writer. He uses false papers, an invented life-story, new clothes, new spectacles or contact lenses, ways of disguising his hair and teeth. For, as he says, his task is 'to deceive in order not to be deceived'.

He styles himself 'the undesirable journalist' and, as far as his targets are concerned, not without good reason. He has played the part of an informer for the security services and the political police, tested Catholic theology and morality by posing as a man who had been making napalm bombs, led the life of a homeless man in a hostel, an alcoholic in a mental hospital, and impersonated a ministry adviser to find out how armed units are available to German industry for factory protection. As a 'German financier of the extreme Right' he discovered plans for a coup in Portugal, and, as a 'tabloid reporter', worked on and exposed the methods of the mass-market *Bild*.

Scrupulous about notes and records, he tapes everything and photocopies all documents that he wishes to quote. As he says: 'I decided to conspire in order to take a look over the wall of camouflage, denials and lies. The method I adopted was only slightly illegal by comparison with the illegal deceptions and manoeuvers which I unmasked.'

Most of his work is published, not in newspapers, but in magazines, booklets or books. Wallraff's investigations consume a great deal of time, more time, perhaps, than many newspapers would grant a staff reporter. But his results are impressive and his methods worthy of more attention than they get.

Social Service

Andy Knott, a hard-driving six-footer with the energy of a threshing machine, became an investigative reporter of the *Chicago Tribune* soon after his graduation from the University of Tennessee. For three months, he worked undercover as an Emergency Medical Technician for five private ambulance companies in Chicago. Then he wrote a six-part series for the *Tribune* entitled Ambulances—Unsafe at Every Turn," Which disclosed scandalously poor maintenance of may private ambulances and widespread abuse of patients. The result major reforms, made mandatory by new state and city laws and regulations.

Andy Knott's campaign, based on his own investigative reporting under the guidance of the *Tribune* 'editors, is one example of the manner in which public service journalism works in the United States. Others of major importance have been a campaign by the *Charlotte (Nonh* Carolina) *Observer* against brown lung disease," created by the cotton dust that is responsible for the deaths of thousands of textile workers; the *Nashville Tennessean's* crusade against a resurgent Ku Klux Klan, based on undercover work by a reporter who became a Plan member, and the *Philadephia Inquirer's* compaign against the reckless disposal of hazardous-waste chemical products.

There are many others of current interest in which newspapers, both large and small, have taken unpopular positions based on principle and carried out investigations against the angry objections of powerful adversaries. The record shows, as well, that the broadcast medial also are going into the field with signal results, as the popularity of the CBS programme *60 Minutes* demonstrates.

How Campaigns Begin : Many campaigns are quite deliberately planned to meet a long-felt community need. Others develop naturally out of news breaks that point to the probability of dangerous abuses. Often, they come about by accident, as witness the following:

> A woman wrote a letter of protest to the *Detroit News,* touching off its campaign to free four men who had been wrongfully convicted of murder in New Mexico. A congressional secretary confided her woes to a symathetic stranger satd next to her on a bus, who happened to be a *Washington Post* reporter, and who proceeded to break the congressional sex scandals. A photographer in Buffalo happened to take a picture of a city truck unloading supplies at a private contracting job, thus revealing a major municipal scandal that rocked City Hall. A penciled notation on a card, found by a reporter for the *Seattle Times,* resulted in clearing a University of Washington professor of charges of Communist activity. A wrinkeld news paper clipping about an Air Force lieutenant who was losing his

> commission because some of his relatives were left-wing sympathizers led to a great television expose by Edward R. Murrow.

A few campaigns, usually the most exciting of all, are brought about by the reporters themselves who delve into a suspicious situation long before their editors are aware of it and, in effect, commit the paper to a public service campaign. This was the story of the Watergate investigation of the *Washington Post*, brought about by Bob Woodward and Carl Bernstein. It was also the way Andy Knott's campaign began against ambulance dangers in Chicago, although in his case the editors grabbed up his idea quickly and supported it.

The Ambulance Story : Knot had been pitching several investigative ideas at his boss, Bernard Judge, the Chicago editor of the *Tribune,* from the time he joined the staff. Finally, Knott came up with a proposal to look into the private ambulance operation, which had brought a Pulitzer Prize a decade previously to William Jones, then a *Tribune* investigative reporter and now the magazine editor. The plan was to take another close look at a much-criticized service, and both Jones and Judge approved it.

The first thing Knott had to do was to qualify fore certification as an emergency medical technician (EMT). Under Illinois law, this meant more than 100 house of classroom work at a local junior college, three hours of field training and at least 10 hours of work in a hospital emergency room. The reporter completed the course successfully.

Support by the Paper : The most important factor Knott had going for him was the full support of a powerful paper. It meant—win, lose or draw-that he would never be defenseless. If he was hurt, he would be cared for. If he got into legal trouble, he would be defended. There was no advance guarantee that he 'd find anything wrong-the ration of successful investigations to failures is about one in five in the United States-but he knew that a washout wouldn't cripple his carrier. He was just beginning.

Was there personal danger? He didn't know. But he realized that it would be no fan riding a racing ambulance through heavy traffic. There were risks and they were a part of the job.

Under the guidance of William Reckentwald, a senior *Tribune*, investigator who also had worked on the original story, Knott took these additional steps while he was studying to be an EMT:

- Examined ambulance company records in Springfield, the state capital, and learned that the private firms billed the state $2 million a year in the Chicago area.
- Checked into Dun & Broadcaster corporate records.
- Reviewed records of suits in United States Tax Court in Washington Federal court in Chicago and Cook Country Circuit Court.
- Made himself familiar with all state and local laws bearing on private ambulances, emergency vehicles and good Samaritan laws.
- Used his first name, Tom, to put together a background as Tom Knott of Georgia, plus references that weren't checked; obtained a ' 'hard card,'' (chauffeur's license) plus the necessary certification from the Illinois Department of Public Health and the Chicago Board to Health.

Then Knott wrote of his employment;

I got a job at the first place I applied and was working on an ambulance less than a week after I first walked in the door. I stayed there about a week and a half. The company was reputable and we used it as a benchmark to judge other companies.

The second company, where I stayed three weeks, was located on and served the South Side of town. I alternated north, south and west to reduce the risk of running into people from other companies.

Quitting one job and moving to the next was not always accomplished with the greatest of ease. It was easy to get a job, for sure, but it was hard to just up and quit.... The hours were exhausting. Most EMTs in Chicago work 60 hours a week, ten hours a day, six days a week. In all, I worked more than 400 hours. After each day, I would return home and write a long memo on the day's activities. These were painfully detailed memos and added up to more than 250 pages by the time I started writing my six-part series.

It was unusual, to say the least, for so young and relatively inexperienced a reporter to be put on a major assignment of this character. But, in the Woodward Bernstein manner, it all worked. Knott recalled:

> Although I wanted to do this story very much. I was not quite prepared for the loneliness of the task. Because I was considered young and green, my editors were very concerned about my performance. When the investigation began, only five people knew of it. When I went undercover, I just disappeared from the office. My peers at the Tribune knew I was doing an investigation but they didn't know what it was about. I had very few people to talk over my problems and concerns with and, to make matters even tougher, I was under strict orders to limit my social life severely. The editors were afraid of bar talk might get me into trouble.

Writing the Story : It all turned out well. Knott did all his six articles before the series went into print. With all his findings and his background of investigation, this is how he led off his first story.

I'm exhausted after a long, tense day of high-speed ambulance riding through the streets of Chicago.

This day began at 7 a.m. when we finally limp back to the garage 13 hours and two ambulances later, we have no beacon lights, no siren, no power steering, no shock absorbers. The brakes are in terrible shape.

My partner, Bob, who is driving, isn't doing much better. He stopped twice to drink beer today and he says he's "popping" Vellum to keep going.

At one point, I thought I'd be killed. With a beer can in one hand and the other on the wheel, he almost lost control of the ambulance as we wove at high speed down a South Side street.

We were "running hot" at the time — lights flashing and siren blaring — even though it was a non-emergency call, I don't know how last we were going. The speedometer didn't work.

On this day also saw fraud and theft. And I can't forget how we terrifet the lunchtime crowds as we zipped down busy Michigan Avenue on the wrong side of the street.

I'm expecting more of the same tomorrow and I'm not sure how much anger I can take it.

Today was by no means my worst day. What I've described happened again and again in the 500 hours. I worked undercover as a certified emergency medical technician (EMT) or five of the city's private ambulance services.

Many of the ambulances are dangerous. In my three months on the, our service to the sick and injured was rarely efficient or safe.

The poor condition of many ambulances was the most immediate mass fault we discovered. The Chicago Board of Health is required to inspect them annually.

But so many elements of ambulance service are bad that it' is hard to say what is the "worst." The problems, which will be examined in detail in subsequent articles, include the following.

Vehicle Condition : Tires werebaid. Brakes were mushy. Safety lights and signals didn't work.

Some ambulances had structural damage or body corrosion. Rain leaked through the roof; road prime came through holes in the floor.

One ambulance I worked in caught fire from a short circuit in the writing while we were carrying a patient. Another fish-tailed and nearly rolled over because its shock absorbers were shot. Another had 3 to 4 inches of play in the steering wheel, making accurate steering difficult.

Patient Care : Patients in private ambulances were cursed, threatened and subjected to rough treatment. A mental patient was allowed to wander unattended. Another had bronchial trouble but was subjected to an EMTs cigarette smoke.

Worst of all was the time when we were transferring an ill man from a hospital to a nursing home and an EMT told me "if his heart arrests, don't do anything. Let him die if his heart stops in the ambulance, just don't tell me."

Equipment Condition : Ambulances I worked in were usually short of bandages, sterile water to cleanse wounds, gauze, oxygen, splints and neck braces. One didn't have any first rate linen.

Soiled linen was used repeatedly. Some ambulances did not carry fire extinguishers or oxygen tanks, both required by the city, or spare tires.

It took an extra 30 minutes to get a woman with a ruptured stomach lining to a hospital because we didn't have a stair chair to get her down a narrow stairway.

Running Hot : Private ambulances consistently run hot, with lights and sirens going, when there is no emergency. On runs I made, it might have been necessary only one time of every five times we did it. At other times, lives were needlessly endangered.

The practice resulted in the death of a 19 year old EMT in September after' dipnoan stubbornly two weeks. The ambulance he was riding in and a car collided at a Park Ridge intersection and the ambulance rolled over. Police said the ambulance was running hot on a non-emergency call.

EMT Attitudes : Most EMTs in Chicago are underpaid, ($3.50an hour is typical) or they work on a piecework basis, which forces them into a frantic pace. The quality of care suffers as EMTs, brutalized by the system, transfer their frustrations to patients.

Though I saw some good EMTs at work, too many were inept. One didn't even know how to take blood pressure readings.

Nothing in my training fully prepared me for what I saw....

Results : Once the Tribune's series ended, changes were swiftly instituted. Governor James R. Thompson signed a bill into law in September 1981, making it mandatory for every ambulance in the state-public and private—to undergo inspection twice year. The Chicago City Council at the same time moved to righting local inspection and regulation laws affecting private and public ambulances. EMT training also was required of ambulance company dispatchers.

The campaign was a classic instance of cooperative effort between a young reporter, directed by knowledgeable editors, and public authorities who acted decisively as soon as the results of a newspaper investigation were brought to their attention.

Investigation of Local Industry : It requires courage, clout and a lot of money to take on a dominant industry, on which the prosperity of a whole region of the country depends. This is what the *Charlotte Observer Aid* when it investigated the incidence of byssinosis, or brown lung, the disease caused by inhalation of cotton dust.

The Observer was well aware at the outset that the powerful textile industry, largest in the Carolinas would fight its inquiry and its findings. But more than 391,500 Carolinians work in the textile industry, one third of them in plants that process cotton. At the time the series was published, 18,000 Carolina workers had been disabled by cotton dust, but only some 320 had received compensation.

This was a typical reaction from one of the leaders of the $ 17 billion industry, W.B. Pitts, president of Hermitage, Inc., who wrote:

> How shameful it is for the Knight family and its organ, the Observer, to take the side of OSHA and the oppressive bureaucrats against the magnificent Southern textile industry. It is sickening to see the gutless minions of the news media siding with a few crying baby Americans who obviously are looking for a handout from the very hand that fedand clothed their families.

Taking the Public's Side **:** Nevertheless, the Observer continued its long inquiry, in which 15 members of its staff participated, and blasted open its campaign against brown lung disease. This is the lead on a summary of the 22 articles. It was written by a staffer, Bob Dragon, who then was 27 and had only been on the paper for three years.

Cotton dust is a killer in Carolina mills.

Already 18,000 Carolina workers are disabled by byssinosis, or brown lung, the lung disease cotton dust causes. Only about 320 have received compensation.

Now six years after the officials oredered mills to clean up, about 115,000 of the Carolinas' 391,500 textile workers remain exposed to dust in cotton mills. Health officials say at least 10,000 North Carolinians still work in dust levels that can kill.

It is a case of deadly neglect.

According to the last week's Observer series on brown lung in the Carolinas:

- At least five textile companies didn't tell some workers they had been diagnosed with brown lung.
- Companies have contested 80% of the 936 North Carolina brown lung compensation claims and virtually all of about 200 South Carillon claims.
- Both industrial commissions have ignored state laws

requiring companies to report on workers diagnosed with occupational diseases such as byssinosis. The North Carolina Commission has violated it own rules by approving company written agreements in which workers forfeited all future claims.

- The commissions have approved compensation in only about 320 of 1,136 claims filed. Settlements often didn't cover lost wages and medical expenses. Some workers died waiting for compensation.
- Some doctors who advise the commissions on brown lung cases also see patients for textile companies; one former South Carolina medical panel member was a consultant for two textile firms...

The End of a Campaign : Editor Richard A. Oppel recalled that within less than a year after the series ran, North Carolina textile workers had received $4 million in compensation for byssinosis, more than had been paid out in the previous nine years. And one mill worker in South Carolina, disabled by brown lung, was awarded $86,000 compensation.

Commission files in both states were opened to the public in response to the Observer's editorial pressure. The North Carolina Labour Commission increased its inspection staff by 11 people and the state's Industrial Commission put on three additional deputies to speed up compensation decisions.

The campaign won for the Observer the Pulitzer Prize gold medal for meritorious public service. The jurors called it an example "of how a newspaper can effectively and dramatically use its editorial resources to expose and draw public attention to an important and previously ignored problem — in this case a disease that disables and kills thousands of workers."

Exposing the Ku Klux Klan : J.W. Thompson, a career Army man who took early disability retirement as a sergeant and earned his living as a cabinet-maker, was a member of the Ku Klux Klan for a year. When he quit, he resumed his true identity, Jerry Thompson, an investigative reporter, and wrote a series of articles on his experiences for his newspaper, the *Nashville Tennessean.*

It was a courageous thing to do. As John Seigenthaler, publisher of the *Tennessean,* wrote some months after the Thompson series was published, "Jerry Thompson always was in danger of discovery and lives today under police protection."

Inside the Klan : This was how Thompson wrote the lead for his Klan series.

The Ku Klux Klan today holds a strange, disturbing attraction for frustrated, fearful middle-income men and women—and a dangerous potential for violence and terror.

I know. For the last year, I have been a Clansman. I have worn the white robe and hood. I have twice taken the oath pledging my life to the Klan. I have twice been "naturalized" into separate Klan empires. I have paid my Clan initiation fees and my Clan dues.

I have fired Clan crosses, collected contributions at Clan roadblokcs, marched in Clan street demonstrations and helped disrupt public order at a public meeting with shouts in a Clan chorus. I have attended KKK den meetings where men armed with pistols and automatic rifles mounted their routine racist rhetoric: "The niggers and the Jews are ruining the country."

Clad in Clan garments, I have picketed the President of the United States, demonstrated against a TV station showing a documentary about the KKK, and been jeered by black citizens. And I have concealed the pistol of an unrepaid fellow Klansman beneath my flowing robes when he thrust it at me as a policeman approached.

Through it all I was acting out a role-working as an investigative reporter for the Tennessean, striving to discover just how dangerous the Clan is, endeavouring to penetrate the secrecy veil that has obsured much of the Clan's life since its founding in Pulaski, Tenn., more than a century ago...

The Findings : These were Thompson's conclusions buttressed by an independent outside investigation by other *Tennessean* reporters and a photographer:

1. The Clan must be disarmed. Many Klansmen routinely carry guns on their public marches and demonstrations. State and federal laws need to be strengthened so that police can deal with this growing threat of violence.
2. The Invisible Emprie of the Ku Klux Clan, headed by Bill Wilkinson of Denham Springs, La., grows more dangerous each day, with a paramilitary training camp near Cullman. This militant faction of the Klan, of which I am a member, bears close scrutiny by the authorities. The Justice Department agrees and has asked federal agencies to cooperate in an effort to combat the danger of violence posed by Low-tension's group.
3. The rival Clan faction, of which I am also a member, the Knights of the Ku Klux Clan, headed by Don Black of Birmingham, is less militant because it is losing members. Still, its wizard, Black, is vehemently anti-Semitic and equally hostile to blacks. A Texas branch of this Clan also operates a paramilitary training team.

Unhappily, despite the expose, very little has been done either to disarm the Clan, close its training camps or reduce the threat of violence. But the *Tennessean* and Seigenthaler, its publisher, have never regretted going into the investigation. Nor has Thompson been sorry that he gave a year of his life to the inquiry.

A TV Investigation : Because television is a visual medium and TV reporters work under severe limitations of time, the investigative job for TV has to be done differently. A two-part series on space weaponry by David Handyman, which was broadcast on successive nights on *The CBS Evening News with Dan Rather,* illustrates the essential points of difference.

Beginning an Investigation : As was the case with Andy Knot's investigation of ambulances for the *Chicago Tribune,* David

Handyman developed the idea for his CBS investigation. He wrote:

This series grew out of some reading I'd been doing on this subject as much as a year before. At the time of the launch of the first space shuttle, I became further intrigued with the uses of military shuttles that were to follow, all of which were shrouded in the deepest secrecy. Looking into the uses of the military space shuttles led me to the much broader question of the nature and use of space weaponry.

CBS Evening News liked the idea and Alan Weisman was assigned as producer.

Investigating a Top-Secret Subject Andelman went on: We began by extensive phone work while a researcher dug up everything published on this subject over the past couple of years (much of which turned out to be somewhat unreliable). In the course of our phoning, we realized that the issue was extremely broad, but potentially far more serious than we had thought. Weapons decisions taken quietly today appeared likely to be nearly irreversible, committing the U.S. and by corollary the Soviet Union to MX-type missile programmes perhaps 10 years down the pike.

We decided, therefore, to outline a three-part series (this way ultimately reduced to two parts), then sat down to figure out whom we should talk within camera (of 25-30 people we had consulted by phone or in person). We settled on six key interviews. I took off across the country to do them (two were in Washington, three in California, one in Boston). Weisman began to work up a series of graphics that were, after all, the heart of the piece, and he rounded up obscure footage of some of these weapon prototypes in action.

I shipped back the interviews as they were done, Weisman transcribed them, looking for the best " sound-bites." By the time I had returned to New York, he had already sketched out an outline of the two parts (where the sound would go, the graphics, etc.) we began work on the detailed scripts. We had been consulting by phone in the evenings after each interview.

The scripts must have go through five or six drafts, each draft being pared down (with 22 minutes in the *CBS Evening News*, our early drafts would have eaten up a third of each show) We then spent a day doing the very complex on camera bridges (shot with two cameras in the main control room of the *Evening News*—we used it as "set," the computer graphic animations we had prepared rolling on the main monitor behind me as I began talking).

Both pieces were finally screened for the executives of the *CBS Evening News* and Dan Rather, too. Dan made some very useful suggestions on where both pieces could be trimmed, there were some negotiations back and forth, and finally both pieces ran on consecutive evenings.

Broadcasting the Investigation : The first of the two Handyman pieces on space weaponry was in effect a primer on space weapons, what they are, how they may be used. The "lightning bolt"—a laser beam of intense light—was one of the potential weapons included, but there were others just as exotic. The principle, however, was to introduce the millions of viewers of the *CBS Evening News to* a complex subject that was going to cost tax-payers a lot of money—much more than most of them realized.

Here is the audio part of the second piece, with the graphics and other illustrations in the video part of the script omitted:

Rather : Speaking of missiles, the Defense Department has just sent Congress its so - called" definitative report" about research into direct-energy weapons, particularly laser weapons. The report is classified, but sources tell CBS News it recommends increased funding to determine just how effective lasers could be against a variety of targets. As David Handyman reports in Part Two of his investigation into the movement toward militarization of outer space, firing lightening bolts through the atmosphere is an idea whose time is coming — rapidly.

David Andelman : Since the early 1960s, the United States has been developing lasers for use by the military. Prototypes have destroyed revolving targets, and airborne targets, and have even been installed in planes for air-to-air combat. But using a laser to fire at a target in space presents some different problems. A land-based laser firing at an orbiting satellite would need huge power and clear skies to hit its target. Without sufficient energy and the large mirrors needed for aiming, the beam would disperse as it passes through the clouds and end up too weak to effect the target. But a laser in space with enough power and precise aiming could conceivably hit a Soviet ICBM as the ascending missile broke through the clouds.

Ffobert Fossum (Defense Research Project Agency): Specifically, we would have in orbit a sequence of lower-altitude battle stations, say on the order of 20, or that order of magnitude number of battle stations. At any one time, several of these would be within visible range and laser-weapon range of a mass attack. A target assignment would be given. One must then acquire on the battle station that particular target, then track the target because both the target and the battle station are moving.

The laser would not fire at the missile's warhead. The beam would lock on to the second stage, the booster, bathing it with intense light, heating it during the ascent and before the warhead has a chance to arm itself.

Senator Malcolm Wallop (R-Wyoming): I honestly believe, from what I`have seen with my own eyes, that we could put together and orbit this prototype satellite within the next four to five years.

Andelman : But the skeptics abound. They say the idea is far more costly than supporters think, that conventional weapons could to the job just as well, and that the Russians could simply harden their missiles or trick the lasers into firing at the wrong targets.

Wolf Gang Ponofsky (Stanford Research Labouratory): You can deploy deceptive screens and alternate targets which fool the sensors and/or serosol sprays which hit the target. You can do all sorts of things with very little weight.

Andelman : Nevertheless, companies like TRW, Rocketdyne, Hughes and United Technologies are hard at work perfecting the mirror' as tracking system and energy sources for the battle stations. Funding for laser technology now runs about $200 million a year. But the Defense Department, in a top-secret report to Congress, is now requesting an additional $250 million over the next five years.

The Soviets too are spending a lot of time and a lot of money developing directed-energy weapons. But there is no hard evidence that they are any closer to an operational system than the United States. And as research of all sorts continues, so does the crucial question: is the dawn of space weaponry the end of the old arms race or merely the beginning of a new one?

Fossum : We have avoided for various policy and national reasons the idea that we should go to space with weapons systems. It is almost investible in my mind that we will have to consider going to space with weapon systems at some time in the not-too-distant future.

William Parry (Former Indersecretary of Defense): I think it would be an extremely desirable objective for the United States to try to nip this space war in the bud, to stop it before it starts. It is still early enough to do that. Now, four or five years from now the opportunity to stop it may be gone. That is, the advances made by both nations by then maybe so great that it is a clock whose hands cannot be turned back any longer.

Andelman : We're really at a crossroads right now.

Perry : I think we are.

Andelman : In accepting the Albert Einstein Peace Prize recently, George Kennan, one time U.S. ambassador to Moscow, remarked that the arms race had reached such grotesque dimensions as to defy rational understanding. The Soviets and the United States, he added, are like victims of some sort of hypnosis, men in a dream, like lemmings headed for the sea. And perhaps he might have added out into space.

The Mirage Bar Story : The investigative art is by no means confined to men, although they are usually given the fattest assignments and the most prominent roles. The great exception is Am Zekman, the Chicago Sun Times's crack investigative reporter, who has run a dozen major inquires with dramatic results. She was the proprietor of the Mirage Bar, which was run by Sun Times reporters to prove that thieves sell stolen goods with impunity. She accumulated the evidence and brought about major reforms in the city's penal system. Although it is taken for granted that reporters will adopt disguises for good reason to obtain necessary results, always with the consent of their paper, the Mirage Bar story didn't with a Pulitzer Prize because some of the board members thought it was "too deceptive."

This raises the issue in journalism of where righteousness ends, in adopting a disguise, and where unethical deception begins. It always has to be decided on a case by case basis by the news organization involved, and there are no set rules by which to judge such a moral issue. In the Mirage Bar case, however, Zekman certainly lost no prestige, in fact, she and here colleagues did win a number of prize and industry wide accolades.

Other women who have done first rate work on investigations, and who have shared Pulitzer Prizes include Ann de Saints of the Boston Globe, Lucent Franks of UP and Mortua JJ. Pulliam of the Indianapolis Star. The evidence is abundant, regardless of disguises, that women investigators do their jobs with as much skill and spirit as men.

Boles Case : The case of Don Boles of the Arizona Republic should serve as a constant reminder to all journalists both of the dedication and the courage that are required of investigative reporters who venture into dangerous situations. The reaction to his murder in downtown Phoenix, while he was on the track of gangland connections with official Arizona, should also serve as an inspiration.

After Boles was killed, 36 reporters and editors from different news organizations came to Arizona and many of them spent up to six months in the state, under the leadership of Bob Greene of *Newsday,* to try to finish the work that the Arizonan had begun. It was a unique cooperative effort, financed in part by most of the 20 news organizations that were represented, to show that no investigative reporter could be harassed or slain without inviting the most serious consequences.

The series of articles produced by the Investigative Reporters and Editors Inc., as the group called its life-was published and broadcast in whole or in part by a number of the participating organizations, but not in Boles's own paper. The charges of links between business and politics and organized crime in Arizona, in a number of instances, bore out allegations that he had first made.

Campaign Objectives : It used to be said that the primary objective of most campaigns was to put wrong dores in jail and get innocent persons out of jail. These, naturally, are the most spectacular results of campaigning. But there are many others, as this discussion has made abundantly clear. It sometimes happens that without any dickered intent, a major public service is performed because a news organization and its staff do their work of informing the public under extreme difficulties and in superlative fashion. This often occurs in the coverage of natural disasters or civil disorders. It results occasionally when reporter, out of sheer conviction, risks life and limit get story that can be obtained in no other way.

In some campaigns, the news stories are quite factual and restrained in tone but the alarm is sounded on the editorial page with thunderous emphasis. This was the case in the successful effort of the *Winston-Salem* (North Carolina) *Journal* and *Sentinel* to prevent strip miners from tearing apart the beautiful hill country of northwest North Carolina. One of the major editorials took this approach:

> The rolling hills and valleys in northwest North Carolina are among the most beautiful anywhere. But the land in She, Allegheny, Likes an Sorry counties

> won't be beautiful much longer if strip-mining gets a foothold in the area.
>
> Strip-mining might get that foothold if landowners and concerned citizens in the north-west aren't careful. The Gabbiest Corporation of America, which has obtained options on thousands of acres in the north-west and in south-west Virginia, is conducting studies to see if gibbosity — a mineral found in the area—can be extracted easily and cheaply from the soil for use in producing aluminum. If the studies prove that strip mining would be profitable, Gibbosity apparently will exercise its options...
>
> One weapon against an unwelcome intruder is a public outcry. Such a protest helped Orange County keep Texas Gibbosity think twice.

If the people of the northwest should allow strip-mining to get a substantial foothold and if large parts of that scenic country side become a virtual wasteland in a decade or so, they will have nobody to blame but themselves.

The point cannot be overemphasized. If a campaign is to mean anything, it must be undertaken with vigor and supported by the resources of the entire newspaper—from Page 1 to editorial, from pictures to cartoons.

This is something that few broadcasters have learned to date in their laudable efforts to emulate the crusading press; it is one thing to do an effective documentary, it is quite another to arouse the public without the editorial intervention of the management itself.

Does Campaigning Pay? : There have been few campaigns of consequence that have added substantially to the circulation of newspaper becomes as wealthy almost overnight as Woodward and Bernstein.

The record shows depressing instances in which campaigners for worthy causes in the press and broadcast media have lost circulation and advertising, become the targets for boycotts and even lost their jobs. The expose is not the royal road to success, by any means.

The *Arkansas Gazette* paid for its championship of school integration in Little Rock with heavy monetary losses and the eventual resignation of its editor, Harry Ashmore. Several newspapers that ran campaigns against unscrupulous used car dealers lost automobile advertising. And in a classic case, the *Wall Street Journal Post* its General Motors advertising because it published information about new models before the auto giant was ready; however, GMJ soon came back into the paper.

One discouraged small-city editor, who tried and failed with a perfectly good campaign, even thought of giving up crusading altogether because it was so little appreciated. And J. Montgomery Curtsy, while director of the American Press Institute, once came across and old Marine editor who refused point-blank to have anything to do with a campaign to improve his community, saying "Son the down town hint worth it."

True, crusading isn't easy. Nor can anything of consequence in a community be accomplished quickly or cheaply merely by viewing with alarm. Most campaigns are won simply by hard, consistent work, backed by a determined editor and publisher. Such was the case in the *Louisville Courier-Journal's* drive to tighten Kentucky's laws against strip-mining, which took four years before the Kentucky legislature finally passed what was then called "the toughest strip-mining legislature in America." More often than not, even a modest crusade takes a good deal longer than either editors or reporters anticipate at the outset.

The issue is not whether crusading journalism pays but whether it is necessary. The answer must be overwhelmingly yes.

Future Prospects

If anything at all is certain about the concluding years of the 20th century and the opening of the twenty first, it is that American society will undergo drastic changes and journalism will have to reflect them. In no sense can it be said that social and economic pressures on this nation are likely to decrease; the outlook is quite the opposite. Even such necessary and long-delayed political reforms as government consolidation, an equitable taxing system and the elimination of towering injustices in the treatment of the sick and the needy, helpless children and the elderly may have a chance of success.

The nation will have need of a more efficient and broadened system for the dissemination of news, ideas and opinions. What we are seeing today in the adaptation of newspapers and wire services to the computer age and the development of the electronic media is only the beginning of the changes that are ahead for journalism. It is useless to speculate on whether there will be giant screens for TV across our living room walls, instant production of newspapers in the basement whenever we want them or production of voluminous statistics from distant data banks at the touch of a finger. The genius of science, interacting with the laws of supply and demand, will determine how much instant journalism we can live, what form it will take and how much we can actually absorb.

There are several things that are more important to the journalist than research and development, much as they are needed in a profession that has been backward for too long in such matters. The first and greatest of these is the continued protection of the freedoms guaranteed in the First Amendment, which are under increasing challenge in times of social change and worldwide political upheaval. For without a free press, the journalist becomes a mouthpiece for government, a lackey of the powerful, a robot who performs mindless duties in a graceless style.

While it is a temporary relief to have the United States Supreme Court strike down judicial gag orders and other prior restraints on publication, no journalist can feel secure if reporters sit in jail in violation of judicial orders to disclose their sources to the authorities and act, in fact, as servants of the government. It is a disturbing, even a threatening trend.

Second only to the perpetuation of the rights of a free press is a reconsideration of the substance of journalism. And that bears upon the preparation and the beliefs of those who are intimately concerned with the identification, gathering, distribution and presentation of the news. Because, whatever definition may be offered, news actually tends to be what the journalist says it is. And the current definition of what the journalist treats as news is simply not good enough. Television and radio will have to be something more than glorified bulletin boards; newspapers; wire services and newsmagazines will be obliged to shape their reports to a greater extent towards areas that more deeply affect the public interest.

Finally, journalism must stand for something if it is to continue to be respected in a democratic society and given constitutional protection, it is enough to be the harbinger of bad tidings; in primitive societies, such messengers were killed and journalists, in modern times, have frequently felt the sting of public animus merely because they did their duty. No less than the holding of public office, the difficult task of informing the public is a trust. It is therefore inevitable that the concept of journalism as a public service is bound to increase in strength. Today, it is a trend. Tomorrow, it will be a necessity.

Important Salient Features of Campaigning and Investigative Reporting

1. Campaigns must have the wholehearted support of the news organization-newspaper or magazine or broadcasting station—or reporters will find themselves helpless to continue. Even though one reporter may be the main investigator, the whole organization must give the inquiry of its backing. And if legal trouble results, the reporter must have a proper defense, supported by the management.

2. Campaigns based on the premise that the press is the watchdog over the public's business should show results. If there is a need for an inquiry, however, it should be undertaken whether there is any advance guarantee of results or not.
3. It is manifestly true that not every campaign or investigation that is undertaken will pay off in a dramatic way. The radio of success to failure is about one in five in the United States.
4. Reporters undertaking investigations of crime or suspicious organizations are always in personal danger and they and their editors must realize it. Don Boles of the *Arizona Republic* was murdered during his crime inquiry. Terry Thompson of the *Nashville Tennessean* remained under police guard for a long time after he became a Clan member for a year and then wrote an expose.
5. TV investigations, because of the visual nature of the medium, usually take a lot longer to complete than newspaper inquiries. On network TV, with the exception of special programmes like *60 Minutes,* the time allowed for national coverage is relatively modest. TV reporters usually have to do a much tighter job of writing than their colleagues in print.
6. The substance of many an investigation is based on examinations of public documents such as land sales, tax records and court actions. The objective, in examining such data, is to determine first of all if there is a *pattern* of suspicious circumstances that might indicate wrongdoing. If the pattern exists, it should be followed up with a detailed inquiry.
7. A campaign or an investigative report should be written in a cairn, restrained manner. This is not the place for type. The lead ought to indicate broadly the nature of the inquiry and the principal results, the reason the

investigation was undertaken, the length of the inquiry and the participants.

8. Whether campaigns are undertaken in the public or private sector, they ought to be so fashioned and so directed as to serve the public interest. In most investigations, both news organizations and reporters will find it to their benefit to work with prosecuting authorities. Except when the prosecutor's office itself is involved in an investigation, it seldom helps to fight the people who will eventually have to decide whether sufficient evidence exists for criminal charges.

13

News of Budget

It is a major duty of newspapers at the local level to maintain a continual scrutiny of the cost of running our cities and states. At the federal level, there are watchdogs a plenty.

But locally, newspapers alone — with very few exceptions — have the staff and the funds to cover local government in all its aspects on a day-to-day basis. Moreover, a complicated budget for a town, city or country, or a school or other political sub-division, cannot be analyzed for worried citizens in 30 to 45 seconds of TV time. It also takes a bit longer than that, and a lot more space and reportorial time, to explain the reasons for budget deficits and projected tax increases.

Story of Budget

The story of budgets and taxes is at the very root of the reporting of local government. The excuse that such accounts are likely to be dull doesn't wash any longer. What happened when New York city faced bankruptcy turned out to be a cliff hanger that produced excitement in this country and abroad. For if the city had defaulted on its bonds and other obligations, financial institutions and individual bondholders would have lost billions of dollars and the credit of the entire state of New York could have gone down the drain as well.

Outline of the Assignment : Nothing is more important to the cause of democratic self-government than a public presentation of the costs of government and the tax proposals through which officials seek to raise the funds to meet those costs. What the public wants to know, and what reporters must establish right off when a new budget proposal is presented, is whether it will be necessary to increase taxes and, if so, what kind and how much.

Without this kind of information, the public is left in the dark and it is possible for unscrupulous or incompetent office holders to play all kinds of tricks with public funds. To be sure, reporters with a good background in standard accounting practices and a knowledge of computer operations can dig into a government budget presentation at the local level and sometimes they can come up with some unpleasant truths that make headlines. But budget reporting, as a rule, isn't all that heroic. It involves a lot of painstaking, step by step journalistic routine and conferences with responsible municipal officials.

Every budget story must be told with regard for detail. In outline, this is the way the story generally develops.

- The total amount to be spent over the next fiscal very (usually from July 1 to June 30).
- The amount of increase or decrease over the preceding year.
- If there is an increase, the ways in which the city will raise the money.

1. New taxes, and if so, what kind and how much.
2. Increased taxes now on the books, particularly for property and business levies, and how much of each.
3. Increases in fees and license charges.
4. Economics such as staff reductions, and how many and how much is to be saved, elimination of services, exactly

which ones and the costs involved, and revision of employee benefits and perquisites;

5. New bond issues, and if so, how much and what will the interest charges be.

- Pay increases or decreases for employees, new hiring, if any.

- The largest departmental expenditures in the budget, with each one listed, and the exact amount by which each is to be increased or decreased. Generally, this involves the police and fire departments and the sanitation services, transportation and street repair and, where the city makes a large contribution of its own, schools and welfare services.

- Statements about the budget by the mayor and/or city manager and budget director and from the political opposition on the City Council or other legislative body.

- Explanation of the debt service item. This is always large sum in most city budgets. It consists of the interest charges that the city must pay to bankers and private individuals who buy city bonds, which are issued in order to raise money for specific projects or to meet various types of deficits. The debt service should be reported as an increase or decrease over the previous year and the story should give the latest charges of interest on the newest city obligations.

Making Tax Estimates : Sometimes, for understandable reasons, public officials are not willing to admit that their spending plans are going to cost the public more money in the form of higher taxes. It then becomes the responsibility of the reporter to determine how much of a tax increase is likely and what areas it will affect, usually property taxes and general business taxes.

Where there are private citizens' budget organizations, their executive directors always are a big help in such situations and generally they permit direct quotation. Failing that, tax estimates may often be obtained from the political opposition but they are likely to be suspect. If reporters try to make a forecast of their own, however, they are on shaky ground because too many variables are involved.

Types of Budgets : The budget outlined here is called an operating or expense budget, which is financed mainly by property and business taxes, fines, licenses, permits and service charges, revenue sharing from state and federal governments and miscellaneous sources.

Some cities also have capital budgets, separate accounts for capital expenditures on new projects such as bridges, roads, buildings and so on that are financed by bonds or other forms of city indebtedness outside the general expense budget.

A more recent innovation is the performance budget, which accompanies the operating budget and explains, generally on a line by line basis, exactly how and why the money is being spent and what the duties of the departments or officials involved may be.

Local Government and Budgets : The two principal types of local government consist of the following.

Major-City Council : This is the most familiar type of local governmental authority. The mayor is responsible for drafting the budget and submitting it to the Council, which then has the authority to make changes, but must finally adopt it before the beginning of the next fiscal year. Very often, the mayor has the services of a senior official who may be termed a city manager or a chief operating officer. In large cities, the office of the comptroller is of great importance in the budgetary process.

City Commission-City Manager : In this type of government, a number of elected commissioners, say five or seven, choose one of their number to be the mayor and also elect a vice-mayor, but the entire commission has the over-riding authority on any specific issue, such as the budget. The commission delegates the day-to-day operation of the city to a professional manager. In a variation of this system, the City Council is the elected body and hires the manager, and that official runs the city, prepares the budget and calculates the amount of taxes that will be needed.

Whatever the system, some single person—either a mayor or a city manager or a budget director — must take the responsibility for making up a budget and presenting it for adoption. This is not just an overnight job but requires literally months of consultation and negotiation between the budget makers and departmental heads on the one hand and affected city groups, such as property owners and business executives and unions, on the other.

Making up an Operating Budget : An operating budget, the most common and necessary type of financial document, consists of two parts (1) proposed revenues and (2) proposed appropriations. Generally, income matches outgo, and that is called a balanced budget. Many city governments operate under laws requiring them to work only under balanced budgets.

Sources of Revenue : The principal source of revenue for most city governments is the property tax. This is expressed in a unit called a mill levy, a mill being 1/10 of 1 cent. In theory, the property tax rate is expressed as a certain number of mills for each dollar of the assessed valuation of a property: in reality, this is multiplied by 100 and it becomes a certain number of dollars for each $100 of the assessed valuation of a property. Suppose a city's property is valued at 200 million, and $ 15 million is calculated to be the amount to be raised by property taxes. Dividing $ 15 million by $200 million makes the mill levy $075 for each $1 of assessed valuation. Multiplying both by 100 makes the rate $7.50 for each $100 of assessed valuation. Thus, on a $50,000 house, the tax would be a whopping $3,750. That is a very high tax rate for residential property in a small to medium size city. Other sources of revenue include business taxes, fines, licenses, permits, charges for services, revenues from other governments such as a share in state sales taxes and revenue sharing from the federal government, and miscellaneous areas of income.

Appropriations : In most city governments, the largest sums are appropriated for the police and fire departments, sanitation and debt service. Recreation, engineering, administration and community development costs are in the second rank of departmental fund totals. Schools, a major item, usually are run on joint contributions from state and country governments as well as local revenues. Among other departmental costs are finance, law, public relations, parks, libraries, community services and various non-departmental functions. Welfare, one of the greatest costs in most governments, usually is carried in large part by the state and federal governments, with minimal contributions from cities. The great exception to that rule is New York City, where, for political reasons, the city has been saddled with the bulk of the cost of sustaining more than a million people on the public assistance rolls.

Coverage of Budget

Budget stories range in total sums for a small community to the billions of dollars. These accounts are usually simply told and care is taken to explain any complications that may arise. This is the beginning of a budget story in the *Vineyard Gazette.* Edgartown, on Maratha's Vineyard, as written by Andrew J. Shanley.

The country advisory board took from the Dukes County news and information bureau and gave to Community Services and the country jail as the board met this week to set its preliminary country budget for the next fiscal year.

This is the first year the board has had final say over the budget and the session Tuesday afternoon showed tension between the board and the country commissioners.

The commissioners had proposed a $42,000 budget for the information bureau. The advisory board cut $ 10,000 eliminating a part time position and money for printing and rent.

The board gave Programmes on Alcohol $5,000 and Visiting Nurses $1,000 more than had been allotted by the commissioners. They also increased the jail budget by $7,000 for a part-time jailer even after the commissioners had included money for one additional jailer.

To balance the budget, the board took $3,000 from the airport budget. The bottom lines assessment figure to the Island towns is $606,3 57 in both the board's and commissioners' budget, which represents level funding for the year ahead.

The board will hold a public hearing on the budget Jan. 21.

Ken McLaughlin, City Hall reporter for the Wastonville (California) Register Pajaronian, took a different tack in describing a final City Council budget session for that city.

After six years on the City Hail beat, my philosophy is to keep budget stories as short as possible and to use as few numbers as possible always make an extra effort with budget stories to add humour and describe the interaction of personalities. In addition, I always try to talk the city editor into running a graphic of a "pie" with budget stories. This is probably the best way to show the people how their money is being spent, which, after all, is really the only reason we report what goes on at these sessions.

A Typical City Budget Operation : The annual budget of Knoxville, Tennessee, which is reasonably typical of most cities of its size in this country, ran around $60 million in the early 1980s and was prepared by Lewis. A Gorham Jr., the director of the Office of Management and Budget, for Mayor Randy Tyree and the Knoxville City Council. Under local law, it had to be in balance.

Situation of the City : At a time when recession had hit hard at the large industrial cities of the north, Knoxville regarded itself as being fortunate. As the home of the University of Tennessee and the Tennessee Valley Authority, its employment record was better than most and it was in a fairly stable position. Moreover, although it was a city of modest size, with 185,000 population, it sponsored a World's Fair in 1982 on a 70 acre site beside the winding Tennessee River and attracted millions of visitors. As an additional boost to its bid for tourism, it continued to be the gateway to the lofty wooded vastness of the Great Smokies National Park.

Analyzing the Budget : The operating budget drafted for the World's Fair year, fiscal 1982, ran to 601 pages and the performance budget, which explained the functions of the various parts of the city government and its beneficiaries, totaled 290 pages. Budget director Gorham gave this advice to reporters who received the two bulky volumes— advice that applies to the analysis of most budgets.

The first thing any reporter should do on receiving a proposed budget is to look at the summary, up front, of income and outgo, the anticipated revenue and the proposed appropriations, and then read the mayor's accompanying message. This is the big picture—the extent of the tiry'scommitments the measures that will have to be taken to bring the budget into balance and the basic decisions on whether taxes will or will not be raised and whether the work force will have to be reduced.

Next, both the covering message and the summary will point to the improvements in services that are being proposed—the addition of more police, for example, and the provision of more city buses.

The name of the game isn't always to damn the government. Sometimes, the government might be given a little credit, too particularly if it performs well in adversity.

Final Budget : After prolonged City Council debate, more interdepartmental negotiations and talks with leaders of union and other employee groups, the final operating budget as adopted was increased to $58,405,684 but it still averted the imposition of new taxes or increases in existing property and business taxes. The total amounted to an increase of 4.8 percent over the previous year's $55.7 million.

Story About the Final Budget : On the basis of these figures and the mayor's letter of transmittal to the City Council, a final story was written based on the Council's adoption of the budget.

The City Council adopted a $58.4 million balanced budget last night for the fiscal year beginning July 1 that provides for pay increases for city employees of up to 10%, eliminates 35 city jobs and calls for no new taxes or tax increases.

The budget is 4.8 percent higher than the current $55.7 million budget, but Mayor Tyree said, "Given a 10% inflation rate and fixed and mandated cost over which we have no control, I believe we have acted responsibly in adopting a budget that maintains essential service delivery and controls the growth of city government."

These were major provisions in the budget:

1. An across-the-board 10% cost of living raise for all non-uniform city employees with annual salaries below $10,000, 7.5% for all non-uniform employees with salaries above $10,000 and $75 a month more for all uniform employees.
2. Elimination of 100% coverage by the city in the deficit—ridden city employee health insurance fund. Employees now will pay 20% of the cost with a $ 100 front end deductible and the city will pay 80%.
3. The Recreation Department is hardest hit in the employee reductions, with some centers being closed. Total city employees now stand at 1,915 a decrease of more than 20% from the 2,407 work force when Mayor Tyree took office.
4. A new police class that may go as high as 50 employees and overtime funding for police work are provided for in connection with the World's Fair.
5. A $421,000 appropriation is provided to match a federal grant of $4.2 million for 30 new buses.

The mayor also announced that a $275,000 budget appropriation would go to 29 social service agencies because "recent disastrous cuts in federal aid make it necessary that we fund these agencies to the fullest extent possible."

Tyree pointed out that the economies provided for in the budget, plus revenues from the World's Fair, made it possible to avoid tax increases, leaving the property tax rate at $6.10 for each $100 of assessed valuation.

Changes in Budget During the Year : It should not be imagined that budgets, once adopted, are then frozen for the entire year. Unexpected costs, such as storm damage and snow removal, can make supplemental appropriations necessary. These and other factors, as well, can throw the most carefully administered budget out of balance and force hard-pressed city administrations to borrow money or to issue tax anticipation notes against income expected in the succeeding fiscal year.

City Hall reporters are well advised to be alert at all times for such changes and to follow up with direct departmental interviews to go to the source of the problem.

The budget routine outlined here for the city of Knoxville and the illustrative news story will differ in degree from the fiscal operations in other cities, but the basic requirement of matching income with outgo while maintaining essential services will be the same for all municipalities, large or small.

That, too, is the reporting principle applicable to budgets for school districts countries and state and federal government subdivisions. But no budget story can ever be done in a fast shuffle. It takes a lot of time, a great deal of care and interminable checking, through interviews with public officials and private groups that maintain a close watch over public financing.

Definitions of Budget Terms : The following definitions of budget terms have been provided by Lewis. A Gorham Jr., Director, Office of Management and Budget, City of Knoxville, based on research by Thomas Sherran, of the Public Administration Programme of the University of Tennessee.

Balanced Budget : This occurs when proposed revenues are equal to proposed expenditures. Many state and local governments require balanced budgets by law.

Block Grants : Block grants are given primarily to general purpose governmental units in accordance with a statutory formula. Such grants can be used for a variety of activities within a broad functional area (for instance, Omnibus Crime Control and Safe Streets Act of 1968, Comprehensive Employment and Training Act of 1973).

Bond Anticipation Notes : This is to temporary borrowing for capital financing. These temporary notes are usually serviced from the proceeds of bond sales and enable the borrower to reduce the cost of interest during construction of large projects.

Budget Expense : Outlay incurred for a specific time for goods and services and chargeable against revenues collected and held by public authorities.

Capital Budget : A plan of proposed outlays that are associated with large expenditures for capital items, usually financed by borrowing. Capital items are dominant features of the physical environment — for instance, buildings, roadways, parks.

Categorical Grants : This type of federal grant can be used only for a specific programme and is usually limited to narrowly defined activities.

Debt Limit : Total allowable government credit obligation.

Debt Service : The amount of principal and interest due on outstanding obligations such as bonds, notes, lease purchases and so forth, in any one year.

Formula Grants : This type of federal assistance allocates federal monies to states or their subdivisions in accordance with a distribution formula prescribed by law or administrative regulation.

General Obligation Bond : Bonds whose payments may be financed by all taxpayers of the issuing government units. They are secured unconditionally by the full faith, credit and taxing powers of the issuing government.

General Revenue Sharing : Advocates of the State and Local Fiscal Assistance Act, passed in 1972, sought to make federal monies available to lower levels of government without the traditional federal controls governing expenditure. It is based on the theory that those units of government closest to their respective interests can make better decisions because they better understand their needs.

Line Item Budget : Consists of authorizing each expenditure line by line, item by item, thus producing a budget format commonly referred to as object of expenditure.

Matching Grants : A financial arrangement under which the grantor agrees to pay some fraction of the unit cost of the recipient.

Mill Levy : Refers to property taxation in mills, which is 1/10 of 1 cent per dollar of valuation, instituted by local government.

Performance Budget : Here, budget data are classified in terms of performance objectives. Criteria are established and monitored throughout the year, such as miles of streets cleaned, response time of emergency vehicles and so forth.

Program Budget : A budgetary format in which line item budget data are rearranged into a programme structure so that, regardless of existing organization location, complementary activities are grouped under common objectives. This helps decision-makers to resolve major policy questions.

Project Grants : This type of cooperative agreement provides federal funding for fixed time periods for specific projects or the delivery of specific products or services.

Revenue Anticipation : Notes or tax anticipation notes refers to short term borrowing by local governments against a current year's property taxes or other revenues.

Revenue Bonds : Bonds issued to finance the acquisition, construction or improvement of revenue producing facilities with their principal and interest requirements payable solely from the revenues generated by the facility. Ordinarily, these are secured only by the subsequent generation of revenues.

Serial Bonds : These bonds are primarily of two varieties, straight serial bonds and annuity serial bonds. Both ordinarily mature in regular, annual installments that are fixed at the time of issue of the bonds.

Zero-based Budget : A budget in which decision units are identified and established by program managers. These in turn require the preparation of several different packages for each of the decision units, which are ranked by priority.

Expanding the Reporting of Government : Most newspapers and the more responsible broadcast organizations see to it that the officials of the mayor and city manager, commissioners, Council members and other top local officials are thoroughly covered.

However, in larger cities, the growing dependence of such authorities on their public relations people tends to remove them from immediate access by local reporters. Now, instead of being tossed into the hurly burly of news conferences, some media-wise officials save their news — and their availability — for much desired personal appearances on local television.

Finding New Sources for News : The news media have changed, too. Instead of letting a reporter sit and await the pleasure of the mayor, whiling away the hours at penny ante in the press room at City Hall, most newspapers insist on enterprise coverage of city affairs. That means reporters get a chance to delve into promising but untouched areas of local government on their own for days at a time in order to produce a special story or series, and most of them welcome it. The growth of the team reporting concept in local affairs has helped open up a lot of different news resources as well.

Once the local reporter moves out of City Hall, the main problem is to find reliable and cooperative officials who will explain the details of their operations. Younger journalist usually depend on reporters already on these beats to break them in, but sometimes that presents difficulties. Journalism, after all, remains highly competitive at every level.

It is basic, therefore, to acquire primary background knowledge of the various forms of government beyond the local level. In countries, for example, the traditional method of government through old and well-established country boards of commissioners is giving way to a country executive-country legislature operation. On the state level, the governor and legislature remain the principal news sources, but the interplay of politics sometimes becomes a dominant factor in formulating state programmes affecting local communities. And in metropolitan areas, forms of government such as the Tennessee Valley Authority and the New York-New Jersey Port Authority cut across state lines and continue to develop formidable powers all their own.

Reporters must be familiar with these systems and their adjuncts. They must also have a knowledge of the pertinent charters and constitutions, plus the source material and daily records that are available for inspection, before they can hope to get a maximum of meaning out of public meetings and news conferences with officials.

It is an old reportorial habit to write stories in terms of persons rather than problems, colourful incidents rather than studied analyses of material in which the public should be interested. All journalists know that it is much easier to sell a story if the name of a controversial official is attached to the lead in some way, such as being for or against a particular proposal. The news media like the specific, abhor the abstract.

State and Public Policy : At the state level, news breaks are infinite in their variety. The public's business often requires chief executives to speak out on a variety of issues. Here, for example, is the way the *New Hampshire Sunday News*, in Manchester, handled an unexpected warning by the governor of the state against fiscal irresponsibility.

Waterville Valley : It is time for New Hampshire to develop a comprehensive approach to its budget problems and stop trying to "cut a little, tax a little, gimmick a little, "Gov. Hugh I. Gallen said Saturday.

Speaking at the annual State Employees Association convention, the governor said the growth of state spending must be reduced. He noted that for nine of the last 14 years, New Hampshire's spending has outstripped its income.

The governor said he would oppose proposals to make selective cuts (such as laying off state employees while leaving agency managers untouched) or passing a "hodge-podge assortment" of taxes to balance the state budget, which may be as much as 70 million in the red.

While the old standby of cut a little, tax a little, gimmick a little may appear attractive, it has been a poor policy in the past and it is a poor policy today," Gallen said.,.

State governors also have to be responsive to public needs and frequently will take the initiative in putting our proposals on everything from environmental issues to consumer affairs. In Utah, the Ogden Standard Examiner sent its business editor, Cliff Thompson, to cover a meeting on power rates — usually a dull subject. But Utah's governor unexpectedly took a hand in the controversy, with this result.

By Cliff Thompson : Gov Scott Matheson says the cost of meeting the state's growing electrical power demands should be fairly allocated to protect residential users from unreasonable rate hikes while encouraging continued industrial growth.

But he admits that won't be easy to accomplish.

Matheson's position was outlined in a letter read to the Ogden area Chamber of Commerce-sponsored meeting Monday between officials of the Utah Power & Light Co. and some of its biggest industrial users.

There was general agreement by both power company executives and industrial customers that Utah Power & Light Co faces a "tough complex" question coming up with $300 million to $400 million a year to build new generating plants for the 1980s.

"I consider utility pricing issues to be one of the major policy items Utahns will face in the 1980s," Matheson wrote....

At the legislative level of state coverage, reporters often have to go with incomplete stories because that is the nature of the legislative process. Where two houses are working on numerous proposed laws midway through a legislative session, almost anything can happen and reporters have to cover themselves. Here, for example, is such a partial story in the *Berkshire Eagle* of Pittsfield, Massachusetts, written by the paper's legislative correspondent, A.A. Michelson.

BOSTON— Even though there are more than 1,000 bills still bottled up in legislative committees, there is talk that the Senate will call it quits for this session at the end of the coming week.

"That's what the Senate leadership told us this week, "Sen. Peter. Webber,R-Great Barrington, said last night.

Rep. Dennis J. Duffin, D-Lenox, vice chairman of the House Ways and Means Committee, said he had heard of the plan "but I'll believe it when I see it. There's a tremendous amount of important legislation pending."

The idea, Webber explained, is for the Senate to go into recess for the winter holidays, not final adjournment. The legislators have only three weeks left in which to act on pending proposals. After that, all bills not acted on in the current session are dead....

News at the Country Level : Many countries in the United States have special authority beyond that of the cities within their jurisdiction and often make major decisions that deeply affect the quality of life in those municipalities.

This is how Barbara Johnson of the *Fort Myers* (Florida) News-Press began a story about beach erosion that could cost county tax payers millions of dollars.

To the sun-drunk sun worshippers who week end on Captiva Island, the furious two year debate over enlarging South Seas Plantation's eroded beach might seem to be just so much environmental esoterica.

But now a companion project by the Captiva Erosion Prevention District to rebuild the rest of the Island's shore line is getting under way. The cost is estimated to be between $7 and $8 million.

District officials are speaking of new island property taxes and country wide tax revenue. The erosion prevention district has applied for state and federal permits to rebuild the island's remaining shore line.

District Chairman RichardButze said the erosion has become a menace to island property owners. On some parts of the island, he added, home owners this year have watched four to ten feet of beach drop into the Guff of Mexico...

In the Milwaukee Journal, sewer funds made news, what was involved was a $1.53 billion anti-pollution programme for the Milwaukee Metropolitan Sewerage District, and it took a certain amount of explaining, as the following story demonstrated.

Country officials, including nearly all 25 members of the Country Board, packed a room in the Court house Friday to hear if a judge would find the country in contempt for defying an order to provide $55.7 million for the Milwaukee Metropolitan Sewerage District.

Circuit Judge Daniel P. Anderson of Sheboygan County had been asked to force the country to come up with the money. Officials warned that the Milwaukee District's $1.52 billion anti-pollution programme would come to a halt for lack of funds if the $55.7 million cannot be paid.

Recently, Judge Anderson ruled that Country Executive O'Donnell and the Country Board must provide the $55.7 million, which they have failed to do. Lawyers for the country argued their client should not have to pay the money pending appeal....

The work of Reporting Teams : Through detailed investigation of land purchases, tax records and other available official documents, individual reporters and reporting teams have come up with a lot of news that could never have been obtained through the old routine of coverage by the beat.

One of the most brilliant investigations in recent years, which was conducted for six months by the investigative team of the *Indianapolis Star*, exposed wide-spread corruption in the Indianapolis Police Department and won the Pulitzer Prize for Special Local Reporting. It resulted in the dismissal of the director of public safety, the removal of the police chief and virtually all ranking police officers, and the defeat at the polls of a prosecuting attorney who was charged with a cover-up of the scandal. Here was the first of more than 400 stories that led to such spectacular results.

Widespread corruption in the Indianpolis Police Department—including graft and protection for prostitution, narcotics, bootlegging and gambling— has been uncovered in a six month investigation by the Indianpolis Star.

Involvement in corruption by dozens of Indianpolis policemen is not limited to taking money, but has led some members of the department into criminal activities, the probe showed.

Allegations of bribery and wrong doing over a period of five years are being investigated by the FBI and other federal agencies Information obtained by the Star has been made available to federal investigators.

The Star investigation showed that vice operations in the city over the last decade add up to an estimated $40 million annual "pie" while the illegal narcotics trade is well over that figure.

The majority of illegal money filters up to high ranking policemen and a few key political figures.

Aided by 28 policemen who— disgusted with what has been occurring — provided statements, tape recording, records or other assistance, the investigation showed that corruption reaches into many areas of the department and includes high ranking policemen.

Eight Marion Country Sheriffs detectives also provided information and other assistance, including statements from persons with direct knowledge of graft.

In all, reporters interviewed more than 400 persons, including a total of 60 policemen plus several former policemen.

There followed 15 itemized charges supported by documented evidence, a careful and well-checked case that stood up for the most part under the most searching examination. Even though two of the reporters were indicted in relation on trumped up charges of bribing police, nothing stopped the Indianapolis Star. The reporters were cleared, the police were not. The investigation was a model for planning, execution and results.

Basic Facts

These are the principal things to remember about reporting on budgets, taxes and local government:

- The first requirement is a basic knowledge of the functions of local government, the manner in which budgets are prepared and the manner in which the need for tax increases is determined.
- If a budget is increased over the previous year, the reporter must determine as quickly as possible where the additional money is coming from. It must be derived either from economies through decreases in staffs and services, increases in existing taxes or the levying of new ones, or the sale of bonds or tax anticipation notes.
- If taxes are to be increased, the first test is to determine how much the property tax will rise and what this will mean to the average home owner.
- Pay increases or decreases for city employees should be noted, with exact amounts wherever possible.
- Where there is an increase in debt service—the amount a city pays in interest on the bonds it issues — the reporter should know how much interest the city now pays on its bonds. (Municipal securities are tax-exempt under federal laws.)
- In writing budget stories, the lead should specify the total

amount of the proposed or final operating budget and report on whether tax increases or new taxes are requested. A summary of the main points of the budget should follow, with the body of the story elaborating on the principal developments.

- The tax levy (called a mill rate) is determined by dividing the sum needed for property taxes by the total assessed valuation of all property involved, multiplied by 100. If the budget allows for a small percentage of property taxes that may not be collected, this should be subtracted from the property-tax total before the final calculation is made.
- Team reporting is often required at the local level if a detailed inquiry is being made into governmental affairs. Since governmental affairs at the state level are even more complicated, such devices as the in-depth report and the "take-out," a detailed account using a feature style approach, are sometimes used to describe such developments.

14

News from Police

Angry, frightened woman telephoned Edna Buchanan, a police reporter for the *Miami.Herald,* late one March afternoon and told of witnessing the kidnapping of engaged couple that had ended in a gang rape. The witness identified one of the neighborhood hoodlums who had been preying on passing cars as well as residents.

"I'm fed up," the caller said. "What happened was outrageous."

Nothing could be done to help the young man, who had been beaten by the hoodlums or his fiancee, who had been sexually assaulted. But Buchanan made it her witness to interview other neighbourhood residents, and she didn't stop until she identified all the suspects. They were arrested, charged with rape, robbery and misuse of a gun in the commission of a felony. The police gave the reporter credit. "Edna's sources," said Police Sergent Mike Gonzalez, "Knew who they were, they did, where they were and who played what role."

Coverage of Police Activities

The story was part of the daily—and often nightly-routine for Buchanan, who has had police news for the *Herald'* for almost 15 years.

"Police reporting is exciting work," she says. "I get to see what people are really like—what makes some turn to crime, what makes some become cowards, and some become heroes. It's great job.

Toughest Beat : The police beat in Miami is the toughest in the country. For some years now, the Florida metropolis has had the highest crime rate of any city in the country, in statistics reported annually by the FBI. And in addition to crime, the beat includes coverage of fires, explosions, accidents of all kinds and rescues as well as departmental policies and charges affecting individual police officers and the activities of cooperating federal, state and local law enforcement agencies.

Any newcomer who is assigned to a police beat — even a beat less tough than Miami's — is going to be tested for courage as well as ability. For historically, that is where city and metropolitan editors generally start their best young prospects. On the *Heralad*, they have the advantage of working with seasoned professionals like Buchanan. But very often they are on their own.

The Daily Routine Here is a summary of the police beat assignment for the *Herald's* police reporters.

- Continual radio monitoring of all police calls and messages.
- Continual monitoring of fire calls and services.
- Hourly telephone checks of federal, state and other municipal departments.
- Close liaison with police public information offices and installation of related teletype, beeper and communications systems.
- Immediate communication with the office by car radio, beeper and walkie talkie.

- The Herald uses wake up calls for reporters plus helicopters, planes, ships and speedboats for reporters and photographers.
- Examination of logs, uniform crime reports and arrest forms daily at police offices in Miami, Miami Beach and the Metro complex.
- Daily examination of booking sheets at the central jail.
- Access to special categories in the *Herald* library on all forms of crime and crime statistics.

The *Herald's* editors have arranged for service by lawyers to back up reporters' requests for the release of information by the police. The lawyers also try to handle subpoenas issued by the courts, at the request of prosecutors or defense lawyers, to gain access to reporters' file and notes.

The newspaper has a policy of following up tips or complaints from citizens, such as the one given to Buchanan, on everything from illict drug trafficking to police brutality, failures of the justice system or outrages in the streets. The paper also keeps files in the newsroom for identification of people involved in crimes, as victims or assailants, including the latest city directories, tax rolls and other helpful data.

FBI's Uniform Crime Reports : The FBI issues each year a thick book entitled Crime in the United States, which is crammed with disheartening statistics. While lists of cities with the highest crime rates are regularly compiled from the book's section called "Index of Crime, Standard Metropolitan Statistical Areas," the FBI itself does not issue such a tabulation and discourages it as misleading for a number of reasons. However, the lists can easily be put together by checking the figures for the crime index total rate per 100,000 population.

While the list varies from year to year, three of the cities that have figured preeminently among the " first 10 " for some years are also the ones that attract millions of tourists annually — Mimani Atlantic City, New Jersey, and Las Vegas, Nevada. With the rate of crime in the average metropolitan area at the beginning of the 1980s set at 6,757.6 per year per 100,000 population, this was the rating of the three tourist centres. Miami, 11,581.8 , Atlantic City, 11,481.3 and Las Vegas, 0,292.3.

Rise in National Crime : The FBI report the decade 1971-80 showed a 54.8 percent increase in the number of serious crime committed since 1971 and an almost 10 percent increase from 1979 to 1980. In fact, the report showed that violent crimes over the decade surged by 60 percent and crimes escalated by 54 percent.

Crimes Defined : The Uniform Crime Reports (UCR) uses these definitions of the eight crimes included in the index.

Murder and Non-negligent Manslaughter : The willful (non-negligent) killing of one human being by another. A total of 50 percent was attributed to handguns.

Forcible Rape : The carnal knowledge of a female forcibly and against her will. Assaults or attempts to commit rape are included, but not statutory rape (with our force).

Robbery : The taking or attempting to take anything of value from the care, custody or control of a person or persons by force or threat of force or violence and/or by putting the victim in fear. Street and highway crime was put at 51 percent.

Aggravated Assault : An unlawful attack by one person upon another for the purpose of inflicting severe or aggravated bodily injury. Attempts are included.

Burglary : The unlawful entry of a structure to commit telony or theft. The use of force to gain entry is not required to classify an offense as a burglary. There are three subclassifications forcible entry, unlawful entry where no force is used and attempted forcible entry. A total of 67 percent of the reported burglaries occurred in residential property.

Larceny-theft : The unlawful taking, carrying, leading or riding away of property from the possession or constructive possession of another. It includes crimes such as shoplifting, pocket-picking and purse snatching, thefts from motor vehicle, of motor vehicle parts and accessories and of bicycles in which no use of force, violence or fraud occurs. The volume of larceny-theft was 53 percent of the crime index total and 59 percent of the property crime total, with thefts from motor vehicles and the taking of motor vehicle accessories as the largest single crime, 36 percent.

Motor Vehicle Theft : The theft or attempted theft of a motor vehicle.

Arson : Any willful or malicious burning or attempt to burn, with or without intent to defraud, a dwelling house, public building, motor vehicle or aircraft, personal property of another etc. The monetary value of property damage due to reported arson was very heavy, the most frequent target being structures which comprised 54 percent of the total.

The FBI reported that 10.4 million arrests were made in 1980 of all criminal infractions except traffic violations, with persons under 25 comprising 70 percent of those arrested for Crime Index offenses. However, only 19 percent of the reported index crimes were cleared during the year, the FBI said, the rate for violent crimes being 44 percent and for crimes against property 16 percent.

Police Reporters' Task : This statistical pattern vividly illustrates the magnitude of the task crime poses for the news media in general and police reporters in particular. For in any self-respecting community, unfavourable publicity affecting the business community always produces dismay. And this is particularly in places like Atlantic City and Las Vegas, which are dependent on attracting millions of visitors to try their luck at the gambling tables, and Miami, as well as other Florida cities, in a state that annually draws 35 to 40 million tourists annually.

But not many newspapers in such areas try to bury the news or omit it entirely. As one editor put it, "This is not something we can keep a secret. We have to face it , report on it and trust that our citizens will be sufficiently angry and determined that they will insist on federal and state action to help reduce the threat of crime." That, in fact, is a substantial part of the anticrime movement throughout the country today.

Stories of the Police Beat : With violence rising in many American cities, large and small, a part of the police beat assignment necessarily has to do with delving into the causes of crime.

In states along the Atlantic Seaboard and the Mexican border, the FBI points out that much crime is drug-related. The drug traffic in itself is so huge as to be almost uncontrollable. In addition, there is continual warfare between narcotics smugglers and loosely organized gangs that vie for local control of illicit drug sales. No large city is immune from this type of mob violence, whether it is New York, Chicago, Los Angeles or Miami.

Then, too, there are major problems related to the massive influx of Cuban and Haitian refuges and millions of illegal immigrants from Mexico. It is no accident the New York police have found that hardened criminals let out of Cuban jails, who joined the mass movement of more reputable Cuban immigrants, were settling in the least accessible areas of the Bronx and preying on their countrymen and others. But in the 1980s, the move to the north had ebbed and most Cuban emigres were settling elsewhere.

Still, the police story can't be told entirely in terms of major drug busts, Mafia type gangland murders, large-scale robbies and other big-time crimes.

Edna Buchanan's bylines, for example, appear on all kinds of stories for the *Miami Herald-fires,* police shoot-outs, features and investigations. Within about one month, the following two accounts were among the interesting and detailed stories, most of them on Page 1, her assignments produced.

A Fire Story : Buchanan received a call from one of her sources at 4 a.m. that several people, all members of the same family, had died in a fire that destroyed their home. It was a stormy night, but she phoned a photographer to meet her and got rolling in her car in the middle of a thunder-and-lightning storm.

"The fire was more than 40 miles away," she recaleed, "and I got lost in south Dade Country farmland in the rainy dark before dawn. I was driving with my gas indicator on empty."

Finally she reached a gas station and was able to get to the firefighters, who had been on the job and had returned to the firehouse, before the shift changed in Leisure City. Then she drove to the charred ruins of the home and talked with investigators, cops, neighbours, friends and relatives of the bereaved family.

"I set out at 9.30 a.m. to return to the office and write for the early edition," she went on. "Back at the office, I interviewed the medical examiner by phone and talked the cops into giving us a rough drawing of the layout of the house and the body positions. In the meantime—in case of argument or disagreement—I got the floor plans of the house from the courthouse. After polishing and writing through for later editions, I left the *Herald* at 9.30 p.m."

A smoldering fire from a worn air conditioner wire ignited a sofa, raced across wall paneling and gutted a Leisure City home in an inferno that killed five children and their small dog Wednesday.

The parents, Redland Construction Co. superintendent John Paul Dixon, 54, and his wife, Baibar, 38, and their two other children, Delbert, 3, and Tracy, 19, were cut and burned but survived.

"A $ 10 smoke detector would have saved five lives," said Metro firefighter Anthony Spadaro. He carried two dead girls, five and six years old, from the house.

He found them in their bed, "beautiful little blonde girls in long nightgowns. One was resting her head in her hands like she was sleeping." Two baby dolls lay nearby.

A neighbour tried to rescue the children but was driven back by two snaring and snapping family dogs, a boxer and a bird dog, who tried in panic to protect the burning house.

Flames shot from every windows the doors were ablaze and a huge column of smoke rose skyward when the firefighters arrived at 2.54 a.m. The trantic parents and screaming neighbours shouted that five children were inside.

There was no sigh of life within the modest 10-year-old, four bedroom home. Rescuers were forced back by flames and heat so intense that it melted the aluminium trim on the house.

A huge pumper equipped with 3,000 gallons of water arrived at 3:03 a.m. The flames were knocked down and fire fighters were able to enter the house in five minutes.

It was too late for those inside.

A windows screen lay atop his body in a back bedroom. His hands were cut. His pet dog, a miniature dachshund, lay dead at his feet.

Wanda Dixon, 6, and John Dixon's granddaughter, Misty Hogan, 5, died in their beds. Two more little girls, sisters Paula and Reba Dixon, three years old, died crouched, wedged in corners, trying to escape the flames....

It is reportorial detail that makes this story. It takes the reader to the scene, of the plight of the shattered family devastatingly real, adds poignant evidence of firefighter's observation that a smoke detector could have saved them all.

Cop's Last Night on the Job : This was a different story, about a violent final night on the job. It is also came alive through Buchanan's drive for detail and more detail. Here is the start of that story:

After a rough and tumble ten-year-career as a Metro cop. Officer James Melvin shot a man Sunday, his last night on patrol.

Melvin, who is moving away from Dade County to South Carolina, wounded one of three burglars he caught in the act, police said.

"He was upset. He wanted to get through a quiet evening his last night on the road," said Metro Police spokesman Pete Cuccaro.

But Melvin, who has won honors for bravery and heroic rescues in the past, was too conscientious a cop to ignore a suspicious truck during his final hours on the job, superiors said.

The truck was a pickup, parked at the rear of the Service Merchandise Mart and the vacated former Treasury Store, at SW 160th St. and US 1.

The truck was loaded with Thurs. and of dollars' worth of stolen equipment, stereo and electronic, police said.

As officers searched the darkened building, they spied two men, identified as Richard Yound and Ernest Holcomb, both 22, hiding in the ceiling work, police said. They added that both refused commands to surrender.

Concerned, Young shouted an obscenity and rolled to one side, reaching into his waistband, police said. Thinking he was reaching for a gun.

Melvin fired a shot, striking Young in the leg. Young is listed in good condition at Jackson Memorial Hospital....

Following up a Story : Police reporting elsewhere in the United States differs only in degree from the intensive work that is demanded of the men and women on the police beat in Miami and other metropolitan centres. The same watchfulness, the same effort, the same dedication and the same professional knowledge and skill are called for the people who handle police news in every city and town, regardless of size.

The routine may differ, depending on circumstances, but the stories are seldom if ever handed to reporters with a flourish and a bow from the participating police officers. If there is one lesson that beginners learn very early on the police beat, it is that they have to struggle—and sometimes even fight—for every fact they get. There is a limit to what even the best police sources can do for the news media, and reporter know it.

A Double Slaying in Kansas : Even if there isn't anywhere near as much crime in Kansas as there is in New York, Illinois, Florida or California, people in Kansas are just as concerned about the rise of violence on the Great Plains as other police news has to be carefully scrutinized.

Anita Miller of the *Topeka Daily Capital*, only a year out of the William Allen White School of Journalism at the University of Kansas, may not have had either the reputation or the experience of Edna Buchanan of the *Miami Herald*, but she worked with the same care and efficiency in developing the facts behind a double slayig. It was sensitive story, to begin with, and Miller explained why:

> My story was a second day story. The first story was sketchy because police hesitated to say anything, since one of their own officers was involved.
>
> It was a double slaying. A girl had been fatally shot by her former boyfriend, and the boyfriend then was fatally shot by a police officer in the parking lot of a major shopping center in Topeka.
>
> I didn't write the first-day story but I felt a follow-up was necessary because there wasn't much of a hint as to how the woman and man were associated. She was only 17 and he was 19.
>
> I happened to know one of the victims and I knew where the two had gone to school, so I began calling people at the school, including teachers, students and counselors. My main goal was to find some friends who might have been with the couple prior to the shooting, or knew what the girl was doing at the shopping center and how the man knew she was there.
>
> Digging for facts on a story like this was really frustrating. For every ten calls I made, only one would come up with good, current information. I was careful about taking down what each acquaintance said until I had a clear picture in my mind of what the girl was really like and the chain of events that led to the shooting.

I didn't use information unless I felt comfortable with the people and had a good idea that they were telling me the truth.

Results of the Follow-Up : When Miller finally wrote her story for *Capital,* she had checked all the facts she used. She didn't do a sob story-it isn't in her nature. The story is straight throughout, with no flourishes and no attempt to do anything more to set out the facts behind a tragedy. Here is the substance of the story she wrote.

A 17-year old Topeka girl who was fatally shot Thursday night at the White Lakes Shopping Center parking lot had recently stopped dating the man who shot her, acquaintances said Friday.

They asserted LindaM. Schneider, 324 Woodbury Lane, had dated Mark. Thompson, 19, 919 S.E. Consuelo, about a year until they broke up two months ago.

"When they broke up she went to St. Louis [and stayed with relatives] to get away," Stacey Moore, 4012 W. 28th, said. "Then she moved back here with her parents about four weeks ago."

Thursday night Miss Schneider was at White Lakes Mall attending her first session at the Barbizon School of Modelling since her return to Topeka from St. Louis. One friend said Miss Schneider had wanted to be an airline stewardess.

Topeka police said Miss Schneider was fatally shot in the head by Thompsons at 8:59 p.m. as she ran toward two police officers just south of the Sears Automotive Center outside the White Lakes Shopping Center complex.

Police said after the girl fell, Reserve Patrolman Gaylon Thompson, 27, a two-year member of the reserve force had fired in self-defense.

Acquaintances of Miss Schneider said she had been invited to attend a party at a friend's house in central Topeka after her class Thursday, but Thompson was not allowed inside when he went to the house. However, he learned that she was at White Lakes and drove there, acquaintances said. The slayings followed.

Are Police Reporter Insensitive? : People unfamiliar with newspaper work in general, and police reporting in particular, often assume that journalists are insensitive to all the tragedies about them on many occasions. A few may be, but most reporters could be deeply affected if they weren't able to seal off their personal feelings by casting a protective shell about their emotions. This, perhaps, may give the appearance of insensitivity to human suffering, but appearances are often deceiving. Miller summed up her own position this way:

> Talking to close friends and the family of a dead person really bothers some reporters, but it has never upset me much. Before I start an interview, I as the people involved if they want to talk to me. I think ti's important to give them a choice. If they refuse, then I don't pressure them. It's always necessary for me to remember that I'm approaching them at a sensitive time and try to be understanding. If they won't talk, there's usually someone else who will be able to give me the information.

The columnist Jim Bishop, once a police reporter on the New York tabloid the *Daily Mirror,* which went to the journalistic boneyard in the 1960s, put the case this way: "I was a crime reporter... A callus grows on your brain. The heart becomes a cool stone. There is a shade of cynicism on the retina." And then, he added, there comes a time when the reporter reads something about the piteous victim of a crime and this happens: "Your throat slams shut and you throw the book on the floor.

Miranda Rule : Under the Miranda Rule, the police are obliged, with certain exceptions, to notify defendants of their right to remain silent and to obtain counsel. The notification must take place upon arrest. It became law when the Supreme Court in 1966 reversed the conviction of Ernesto A. Miranda, a 25-year-old mentally retarded Arizona truck driver, because he had not been warned of his right to counsel or that his statements might be used against him before he confessed to raping an 18-year-old girl. Miranda had been serving concurrent sentences of 20 to 30 years.

Chief Justice Earl Warren held for the 5-4 majority that police must inform criminal suspects, when arrested, of their right to remain silent and to obtain counsel. While the Miranda ruling remains on the books, it has been weakened by subsequent high court decisions. In 1971, statements made by an accused person before being informed of his rights were admitted under cross-examination. Four years later, statements made by an accused person after being informed of his rights were admitted as rebuttal testimony. And in 1976, the Miranda rule was held inapplicable to grand jury testimony.

Arrest Procedures : In brief outline, is what happens when an arrest is made.

- The suspect maybe brought in on a complaint or a warrant or he may be seized at the scene of a crime. But until formally charged and booked, he cannot be said to be under arrest.
- The booking consists of recording the suspect's identity, address and vital statistics in a large record together with the alleged crime, time and place of the arrest and the name of the arresting officer.
- The suspect is searched, his property is enumerated, sealed and given to the property' clerk for safekeeping.
- The Miranda card, notifying the suspect of his constitutional rights, is read to him. He is informed that he may remain silent, that he may consult a lawyer or, if he doesn't have one, a lawyer will be provided. Before he can be questioned by police, he must sign a paper waiving these rights.
- If he signs, the police question him and put together a formal arrest report. In any case, he is photographed, fine printed, told he can make a telephone call and then he is put in a detention cell.

In some cities, notably New York, there is an arrangement either in a day court or in Night Court, as soon as possible after a formal complaint is drafted by a member of the prosecutor's office. The suspect then is given a chance to enter a plea. If the plea is not guilty, the presiding magistrate or judges sets bail.

Some defendants-depending on the charge and on their record, and on the amount of security company after the hearing and thereby obtain release. If they can't raise bail, they are held in jail.

The prosecutor's office must now determine whether the evidence against the suspect is strong enough to warrant holding the suspect on a felony charge, in which event a case must be presented to a grand jury and an indictment must be returned, or whether to proceed to trial in a lower court on a misdemeanor, a lesser charge.

It is at this point that the courts take over. If it is decided to proceed with the misdemeanor charge, generally the trial is scheduled in a lower court with out a jury. But if the felony charge holds good, and an indictment is returned, the suspect must await trial before a judge and a jury. Or, through their lawyer, suspects may plea bargain with the prosecutor's office and consent to a guilty plea on a lesser charge.

In any event, once an arrest has been made, the police and court procedures are intricate and time-consuming. Generally, if the case warrants it, the reporter who was in on the arrest follows through to at least the preliminary hearings in the lower courts. Once an indictment has been returned, particularly in larger cities where there are regular court reporters on daily assignment, they take over the story.

The Guidelines

Some reporters often have to go behind the news. The following safeguards are, therefore, in the coverage of the administration of justice.

Arrests : It is a serious matter to report that a person has been placed under arrest. When such a report is made, the exact charge against the arrested person could be given and it should be documented by either a record or attribution to a responsible official. If such documentation cannot be obtained, the reporter had better to check the facts. The person in question may not have been under arrest at all. There are euphemisms in police work such as "holding someone for questioning," asking witness to appear voluntarily to cooperate with an investigation" and simple statements which indicate the person is being detained but may or may not be subject to arrest. In many states an arrest is not formally accomplished until a prisoners is booked. The news, in any case, must be handled with care.

Accusations : It is commonly written that someone is being "sought for robbery suspected of arson or tried for murder This is journalistic shorthand, which has gained acceptance through usage, but it is neither precise nor correct.

Persons are" sought in connection with a robbery," unless a charge has actually been made, in which case they are "charged with robbery." Persons under suspicion are not necessarily going to be charged with a crime and it is generally not privileged matter to indicate that suspicion is attached to any individual by name. Where the police suspect someone, but lack proof, that person may be held as a material witness — which is far different from being accused of a crime. Therefore, cases of suspicion are not usually given too extensive and detailed news treatment if no privileged material is available for use. The practice of reporting that a defendant is being "tried for murder," while widely used, is obviously prejudicial and could be more accurately, if less dramatically, stated, as "being tried on a charge of murder," or "on a murder indictment."

Confessions : The use of the word "confession" to describe statements made by a person to the police or to prosecuring authorities is dangerous when it is not a matter of public record. The fact that a police chief or a prosecutor has claimed to have a confession, except in open court, may be used only at the risk of the news organization. Most press-bar voluntary agreements forbid the use of confessions until they are admitted in open court. The records are full of supposed confessions that backfired later for a variety of reasons and of persons who admitted crimes they could not possibly have committed. Unless and until it is established in fact that a person has confessed, approved procedure for reporters is to use such terms as "statement," "admission," "description" or "explanation." They convey the shade of meaning that is warranted by circumstances and do not subject the news organization to unnecessary risk.

The reporter must always remember that under the law individuals are presumed to be innocent until they have been found guilty.

Investigations : Certain stages of police investigations require secrecy in the public interest. This also pertains to some of the aspects of prosecutions and trials. The secrecy of the grand jury room and of a trial jury' s deliberations are soundly based on public policy. Except under the most extraordinary circumstances, no reporter and no news organization have any right to interfere and few have ever attempted to do so.

Often, during the course of investigations, reporters are confined to listing the identities of witnesses who have entered or left a police station or g rand jury room, if the names can be obtained. They have every right to try to interview such witnesses, if the circumstances are favourable, before and after appearances of this kind. But it is the business of the prosecution, defense lawyers and the witnesses themselves to decide whether or not they should talk.

For this reason investigations in their earliest states, are likely to produce a crop of speculative reports without much basis in fact unless editors insist on sounder reporting. Clever, publicity conscious investigators can often hopelessly prejudice the position of hostile witnesses and others who oppose them if the news media do not hold rigidly to their code of presenting both sides of the story. That is why no claim by any investigators, regardless of their position and personal prestige, should be accepted and published at face value without some effort by a reporter to determine the soundness of the statements that have been issued.

Cases of Violent Death : Nowhere is there a greater tendency to jump to conclusions in the field of crime reporting than in the initial reporting of a violent death. The amateur reporter is invariably in a hurry to characterize the event as a suicide or a murder when it may be an accident death. It is advisable, therefore, to report only what is known and avoid speculation in the absence of an official verdict by a coroner, medical examiner or some other competent authority.

An apparent suicide is one of the most difficult crime stories to handle. If the police report that a man was found shot to death with a bullet in his right temple and a revolver in or near his right hand, the story should be written in exactly that way. In the case of a police finding that someone "jumped or fell" to his death, the reporter should not go beyond the facts but use that phrase. If a woman is found dead in bed with an empty bottle labeled sleeping tablets beside her, no conclusions should be drawn.

In all such cases, it is proper to note any other circumstances that have a bearing on the story, particularly as to whether notes were left. It may not always be proper to publish such notes, even if the text is made available by the police, unless the material is privileged. Moreover, unless there is a formal announcement of suicide by a responsible authority, the news account can do no more than to note that an investigation is being made to determine whether the death was a suicide.

When violent deaths occur without any indications to whether they may be accidents, suicides, murders or combinations of all three, the story should report the identities of the victims and the manner of their deaths. It is usually fruitless to try to unravel such a mystery in a newsroom. That is the job of the police and the prosecuting authorities. In the absence of any word from them, a factual account of the event must suffice.

A murder investigation often tempts reporters to venture into recalms for which their profession has not really equipped them. Because a few reporters have achieved fame through phenomenal exploits, all reporters are scarcely justified in trying to play detective when a newsworthy personage has been "done in." Not many even attempt to do so because there is simply not enough time for the routines of both journalism and police work on a fast-breaking story.

Precautions : There are a few fundamental precautions of which reporters must take account.

The first is that police and prosecutors rarely will give them information on a silver platter. That means a tremendous amount of interviewing and research must be done in a very short time so that a coherent story may be written.

The second is that there can be no guarantee of police accuracy, in fact, an impressive body of evidence can be amassed to the contrary. That means police versions of names, addresses and other facts must be checked.

The third is that police and journalistic terminology are not necessarily identical. The legal term for a slaying is a homicide, but many news organizations loosely and incorrectly refer to such crimes automatically as murder. In a grand jury indictment the homicide eventually may be defined as first or second degree murder, depending on whether there was premeditation, or first or second degree man-slaughter, depending on whether there was provocation or negligence. Since man-slaughter is not murder, care must be used in defining a homicide. Indictments charging murder have been found to be deficient in the past, so writers should be precise in their statements whenever they refer to the legal basis of any charge.

Assessment of Blame : Whenever there is a fist fight, shooting or collision involving police action, it is only human to wonder what happened and who was at fault. Often a trial can determine this, therefore, most reporters use as many versions of the incident as there are witnesses if such extensive treatment is warranted.

Such accounts begin with a statement that two men had a fist fight in a night club, or that there was a shooting match, or that two automobiles collided. The body of the story then documents the non-committal lead, giving such versions of the event as are necessary. The attribution of documentation of this type always presents a problem for writers who want to avoid using "he said," or "she said," or "the police said" in every sentence.

There are several ways of doing this. One is to quote the various versions, if they are briefly enough. Another is to write, "The police version of the incident follows," and then report it without further attribution. In any case, unless there is some official assessment of blame, it is usually not necessary for the reporter to try to act in such matters.

Identification : The identification of persons in crime stories sometimes leads to trouble, no matter how carefully it is checked. Confusion of persons with identical last names, mistakes in middle initials, mix-ups in addresses, misspellings of names and police errors all conspire against the reporter. There is no real safety in the familiar formula "The suspect gave his name as..." or, "The prisoner was identified as ..." If the identification is incorrect, the reporter and the news organization are in trouble.

It is usually a good rule, in stories that warrant it, to include material showing how the identification was made — by papers in the person's possession, by friends or relatives, or by other means. If there is any doubt, the reporter will find it does no harm to add a clause or even a sentence indicating that the identification was partial and remained to be checked. No news organization need regard itself as an oracle whose word is final, when the public knows that many things are possible between the commission of a crime and the conviction of a defendant.

Civil Disorder : The coverage of civil disorder imposes major responsibilities on journalists. On the one hand, they must exercise the greatest care not to spread rumors. On the other, they must expose themselves to danger if necessary to determine the magnitude of any street incident. But whatever they do, they must always be conscious that careless reporting or the provocative appearance of still or television cameras can cause untold harm in a tense situation, particularly in the crowded inner cores of many American cities.

Restraint in Conduct : The conduct of the journalist at the scene of action must be circumspect. A hard-hatted, swaggering white reporter in the center of an angry black community can provoke trouble. A television cameraman training his instrument on a floodlighted crowd, is likely to get more action that be bargains for when fighting has broken out all around him. Nor is there any great sense in sending an armored truck bearing the name of a news organization into a trouble area. These are the things that cause the news media to be blamed for spreading disorder. Complete coverage is desirable at all times, but no one is thereby justified to pay on a circus like performance.

Restraint, such as was maintained in the face of wholesale disorders by street gangs in Detroit, is a necessity in reporting policy.

Defining a Riot : In both written and oral reports of any incident, every effort should be made to arrive at accurate evaluations. An isolated act of vandalism, or a street fight between two teenagers in the midst of a crowd, must not be called a race riot. And if shooting is heard in a crowded neighbourhood at night, it is not automatically "sniper fire" until an investigation determines that snipers are at work. Nor are all fires the work of arsonists. Looking, too, should be carefully defined. Great damage can be done if radio, television and published wire service and newspaper reports exaggerate a few small incidents. Consequently, in the early stages of any civil disorder, the basic rule is to work and report with the greatest restraint.

Necessarily, once a news organization's editors have evidence to show that they are dealing with a riot of major proportions, there is no justification for not making a complete report available to the community at large. When reporters see arsonists setting fire and looters carrying merchandise from wrecked stores, these things must be communicated. Yet, the need for restraint and patient inquiry cannot be abandoned even in such circumstances.

For when shooting breaks out, the reporter is never justified to leap to conclusions that all the damage is being done by demonstrators or that race is aligned against race, littery police and National Guardsmen have been known to fire away at almost anything that moves, sometimes with unfortunate results.

Reporters have to be more patient and more circumspect.

Short Takes : These are the basics of covering the police beat:

- Police reporters check police and fire department radios, arrest records (where available), departmental liaison officers and associated sources. When they spot a story worth going out on, they call their city desk and make suitable arrangements.
- Police reporters do a lot of interviewing at the scene of a crime, a faire, an accident or other incident on a police beat. The heart of their work depends on a good deal of accurate detail and good quotes.
- Police reporters can't afford to be a part of the big blue machine. They must maintain their independence and investigate at once any story that indicates police negligence.
- There is no such thing as going with first police reports without checking the facts. Police reports themselves may not be accurate.
- Some stories, in which important angles are left hanging, must be cleaned up with second-day and sometimes third-day reports. A once-over-lighty isn't sufficient.
- Sometimes it pays to go deeper into a story that indicates a profound human conflict. Such stories may be told at first in three or four paragraphs. But if the police reporter suspects a much better story lies behind the initial report, he or she should try to sell the idea to the city desks and get help.
- There are restraints on the coverge of crime news. All suspects must be read their Miranda rights — their right

to remain silent and to be represented by a lawyer. In some states, under voluntary Press—Bar Guidelines, there are agreements that reporters will not use a defendant's prior police record and other damaging detail in the arrest report. What can and cannot be used should be checked with the city desk.

- Police reporters must be familiar with the department they cover, its regulations and procedures, and must have a good working acquaintance with criminal law.
- The greatest care must be taken in reporting arrests. Sometimes people are detained for questioning, asked to give help to the police or help as material witnesses. But these actions are not arrests and it is libel per se to report that such people are under arrest. The test for an arrest is twofold: (1) The subject must be booked and formal charges must be lodged, and (2) both the booking and the charge must be attributed to a responsible police official.
- Similarly, in the event of a civil disturbance, no reporter should call the exchange of a few blows a riot. And particular care should be exercised never to term a disturbance a race riot, which is a major civil calamity.
- Reporters should beware of announcing confessions. Generally, what is done is to report that a suspect has made a statement, made admissions or given an account of the crime to the authorities, and the source of that intelligence should be named and identified by department and rank.

15

Sports News

This is the era of big-time college football, created in large part by the willingness of the broadcasting networks to spend millions of dollars on nationally televised games. It is also the era of the million-dollar a year professional athlete, enormous stadiums, fanatical fans and gamblers who will do almost anything to avoid losing a bet.

Typical Combination

Such a combination is bound to add up to trouble, sooner or later, but it isn't often that either the sports pages or the sportcasters reflect so damaging a reality. In the mythology of the sports world, sports reporters are supposed to confine themselves to the stories of who won and who lost, or game called on account of the weather. When they don't, it's news.

At a meeting of the American Society of Newspaper Editors, Charles Bailey, editor of the Minneapolis Tribune, put the case this way.

I have a feeling of unease when I think about sports, both college and professional, in terms of the fact that we are not really doing a job of reporting on the true conditions. I am talking about college football in particular, but also most college sports, the money involved and the practices involved. One has a hard time getting sports writers interested in digging into that story.

Brent Musburger of CBS Sports responded with the not-so-original observation that most communities believe sports writers "should not touch this grand entertainment" and went on:

It is very unfortunate we are so hypocritical at the college level. Take a look at the money that is being generated by college athletics in terms of television contracts and tickets that are sold for those arenas. You wonder why athletes aren't paid in some way. Even if the Minneapolis Tribune does a story or CBS goes in with 20 minutes in one, two or three different schools around the country, we are not going to change a thing. They are going to be back out there giving cars away, giving jobs to parents, because there is so much money at stake. It is an economic issue. They just ought to be honest with it and deal with it in some way.

Hometown Story : Musburge's reference to hometown pride in local stories heroes was at the base of an outpouring of resentment in Tucson, Arizona; when the local Arizona Daily Star began digging into rumor about the alleged mishandling of the financial affairs of the University of Arizona's football programme. Some large businesses canceled their advertising in an effort to stop the inquiry, editors of the paper said, and other started a boycott.

Despite these efforts to stop the inquiry, the two city-side reporters who were conducting the investigation, Bobe Lowe and Clark Hallas, broke a series of stories after working for three months, bringing about the resignation and indictment of the university's football coach on charges of financial irregularities in the football recruiting programme. However, when the coach was brought to trial he was acquitted. Even though the reporter were awarded the 1981 Pulitzer Prize for investigative reporting, it did not endear them to the loyal supporters of the Arizona Wildcats. The coach's acquittal, coming as it did after the award of the prize, demonstrated once again that it is one thing for a newspaper to publish charges and quite another to persuade a jury to believe them.

Changes in Sports Reporting **:** Sports editors and reporters are well aware of the criticism that has come their way. In Boston, there was no effort to play down or cover up a criminal investigation into a point-shaving scandal that rocked the Boston College basketball team. As a result, a youthful Boston College basketball player was convicted and sent to jail for ten years. Nor have sports editors always been complaisant about the rumors of wrong-doing in collegiate and professional sports. Years ago, Max Kase, sports editor of the *New York Journal-American,* won a Pulitzer Prize Special Award for turning over information to the district attorney of New York County about a looming basketball scandal. As a result, several local college players were convicted and sent to prison.

But then, New York and Boston aren't as likely to develop hometown pride in local athletes as are smaller communities. And in the big cities, there is less opportunity for booster organizations to bring pressure on the local news media not to interfere in the affairs of local colleges or universities.

Without much doubt, the emergence of television as a dominant influence in the presentation of sports to a mass public has made a difference in the public's perception of right and wrong. As George Solomon to the *Washington Post* has said, "TV buys events. TV puts on the event. And to make TV look good and self all the commercials, the sport must look good."

Brenl Musburger of CBS believes the charges to be overstressed. He says, "To a large extent we are in the entertainment business, which leads me directly into what we do as networks. Yes, we have to buy events. Then we have to make a profit out of them. So we have to attract an audience. And, yes, there is a certain amount of type that goes into it"

Still, Musburger argues, newspapers also try to present the news in as appealing a way as possible because they, too, have to maintain circulation to attract advertisers and they, too, have to make a profit to stay in business. True enough, but the difference is that the newspapers don't pay large sums of money to put on national sports broadcasts. In consequence, to quote Solomon, "A lot of editors are demanding the same standards from sports reporters and sports journalists as they do from everyone else— that is, aggressive reporting, looking behind the scenes, digging, being a true reporter."

The Cult of Privacy : In professional sports, where outstanding athletes can earn enormous sums of money in a relatively short time, sports writers are under even greater handicaps. Because there is a tendency to criticize those players who collect millions and give substandard performances, the cult of privacy has taken firm hold among many teams. Once it was taken for granted that sports reporters and TV cameras would be welcome in team locker rooms or at practice sessions. But not today. Access to athletes in locker rooms is severely restricted by most professional sports teams. Dave Anderson of the *New York Times* says:

> When I was covering the [New York] Jets 10, 12 years ago, you could virtually walk into their locker room during the week at any time. You could go into a locker room before a game up until an hour before. You could walk on the practice field and stand behind the huddle in the middle of the field. Today, virtually all of that is gone. There is no way you can walk out on a practice field of any team. You can stay on the sideline.... During the week, may teams have situations whereby you are only allowed in the locker room, let's say, an hour or a half hour. You have to make appointments with players.... The coaches seem to think the more secrecy they have, the better. To me, the more secrecy they have, the worse it is.

In the major league baseball, star players of the caliber of Steve Carlton and Dave Kingman have refused for years to speak to sports reporters and have gone their own way. And some younger players have had a powerful urge to imitate them.

The problem, therefore, is to obtain access to the millionaire athletes and their colleagues, and not every sports reporter is successful. The athletes appear to divide reporters into "good guys" — that is, cheer leaders and "bad guys"— those who try to do an honest day's work.

There are some coaches, athletes and club owners who still resent women sports writers and try, by various means, to make it difficult for them to obtain access to athletes. But few women are fainthearted enough to be put off by such phony excuses as male modesty in locker rooms. Nor have women sports writers turned out to be the problem that some of their male colleagues predicted they would be. There still aren't very many of them.

Making a Beginning : It is a long way from such major concerns among the top figures in the sports reporting field to the beginner who wants to break into sports reporting for a newspaper or broadcast organization. Yet sports is almost a common denominator among working journalists today. Many of them had their first task of journalism covering sports as stringers at the high school level. And few have forgotten their experience.

Getting a Sports Job : In a lot of American cities, high school sports have a wide following and particularly in communities without college or professional teams, are a dominant community activity. On any autumn Saturday afternoon, thousands of people turn out to watch high school football. In many places, too, basketball is a magnet that draws towns people to high school gymnasiums. Such sports as baseball and track traditionally have lighter attendance, but all are reported on in the local papers and local broadcast media.

Beginners generally inherit stringing jobs in high school from graduating classmates. Or, if they are particularly enterprising, they may find a nearby publication of station that gives no coverage to a high school within the general circulation area and win the assignment. At any rate, the first time they report on a game, they may be told that the paper or station wants only the final score and how the victory was achieved. Then someone in the office writes a roundup including this information.

As the new comer proves trustworthy, the assignments improve. In addition to the final score, other details are requested—the number of people attending the game, an interview with the winning coach or the player who scored the deciding points, plus a summary of the scoring by both sides. Once again, that story may be written by somebody else in the office.

It sounds so easy to do these things. But actually, as all beginning sports reports learn, it is almost as difficult to pin down sources at the high school level as it is to gain access to the big-time professionals. The reasons are apparent. Coaches, for the most part, don't trust the judgement of youngsters to report what they say and — if they comment at all — it will usually be in pleasantries with little news value. The same is true of officials at the games and those teachers who have a special responsibility for athletics. Players, too, are often cautioned to say as little as possible on the air or for publication, to avoid making some statement that can be seized upon by a future opponent.

Working at the High School Level : From these experiences, the beginner will learn persistence if nothing else. And that will be all to the good. But there will come a day when an assistant sports editor tells the beginner to write the story and bring it to the office or, better still, to come to the office and do the piece under supervision. That is always something to be remembered, even if the copy is heavily edited and bears little resemblance to the original.

Most young and inexperienced sports writers make the same mistakes. They deal in cliches instead of writing simple, straightforward English sentences. They load their copy with expertise, or what they believe to be expert comment, all of which is us..ally eliminated. And, worst of all, they betray a partisanship for the home team that makes their credibility suspect to anybody who merely wants a fair account of what happened.

The process of learning to write a sports story, therefore takes time. Except in rare instances, beginners can't learn to do it well overnight. It helps to read the work of outstanding professionals. Above all, the job is learned best by continual practice.

Daily Sports Coverage : Every year, depending on the size of the paper and the rate of turnover, a certain number of stringers are offered regular sports jobs. It is far more difficult to make a beginning as a sports broadcaster, because these jobs are even more limited. The progression is usually through the sports broadcaster, because these jobs are even more limited. The progression is usually through the sports pages of newspapers in medium-size cities. Such papers, though, rarely hire more than one youngster a year. Very small dailies do not have enough staff turnover to warrant expectation of jobs for beginners, and the big metropolitan papers prefer to take on people with experience.

For the lucky ones who come up through the system and land regular jobs, the routine of daily sports coverage can develop into a pleasant life. Newcomers generally are assigned to writing the same high school sports they covered as stringers — in easy way of breaking in. The next step in the progression is to handle college sports if there is a nearby institution of higher learning. It takes a while to graduate to professional sports coverage, particularly if professional teams are outside the papers circulation area. But when the new comer does get a professional assignment it generally is to do either a colour story on a major contest or to handle the play-by-play.

Regular beats-following a particular baseball or football team through the season — aren't practical for a small sports staff. Reporters may handle several different sports in single week and have to adapt themselves to local conditions.

Interviewing Sports Figures : Bob Matthews, sports columnist for the Rochester (New York) Times Union, has these suggestions for interviewing sports personalities.

- Make sure your first question is a good one so the subject will know you have something on the ball.
- Always be on a first-name basis with every player on a pro team. Sooner or later, one of them will good up and it's sports writer's job to ask him about it. Nothing turns off an athlete faster than a reporter who hasn't said hello to him all season but is quick to arrive after a costly error.
- Try for specifies. Don't settle for generalities. Ask why the center fielder dropped the ball in the last half of the ninth, enabling the opposition to score the winning run.
- I have one pet question I often ask athletes. "What do you think of sports writers?" They usually have definite opinions and branch off into how they've been misquoted,

misrepresented, etc. It's a good way to build rapport and can lead to some good exchanges.

- Before I interview a national sports figure, I often phone a sports writer in his particular town for background and tips on how to approach the subject.
- Invariably there's a question I forget to ask or a point that needs clarification. So I always ask where the subject can be reached later in the day, just in case he's needed.

Patterns of Sports : There most of the sports public knows the final score of the game from radio of before the paper comes out, sports writing in the TV age is different in many ways from what it used to be. Dave Anderson of the New York Times says.

A lot of my colleagues really seem to resent television. I may be different, but I enjoy television for this reason. I think television creates sports readers. Any time people see an even on television, they invariably want to read about it next day. To name the beauty of television is that as soon as the game ends, they go off....As soon as they go off, that's when we go to work. That to me is the great value of television on the sports business.

Other newspaper, magazine and syndicated sports writers have been pleasantly surprised by the self-evident truth that Anderson expressed. And they have adapted to the new dispensation by using many of techniques of the feature writer— the bright anecdote, the sharp quote, the interview with all concerned in a disputed play or a disputed decision, the description of a part of the contest that television down played. Relatively few editors now want the fast summary lead on the final score; instead, they ask for the way it happened and the answers to all the questions the fans will be raising that night and the next day.

Damon Runyon, Bob Considine and Jimmy Cannon — three of the old-time greats in the sports writing business— would have been very much at home in today's sports pages. As the saying goes, they always played the angles and wrote the story for all it was worth.

Telling the Sports Story : Anybody who undertakes to write about sports must have an intimate knowledge of the assignment. The three greatest necessities are accuracy, restraint and decent respect for the English language.

Sports followers invariably pride themselves on being experts. They like to hear and rear about "inside" strategy, just as the literacy gossip endlessly about the famous people on whom characters in a sensational new novel are supposedly patterned. However, some games are more easy to describe than others — and that depends on the patterns of the sport.

Simple Game

An essentially simple game like baseball is easy reported. The game's play-by-play, the result and the reasons for it can be quickly summarized, then documented with a description of the key plays. A few other details, and the account is complete enough for a post-game electronic round-up. But the written sports story must be different and it must have more detail.

Boxing and horse racing, too, have essentially simple patterns and need not be told in too complicated a fashion. What matters, particularly in television, is the detail that makes the tiny images on the small screen come alive— the blow-by-blow in a fight and the "call" in a horse race. By comparison, accounts of competitions in crew, swimming, tennis, polo and golf are handled with relative ease.

In football, however, the pattern of the game becomes increasingly complicated and difficult to follow. The effort of a play-by-play commentator here must be to simplify, wherever possible, and to explain to the viewer what happened and why it happened instead of prattling excitedly about the confusing technicalities. In a summary, oral as well as written, it becomes necessary to analyze the result, to select the principal plays and to give the public a sense of participation in the reporting. The writer, especially, must emphasize anecdote and detail.

The many events in track and field, each with special complications, also require a good deal of guidance from professionals who are intimately acquainted with the sport. This is particularly true during the spectacle of the Olympic Games every four years; inexpert hands, such reportage may be the worst, rather than the best, of the year because some American Commentators and reporters know only the United States' competitors as a rule and tend to give the results of each race as a triumph of American righteousness or a blow to the Stars and Stripes. Actually in any track meet, the reporting can be done very nicely— and interestingly if the expert— for the day studies the teams in advance, looks up the necessary background and records and comes to the field an hour before the meets starts to do a final checkup. To wait until the first event begins is to bog down completely in detail. But if it is known in advance that the pole vault, the mile run and the hurdles are likely to develop the most interesting contests, then the meet becomes a relatively easy matter to cover. What can never be anticipated is the unexpected event, such as the murders of Israeli athletes by Arab guerrillas that made so tragic a spectacle out of the 1972 Olympic games in Munich, the wholesale withdrawal of black African nations from the 1976 Games in Montreal and the 1980 American boycott of the Moscow Games.

As for basketball, with its seven-footers and its statistical labyrinths, this is less a job for a sports reporter than for a certified public accountant. It is hard to follow on television and even worse to describe in print, but it has such a large and devoted following that it receives major coverage.

It is clear, therefore, that the patterns of sport have much to do with the pattern of sports journalism. The big-money sports such as horse racing, boxing, baseball and football are the ones with the most pubic appeal in general, professional sports have the widest following. But college sports also attract millions of followers, and the TV contracts are much sought after.

New Interests : Two developments have broadened the audiences for both the sports page and sports events on the tube. One is the rise in participation for women's sports and the broader attention and funding that universities have given to them. In some parts of the nation, the excitement over women's sports, even at the high school level, has become a matter of consequence.

The second break in the traditional sports pages has been the interest in such audience participation events as stock car racing, motor boating and sailing, hunting and fishing, skating and skiing and the like. Such events are not easy for TV to cover, and therefore offer something to newspapers that can interest their readers. The boom in soccer, so long considered a "foreign" sport, benefits all the news media.

Writing Techniques : The incomparable Red Smith, viewing an Army-Navy football game at Philadelphia, began his account as follows:

> As some churlish historian of America's great undergraduate pastime wrote years ago, "it was an ideal day for football — too cold for the players". For 100,000 citizens of assorted nations, including Russia and Monaco, whose chattering teeth rattled like castanets upon the necks of bottles in Municipal Stadium yesterday, that just about sums up the match of Army and Navy.

Eventually, Smith got around to mentioning the size of the Army's victory, 22-6, which wasn't particularly important to him because everybody who read him knew it anyway. What was more important to his readers was his point of view.

The entertainment seemed flat by comparison with Army — Navy contest of the past. It was just too perishing cold. Reluctant to quit a slugging match which they had travelled many miles to watch, the customers nevertheless started making their numbed way toward the exits when the first half-ended, longing for a warm hotel room with the guy across the courtyard beating his wife....

Unlike Red Smith, most sports writers and commentators immerse themselves in technicalities to such an extent that they often forget entirely about the game itself and the people who contest it and who watch it. The electronic reporters becomes slaves to their equipment. The newspaper reporters worry about writing three separate accounts of a single event in order to cover all editions of a newspaper— a time consuming and expensive procedure that provides no advantage in these times of instant communication.

Multiple Techniques

The technique of doing multiple stories of one sports event is still practiced in a large section of the daily press, the essentials are recorded here without assurance that they will survive many more years.

The Advance Story : The advance begins with a situation lead, relating that two teams are facing each other or that a field of seven horses is ready for the big race of the day. The remainder of the story merely discuses the background of the event, gives whatever detail there is on the participants and the crowd, and winds up in such a way the running account of the early part of the game can be added on. If the contest is under way before the edition closes, a brief high insert can give the early scoring. Necessarily, even in an, early edition, the advance is bound to look foolish. It assumes that the public is entirely dependent on the news paper to find out what happened and will buy a later editor to get the full details. This used to happen, but it hasn't for many years. 2.

The Running Story : Depending on the style of the paper, the chronological story of the game is told as B copy (or B matter) or merely slugged "Running" or "Play-By-Play." As an edition approaches, a two-paragraphs lead is written by the reporter at the scene or by an editor in the office and put on top of the opening of the chronological account. Once the event is over, a final wrap-up lead is written and the details of the end of the game are put at the bottom of the piece.

If the running story is well done within reasonable space, it should stand. But frequently, sports writers have the urge to do the whole exercise over again on the dubious theory that they will produce magnificent prose the second time around. Unfortunately, it rarely turns out that way.

These are trying circumstances for any journalist. If the objective is to keep pace with radio and television, it is impossible to attain. If it is to "save space" for the final story, the theory is lacking in practicality. Such saved space is always wasted space. The news magazines manage to do pretty well with their weekly summaries of sports and do not arouse great feeling among the sports-minded public that it is being cheated. Sooner or later, the newspapers will come around to the obvious-that the best way to do a sports story is to wait until the event is over and then give it the well-considered treatment it deserves. Few sports events are big enough to calf for edition-by-edition coverage against electronic competition.

Statistics : The sports fans of the nation love statistics, and most sports pages provide them in abundance with columns of box score averages, racing detail, league standings and the like. Every reporter must learn at the outset how to keep an individual set of statistics and make sure they are accurate. But the wisest reporters know when to stop loading a story with ' 'stats" and depend, instead on the beauty and utility of t he English language. Too many statistics can kill a story. Too few will make it unusable. The trick is to find a practical in-between point.

Basics Facts

Here are some of the basics that should be remembered about sports reporting:

- Sports reporters are measured by the same standards as all other reporters. They have to do more than just report the score; it is their business to be aggressive to dig for the hidde story, to make sports pages mean something more than a repository for columns of agate results.
- One of the foremost problems today is access to athletes and locker rooms, at both the professional and the amateur levels. Reporters have to make it their business to ask the tough question— which means that they can't let themselves be turned aside by a stern locker room janitor.

- Most beginners in sports get their first job stringing for a neighbourhood paper and reporting high school scores. The high school sports beat is a testing ground for the next generation of sports writers. Usually, the best of the stringers gets first crack at an opening for a high school sports reporter and the progression starts there.
- The three necessities for a sports writer are accuracy, restraint and a decent knowledge of and respect for the English language. Phony expertise and cliche-ridden writing are the principal faults of new comers.
- In a contest featured on TV, the newspaper sports writer has to emphasize something other than the score, even though the score does have to be repeated high up. This can be anecdote, a sharp quote, an interview or an explanation of some occurrence that was fuzzed up by the TV reporters.
- In the thousands of contests that sports writers cover with little or no broadcast competition, the emphasis is still on writing the story straight and featuring the manner in which the game was won or lost. But even here, the feature approach always helps and—except for the brief summary story-good quotes are mandatory.
- Keeping statistics is an important part of a sports reporter's or and he or she should devise a system that can be quickly scanned and summarized at the end of the game. Too many states will spoil a story; too few will make it unusable. The point is to find the happy medium.
- Everybody in the business emphasizes sports writing styles. But mostly, this refers to the elite-the columnists and commentators who speak and write pretty much as they please. The young sports staffer is bound to the same rules that cover all reporters, however, and should not deviate from them without permission.

Bibliography

Almond, Gabriel A. and Coleman, James S. : *The Politics of the Developing Areas*, Princeton University Press, Princeton, 1960.

Altschull, J.H.: *Agents of Power: the Role of the News Media in Human Affairs*, Longman, New York, 1984.

Baker, R.K., and Ball, SJ.: *Mass Media and Violence, Report to the National Commission on the Causes and Prevention of Violence*, 1969.

Bell, D.: *The End of Ideology*, Collier Books, New York, 1976.

Berelson, B.: *Content Analysis in Communication Research*, Free Press, Glencoe, Illinois, 1952.

Bhatt, S.C.: *Indian Press Since 1955*, Publications Division, Government of India, New Delhi, 1997.

Bhattacharjea, Ajit: *Emergency and Media*, Mainstream, 1999.

Blumer, J.G.: 'The Political Effect of Television' in Halloran, J.D., *The Effect of Mass Communication*, Leicester University Press, Leicester, 1970.

Chaffee, S.H. and Berger, C.R. : *Handbook of Communication Science*, Sage Publications, Beverly Hills, London, 1987.

Chaney, D.: *Processes of Mass Communication*, Macmillan, London, 1972.

Cohen, B.C.: *The Press and Foreign Policy*, Princeton University Press, Princeton, N.J., 1963.

Cohen, S. and Young, J. : *The Manufacture of News*, Constable, London, 1973.

Czitrom, Daniel J.: *Media and the American Mind: From Morse to McLuhan*, University of North Corolina Press, Chapel Hill.

Davis, Howard and Walton, Paul : *Language, Image, Media,* Basil Blackwell, Oxford, 1983.

Davison, W.P.: *Mass Communication and Conflict Resolution,* Praeger, New York, 1974.

De Fleur, M.: *Theories of Mass Communication,* David Mckay, New York, 1970.

Dewey, John: *Democracy and Education,* Macmillan, New York, 1961.

Eaman, Ross A.: *The Media Society: Basic Issues and Controversies,* Butterworths, Toronto and Vancouver, 1987.

Febvre, L. and Martin, H.J.: *The Coming of the Book,* Verso Edition, London, 1984.

Fiske, J.: *Introduction to Communication Studies,* Methuen, London, 1982.

Gerbner, G (ed.): *Mass Media Policies in Changing Cultures,* Wiley, New York, 1977.

Gramsci, A.: *Selection from the Prison Notebooks,* Lawrence and Wishart, London, 1971.

Gupta, V.S. and Agarwal, Vir Bala: *Media Policy and Nation Building,* Concept, New Delhi, 1996.

Hovland, C.I., Lunsdane, A. and Sheffield, F.: *Experiments in Mass Communication,* Princeton University Press, Princeton, 1950.

Innis, Harold Adams: *Empire and Communication* (Rev. ed.), University of Toronto Press, Toronto, 1972.

Kivlin, Joseph E., Roy, Prodipto, Fliegl, Frederick C. and Sen, Lalit K.: *Communication in India: Experiments in Introducing Change,* NICD, Hyderabad, 1969.

Kornhauser, W.: *The Politics of Mass Society,* Free Press, New York 1968.

Kreiling, A.L.: *The Making of Racial Identities in the Black Press,* Ph.D. Dissertation, University of Illinois, 1973.

Marcuse, H.: *One Dimensional Man,* Routledge and Kegan Paul, London, 1964.

McLuhan, M.: *Understanding Media*, Routledge and Kegan Paul, London, 1964.

Merton, R.K.: *Social Theory and Social Structure*, Free Press, Glencoe, Illinois, 1957.

Natarajan J.: *History of Indian Journalism*, Part II of the Report of the Press Commission, New Delhi, 1955.

Paletz, D.L. and Entman, R.: *Media, Power and Politics*, Free Press, New York, 1981.

Peterson, R.C. et al.: *The Mass Media and Modern Society*, Holt, Rnehart and Winston, New York, 1965.

Scarfe, Allan and Scarfe, Wendy: *JP: His Biography*, Orient Longman, New Delhi, 1997.

Seymour-Ure, C: *The Political Impact of Mass Media*, Constable, New York, 1973.

Snow, R.P.: *Media Power*, Sage Publications, Beverly Hills and London, 1984.

Szalai, A. et al.: *The United Nations and the News Media*, UNITAR, New York, 1972.

Voos, H.: *Organizational Communication: A Bibliography*, Rutgers University Press, New Brunswick, N.J., 1967.

Williams, R.: *Television, Technology and Cultural Forms*, Fontana, London, 1975.